# Yale Agrarian Studies Series

JAMES C. SCOTT, SERIES EDITOR

The Agrarian Studies Series at Yale University Press seeks to publish outstanding and original interdisciplinary work on agriculture and rural society—for any period, in any location. Works of daring that question existing paradigms and fill abstract categories with the lived-experience of rural people are especially encouraged.

James C. Scott
*Series Editor*

Christiana Payne, *Toil and Plenty: Images of the Agricultural Landscape in England, 1780–1890* (1993)

Brian Donahue, *Reclaiming the Commons: Community Farms and Forests in a New England Town* (1999)

James C. Scott, *Seeing Like a State: How Certain Schemes to Improve the Human Condition Have Failed* (1999)

Tamara L. Whited, *Forests and Peasant Politics in Modern France* (2000)

James C. Scott and Nina Bhatt, eds. *Agrarian Studies: Synthetic Work at the Cutting Edge* (2001)

Peter Boomgaard, *Frontiers of Fear: Tigers and People in the Malay World, 1600–1950* (2001)

Janet Vorwald Dohner, *The Encyclopedia of Historic and Endangered Livestock and Poultry Breeds* (2002)

Deborah Fitzgerald, *Every Farm a Factory: The Industrial Ideal in American Agriculture* (2003)

Stephen B. Brush, *Farmers' Bounty: Locating Crop Diversity in the Contemporary World* (2004)

Brian Donahue, *The Great Meadow: Farmers and the Land in Colonial Concord* (2004)

J. Gary Taylor and Patricia J. Scharlin, *Smart Alliance: How a Global Corporation and Environmental Activists Transformed a Tarnished Brand* (2004)

Raymond L. Bryant, *Nongovernmental Organizations in Environmental Struggles: Politics and the Making of Moral Capital in the Philippines* (2005)

Edward Friedman, Paul G. Pickowicz, and Mark Selden, *Revolution, Resistance, and Reform in Village China* (2005)

Michael Goldman, *Imperial Nature: The World Bank and Struggles for Social Justice in the Age of Globalization* (2005)

Arvid Nelson, *Cold War Ecology: Forests, Farms, and People in the East German Landscape, 1945–1989* (2005)

Steve Striffler, *Chicken: The Dangerous Transformation of America's Favorite Food* (2005)

# Imperial Nature

The World Bank and Struggles for Social Justice
in the Age of Globalization

MICHAEL GOLDMAN

Yale University Press    New Haven and London

Published with assistance from the foundation established in memory of
Amasa Stone Mather, of the Class of 1907, Yale College.

Chapter 4 is a revised version of "The Birth of a Discipline: Producing
Authoritative Green Knowledge, World Bank-Style," from *Ethnography* 2:2
(2001): 191–217. Published by permission of Sage Publications.

Chapter 5 is a revised version of "Constructing an Environmental State:
Eco-Governmentality and Other Transnational Practices of a 'Green' World
Bank," from *Social Problems* 48:4 (2001): 499–523, © Copyright 2001 by
the Society for the Study of Social Problems, with permission.

Set in Minion type by Integrated Publishing Solutions.
Printed in the United States of America.

ISBN: 0-300-10408-1 (cloth)

A catalogue record for this book is available from the Library of Congress
and the British Library.

The paper in this book meets the guidelines for permanence and durability
of the Committee on Production Guidelines for Book Longevity of the
Council on Library Resources.

10 9 8 7 6 5 4 3 2 1

# Contents

# Preface

The World Bank is a fickle place to experience and comprehend. Mental maps mislead, directional signs baffle, and paths through it confuse and confound. Many of the Bank's best intentions seem to backfire in the most disastrous ways, and yet the debates on these disasters tend to reduce the problem to a simple assignment of blame. Every decade of the World Bank's existence has been marked by both major improvements in the techniques of development and new types of colossal failures. In the process of improving development—that is, helping the world's poor improve their livelihoods—so much gets generated in the way of development experts and expertise, research institutes, and worldwide professional networks. The world today is saturated with new knowledge-producing sites on the theme of development inside governments, universities, and business communities. For government officials in Africa, Asia, and Latin America, development has become one of the most time-consuming, and yet potentially lucrative, business opportunities on the horizon. Development has invaded the language, thoughts, and images of people in both the North and the South. Consequently, one can hardly imagine the world today except through the lens of World Bank-style development. As the chief arbiter of development, the World Bank has become so much a part of our everyday lives, with its practices and effects so highly dispersed across the world, that it is difficult to know precisely where the World Bank starts and where it ends (Kumar 2003). Such features make writing a book about this world-renowned institution no easy task.

Although I am not sure when my first encounter with the World Bank took place, I certainly became aware of the institution while living in the Thar desert in western India, along one of the world's largest irrigation canals, built on World Bank plans and capital. Described by the World Bank as an exemplary "sustainable development" project, it was designed to bring Himalayan mountain water and then affluence to the harsh Indian desert. What startled me most as my research took shape was the enormous gap between World Bank depictions of the Thar desert experience and my own observations. Did the blazing desert heat obscure the obvious? Official reports wrote glowingly about this project with the eye of a fascinated child in awe of the grandeur of the accomplishment— a thousand-kilometer-long canal irrigating two million hectares of sandy desert and turning them into lush farm fields. Along the main canal arteries, wealthy landowners produced high yields of export-quality crops. But just down the waterway, the majority of small landowners suffered from an absence of water, sand-choked canals, failed crops, high indebtedness, and government negligence.

To take just one example, the canals I saw were marked by constant shortages of cement, a crucial ingredient for lining the canals to keep them from leaking precious water. Without cement, large swathes of the fields alongside the canal became waterlogged and salinated, making it impossible for many farmers to grow crops. Small farmers went bankrupt and had to leave their land. Was this sustainable development? Walking down the many arteries of the canal, farmers would point out which canals were unlined, and who was getting water and who was not. Yet, seemingly oblivious to the views of tens of thousands of desert dwellers, Bank and government documents repeatedly reported that the canal system was properly lined and that water was being allotted equitably. While having tea with a local official in the engineer's home, I would be told one story, but when we walked to a canal I would observe the opposite. This occurred again and again.

In prosperous neighborhoods of the city of Jaipur, project engineers and government officials were building palatial homes with an abundance of cement, much of it retrieved from canal supply warehouses at night. Did this incongruity persist because World Bank officials slept at night? The crime was not the theft per se but the fact that the supposed beneficiaries of this development project were forced to abandon their allotted land. Once animal herders, weavers, traders, and farmers of rain-fed agriculture who lived off communally managed village lands, these desert dwellers were transformed into a class of landless farmworkers—sharecroppers, indentured servants, and part-time laborers. They fell into debt, were displaced from their lands, and became laborers on the land of the wealthy. The employers, for their part, did not rise to the top through some natural selection process or entrepreneurial spirit. They were well-connected property owners from the city and large farm owners from the Punjab, or government officials and engineers who ran the development project.

One did not need to be Sherlock Holmes to piece together the evidence; it was the talk of the town. The *chai wallas* (tea sellers) and *patwaris* (village revenue collectors) knew the story inside and out; it was as present in daily life as was the blowing sand. Yet World Bank reports repeatedly proclaimed the project a resounding success for the poor and for the environment. Whereas I am regularly told that the project of development uplifts the poor and restores the environment, too often I see it impoverishing the majority and enriching the few.

Many commentators on development—scholars as well as Bank officials—argue that projects often fail because of corruption, a social disease endemic to the third world. These inevitable aberrations, which the project of development works to eliminate, occur during the transition from tradition to modernity. To observers, development is a post–World War II technical achievement that transfers capital, expertise, and technologies from the North, that is, the advanced capitalist countries of the Northern Hemisphere, to the "undeveloped" South. The dictionary defines "corruption" as a debasement, perversion, or decay; it is a dishonest act, and its meaning implies that corruption represents a deviation from an otherwise dominant norm of ethical practices in society. Corruption, so defined, is the exception to the rule.

But what if governments and development agencies prosper financially and politically from a project, what if their professional staffs are all "on the take" in the sense that their salaries depend on the idea of development and its premises? What if a region's capitalist class invariably becomes enriched and empowered through development projects? What if this thing called "corruption" is not the exception but the rule and as such defines the political economy of development? Then it should be logical that the prevailing paradigm of development needs reexamining. As became increasingly evident to me, this process occurred *through* such development schemes, not in spite of them.

From these early experiences with the World Bank, I learned that development cannot be measured by such simple data as increases in yields or gross domestic product. Instead, development should be understood as a complex set of practices woven into the fabric of everyday life, both in poor districts and wealthy ones, in the global South as well as the global North. After all, most of the capital lent to Southern governments in the name of development funnels through Northern banks to purchase goods from Northern firms, ranging from tractors to turbines to the expertise of professional consultants. The surplus to pay back the loans and their accrued interest is produced through the back-breaking work of people like the Indian farm laborers I studied. Part of that farm surplus goes straight into the coffers of Northern firms as repayment for farm inputs, dams, and electricity projects. The role of the World Bank is pivotal for Northern wealth accumulation. The Bank raises most of its capital from Northern corporate investors in search of high returns, and its loans purchase goods and services mainly from Northern firms.

Whatever the original intentions of the Bretton Woods agreement may have been, over the past few decades, the primary effect of World Bank lending and policies is that much more capital flows *out* of borrowing countries and to the World Bank, IMF, and Northern-based banks than in. One alarming statistic that has hardly changed since the Bank's inception more than sixty years ago is that much of the capital lent by the Bank passes through the hands of Southern governments and travels directly to firms in the North, the main actors who do development, and who supply the capital goods and services for large projects. That is, the most important beneficiaries of development live in the North and not in the South.

Hence, World Bank-style development is not only, or even principally, about the perceived "lacks" or "poverties" of the people of the South. Crippling debt, rising income inequalities, and exclusion from such basic goods as fertile land, health care, and clean water are as much the result of development as they are attributable to the fundamental inequalities built into the global political economy.

So why has development become such a laudable enterprise? Why are projects such as this irrigation fiasco seen by development specialists as exemplars of environmentally sustainable development? The canal project I studied was packaged as a success story to school children in the North. Slide shows and teaching guides told the Olympian story of the World Bank "greening" the most inhospitable environment in the world, the desert. (Tellingly, as public protest in India rose and filmmakers produced documentaries dispelling these myths, the Bank pulled them from the shelves.)

Finally, why has the World Bank, the leading proponent of the "project of development," become the world's most powerful international institution? How did development become so central to North-South relations? Why has the Bank become the obvious choice to fix our so-called global problems, from rural poverty in India to the "rebuilding" of Afghanistan and Iraq? It has become easy to recommend the Bank for these awesome tasks because the Bank itself has already defined our global problems and has in place global experts with their toolkits of solutions. Where would we be without the World Bank? What alternatives do we have?

When I presented my research on this inequitable canal project to an academic audience in the United States, a veteran sociologist in the front row barked his exasperation at me:

Enough with these papers on how the poor get screwed over by the World Bank! Tell us something about how this institution works, how its so-called experts can possibly design such schemes, and how these practices have become the norm? These were big questions, and ones that I could not answer. But his challenge and questions stayed with me, and prompted me to embark on this book. I decided I had to study the Bank from within, by conducting research *inside* World Bank headquarters, the belly of the so-called beast. Since Bank staff do not spend all their time in Washington, D.C., neither did I as I gathered material. This book is the result of my long journey through the intestines of one of the world's most powerful institutions. My research took me to unexpected places—to remote research institutes, run-down government agencies, international conferences, and mountain dam sites. It also brought me back to my own professional networks of development professionals, environmentalists, anthropologists, and economists. As I learned from experience, this wily beast certainly gets around.

When I talk about my research on the World Bank, I frequently get asked, "How did you get access?" Did the Bank stonewall me as it does angry citizens demanding "the truth" about its projects? We are well aware that the people whom the Bank wants "to develop" are always the last to know about Bank projects or policies. But what about an academic professional, such as myself? Remarkably, despite the high level of security and their busy travel schedules, few Bank staffers refused my request for an interview; no one slammed the door in my face. Some even seemed eager to talk about their work and worldviews. Interviews often carried over into lunch. Some staff invited me to attend their workshops, staff trainings, and weekend retreats. One invited me to observe his project in Lao PDR (or Laos), which I did. Another senior official offered me an office and secretarial support! (Tempting, but no thanks.) I asked Bank staff members about their new mandate of environmental sustainability and about how the World Bank was retooling itself in light of vociferous social movement pressure. These questions were asked during a tense period when World Bank staffers were receiving relentless criticism from all over the world, a time when senior Bank management pushed a series of dramatic reforms within the institution. Of the many staff I interviewed, a common narrative was never far from the surface. Interviewees repeatedly portrayed themselves as honest reformers working against the grain and against inertia in a troubled and Byzantine organization. They strove to make the Bank more responsive to public demands that it become more participatory, and more alert to indigenous peoples' rights and to the pressing issue of the environment.

I also learned that World Bank staff needed people like me as much as I needed them, in large part because the Bank and its staff need to get their version of the truth out. The Bank cannot possibly carry the responsibility of its enormous tasks without seeking public support and legitimacy. It must deploy professionals around the world to help mainstream Bank-style development into government agendas, investment portfolios, civil-society activities, and the global political economy. Bank staff cannot do the job alone or by relying solely on the Bank's financial muscle. Historically, the Bank has always had access to much more capital than it can lend and has always suffered from a demand deficit for its capital and services. To survive, the Bank needs willing borrowers and willing promoters. After all, there are many reasons to *not* borrow from the World Bank: the irrigation canal fiasco with its huge debt repayments and high social and ecological costs is only one example. The fact that borrowers are now paying much more *back* to the World Bank than the Bank lent to them is another. Hence, the World Bank needs a hospitable climate of opinion; it needs professional support, it needs scientific support, and it vitally needs the consent of civil society. The Bank works like a major, publicly traded corporation, in that "market confidence" is its most important asset and its source of greatest vulnerability. It generates confidence in part through the high rates of return on the global bonds it floats; it also generates confidence through the global science and culture of development that makes the development industry seem essential and natural to the solving of the problems of individuals, industries, nations, and the world. It hopes to place itself, and professional elites worldwide, into the center of this globalizing narrative—as a hero, not a goat. But to do so requires people's confidence in what it sells and their participation in the Bank's own expanded reproduction as a global authority with few peers. Without our participation, in sum, the World Bank would be impotent.

By taking seriously what the Bank does and says, I learned that one of the Bank's greatest accomplishments has been to make *its* worldview, *its* development framework, and *its* data sets the ones that people around the world choose above others. This is one reason why the Bank's influence continues to grow, even with mounting pressure from critics. For example, fifteen years ago, environmentalists were up in arms about the Bank's large-scale dams, rain forest colonization schemes and logging projects, and "greenhouse-gas-producing" power plants. Today, by contrast, the world's largest environmental organizations are now the chief cosponsors of World Bank energy, land colonization, and forestry projects. Why did its foremost critics jump on the bandwagon? How did environmental organizations actually help the Bank *expand* its spheres of influence to places in the South it could never before go? I would argue that the World Bank could only legitimately speak of environmentally sustainable production once Northern environmental experts and activists enabled it to do so.

But following the words and promoters of Bank-style development tells only half the story. After all, Bank staff are not only selling the knowledge, reputation, and deeds of the Bank; they are also selling the use of capital, which concretely translates into dollar-based loans to dollar-poor countries to purchase commodities and services from firms residing largely in the North. The reason this book is not about hunger and poverty is because these are not the Bank's primary interests (although they are its primary *business*). Its staff spend no time with the hungry or poor—they themselves admit it would be foolhardy to send highly paid loan officers, who fly on business-class tickets, stay in five-star hotels, and are accompanied by staff assistants, to sit and chat with itinerant laborers and street dwellers about the structural barriers that keep them from meeting their basic needs and facilitating their desires. In the Bank's own institutional linguistics, this would not be "cost-efficient."

As the Bank's chief pollution adviser once explained to me, he spends very little time responding to queries from concerned citizens or NGOs (nongovernmental organizations) about pollution problems or resource scarcity for the poor. Most of the time he spends with the so-called public is devoted to trying to satisfy the demands of Northern ministers of industry or executives of Northern firms. Badgering him by phone and through office visits, ministers want an explanation as to why the goods and services of their country (and firms) are not being purchased with Bank loans. Executive salespeople are peddling the latest industrial technologies, which may mitigate some pollution problems but may also worsen others. He hesitates to buy their hardware because it comes at German prices with German engineers and German replacement parts for Indian clients with only rupees in their accounts. He finds that in the case of waste-water treatment plants, many European-made plants are idle because of the prohibitive costs of maintenance and replacement parts. Why not promote indigenous solutions to these development problems, he asks. India has its own waste-water treatment solutions that are much cheaper, he explains in frustration. Yet the Bank persists in selling Northern power plants, wastewater plants, and dam turbines to governments across the global South. Moreover, it insists on privatizing Southern airports, power sectors, and industries whose bidders are indifferent to the needs of the poor majority. And it demands that the services of such firms as Bechtel, PricewaterhouseCoopers, Dutch Shell, Enron, and Vivendi are the ones purchased with Bank loans. The World Bank is, after all, situated within a global political economy that has been perpetuating such cozy corporate-government relations for a very long time, at least since colonialism and the birth of market capitalism.

Although this is the practical reality of the World Bank's operating environment, we prefer to think in a less self-serving rhetoric. The most important accomplishment of the World Bank, and the main theme of this book, is how it manages to pursue its day-to-day activities while focusing the public's gaze on the grand illusion of development. This is not simply a shell game. The chasm between rhetoric and reality is common to many public bureaucracies. What is unprecedented is its practice on a world scale with such tremendous global consequences.

This book can be read as an adventure travelogue through one of the most powerful and undemocratic institutions in the world, one that determines currency prices in Mexico City, water rates in Johannesburg, and possibly even the direction of the flow of the Mekong River—in sum, the fates of millions of people—based on an economic "science" it produces within the context of capital-intensive deal making. This book can also be read as a sociological inquiry into the remarkable transformation of the World Bank into a global "knowledge bank," one that uniquely and effectively produces the research institutes, ideational frameworks, data sets, professionals, networks, government and nongovernment agencies, and policies that are influencing the trajectory of North-South relations today. By emphasizing the Bank as simultaneously global lender, policy maker, civil-society actor, and knowledge-producer, I focus on how it has been able to become hegemonic, or the way in which it has successfully determined the parameters in which we speak and act in the name of development. In spite of its long list of abysmal failures and destructive effects, the Bank remains the primary global player in countries in the South, as well as, though less obviously, in countries in the North. No matter what one chooses to emphasize in analyzing World Bank power, the dangers of leaving such authority unchallenged are enormous. As one longtime World Bank consultant observed in his recently published diary on his assignment in Sierra Leone:

> There are times when an economist tells [a borrowing] Government, "If you raise the price of grain to the farmers, certainly the immediate result will be that 200,000 children per year will die." . . . [But] that, after perhaps three years, the increased price will mean a higher income in country areas so there will be, perhaps, 400,000 fewer deaths among

farmers' children. . . . It is not pleasant to have to make such recommendations, but it goes with the job. . . . Making the decision does give you a kick, though. It is a big decision, an important decision that will kill many people and save many people. The fact that you make the decision, on your own judgment rather than on hard fact and theory, makes you feel important, powerful. I recognize that the power is addictive.

A lot of the World Bank economists are exposed to the same temptation, the same addiction. In fact, it may be that the organization as a whole is addicted. It does seem to go out of its way to make decisions that will cause millions of deaths or save millions of lives over the years, basing these decisions on judgments, rules of thumb, and political dogmas like the Free Market. It does come to believe that harsh remedies are more likely to cure. (Griffiths 2003, pp. 175–76)

How did one institution based in Washington, D.C., acquire so much power and make its power and knowledge seem so natural and so logical, allowing it to transform people's lives all over the world? Rather than a study of addictive personalities or fundamentalist theologies, this book instead tries to explain how transnational structures of power, knowledge, and capital are produced; how they become hegemonic; and how they are challenged. I hope readers can gain from these pages a better sense of how "the project of development" gets generated, how it fuels highly uneven and unstable relations of capitalist production, and how it is becoming a trigger for mass mobilization of people fighting against a commodified and inequitable world, and for social justice.

# Acknowledgments

Through the luxury of time, I have learned from many people. At the University of California–Santa Cruz, I was fortunate to have worked with James O'Connor when he began the pathbreaking journal *Capitalism, Nature, Socialism,* and a group of us traveled uncharted territory together. Jim's insights fueled an era of innovation on ecological Marxism, political ecology, ecological history, as well as a re-engagement with the works of Karl Marx and Karl Polanyi. To Jim, I owe the book's title and much, much more. Thanks to two generous postdoctoral fellowships, the S.V. Ciriacy–Wantrup of University of California–Berkeley, and the John D. and Catherine T. MacArthur Fellowship in International Peace and Cooperation, I was able to conduct my research in Washington, D.C., and beyond, while living in Berkeley, where I learned from brilliant scholars, such as Michael Watts, Nancy Peluso, Donald Moore, Dick Norgaard, Ian Boal, Louise Fortmann, and Rachel Schurman, who collectively started the now legendary Berkeley Workshop on Environmental Politics. Gillian Hart and Michael Burawoy deeply influenced my work and have offered exceptional comments on the manuscript as well as inspiration from their own scholarship on manufacturing consent, global ethnography, and disabling globalization.

In Washington, D.C., there were many people inside and outside the Bank who helped me enormously, but I think I should leave them unnamed, with respect and much thanks for their support. Devesh Kapur taught me much about the Bank, although he must not be held responsible for the way I turned on their heads many of his lucid and thoughtful interpretations. The project continued through my move to Urbana, where my colleagues and graduate students gave me tremendous intellectual and comradely support, in particular Tom Bassett, Steve Brechin, Zsuzsa Gille, Julian Go, John Lie, Faranak Miraftab, Zine Mugabane, William Munro, Rachel Schurman, Charis Thompson, Jan Nederveen Pieterse, Andy Pickering, Winnie Poster, Ken Salo, and David Wilson. Together we started an innovative Transnational Studies Seminar series. Tom and William kept me on my toes on our prairie runs, talking through ideas and non-ideas alike. Thanks also go to my intelligent and creative graduate students at Illinois who taught me much about the world. One in particular, Yildirim Senturk, proved to be a superb research assistant, and helped me immensely with this manuscript.

New Haven became a temporary haven for me, where for one year I could work through many of these ideas. Thanks go to Jim Scott, who gave me the confidence and inspiration to (try to) write a good story, and to do it surrounded by wonderfully supportive fellows: Harry West, Liz Oglesby, Vupenyu Dzingirai, Guillaume Boccara, Rachel Schurman, Subir Sinha, and some great locals, such as Eric Worby, Kamari Clarke, Kathy McAfee, Arun Agrawal, and Kay Mansfield who kept the Program in Agrarian Studies the special place it is. (The year at Yale was also sponsored by a University of Illinois's Center for

Advanced Study fellowship, where I was generously allowed to be a resident fellow *out of residence.*) In Thailand, Witoon Permpongsacharoen and the dedicated TERRA gang were extremely helpful and inspirational; in Laos, many people assisted me, but it is best that I not name them; in South Africa, Patrick Bond and his comrades; in India, Shashi and Laxmi Tyagi, A. B. and Rani Bhardwaj, the late Sanjoy Ghose, the Institute of Development Studies–Jaipur scholars, especially Surjit Singh and S. Ramanathan; in Chile, Daniela and Arturo Alvestigui. I could go on.

I would like to offer my heart-felt appreciation to some of the close readers of various chapters and drafts—Ron Aminzade, Tom Bassett, Karen Booth, Jeffrey Broadbent, Fred Buttel, Kate Dunnigan, John Bellamy Foster, Jonathan Fox, Phil Hirsch, Aviva Imhof, Sheila Jasanoff, Nina Laurie, Helga Leitner, Larry Lohmann, Marybeth Martello Long, Patrick McCully, Donald Moore, Ken Salo, Allan Schnaiberg, Ben Schurman, David Smith—as well as for the patient and diligent support from Jean Thomson Black, Eliza Childs, and Laura Davulis at Yale University Press. Fred Buttel, Michael Burawoy, Jim Scott, Gill Hart, and John Lie have all given me immeasurable support in helping me overcome many career hurdles. Many friends and family wisely had no interest in reading drafts, and I thank them for their gifts of sustenance: Barbara Laurence, Ethan Canin, Barbara Schuler, Steve Sellers, Allison Pugh, Karen Rhein, Eric Blanpied, Paul and Barbara Schurman, Bert Schurman, Josh Schurman, David and Ronda Goldman, Vivian and Steve McClure, Monica and Mark Abrahams, and the transcendentally joyful Eli and Nadia Goldman.

Most of my gratitude, however, goes to my parents, who, sadly, were never able to see this book in print, and to my wife, Rachel, who helped me every step of the way. My parents were the product of what Eric Hobsbawm called the "age of extremes," survivors of a place and time that did not bode well for people like themselves. As a consequence, my father, for one, was a person of very few words. For what they had to experience in Germany, and the enduring pain afterwards, there really were no appropriate words. Hence, I was educated in family social history through nonverbal communication. In time, I learned that it may be possible to find words to explain the depth of social injustice, but also its absolute limits: meaning is inevitably lost in translation and in the distance from the experience. My parents spent their life energies keeping me at arm's length from such horrors; yet in spite of their efforts to protect and shield, I learned from them that ultimately the depth of such suffering and injustice can never be experienced alone. For better or worse, it is always a shared social experience. This was their greatest gift to me. And it has been one of Rachel's most precious gifts to show me how to bring these experiences, and many others more joyous, to life. I dedicate this book to her.

# I

# Introduction:
# Understanding
# World Bank Power

*The purpose of this training seminar is to try to create
an epistemic community in Africa so that you can have
more power with your governments when negotiating for
institutional reform. You won't feel alone. We'll help you set up
networks and share information. You will be able to say to your
bosses: "Hey, but that's how they're doing it next door, and
look how successful they are." We are prepared to offer you
support. . . . And when you return home after this workshop,
we would like you to initiate your own training workshops
on environmental economics. This way we can change
decision-making in your countries.*

—*Training workshop coordinator, Economic
Development Institute, World Bank, June 1995*

In June 1995 I was an observer in a two-week training workshop on "environmental economics and economy-wide policymaking" at World Bank headquarters in Washington, D.C. Most of the invited participants came from Anglophone Africa—Ethiopia, Tanzania, Zambia, Zimbabwe, Nigeria, Kenya, Uganda, and South Africa—and two from Russia and Chile, countries that would be hosting future training workshops.

Every two hours for the next two weeks, new learning modules were presented by experts from the World Bank, the U.S. Environmental Protection Agency (EPA), Worldwatch Institute, and other Washington-based agencies. The workshop started out with a learning module on "imagining a global future," followed by sessions on environmental cost-benefit analysis, writing National Environmental Action Plans (NEAPs), the benefits of structural adjustment for the environment, and applying the concept of natural capital. The case studies were mostly from the United States, Europe, and Asia. Many were on the management of industrial waste, urban air pollution, and forest logging. In one of the few illustrations from Africa, a senior Bank official, drawing on his research in Zimbabwe, explained that if highly inefficient cattle grazing were replaced with wildlife preservation—that is, eco-tourism and game parks—it would create a win-win scenario of both a sustainable environment and a high-growth economy, never mentioning the "value" of cattle to the rural people's culture, environment, and survival. When another senior Bank official explained that "all environmental problems can be mitigated by microeconomic tools," the audience was silent. "That's how we find the true value of nature," he said. Ten minutes later, over British biscuits and tea, the lounge was lively with conversation on the relevance of these lectures. After a round of amused chatter on the inapplicability of the Bank's models and assumptions for Africa, a South African professor from a major urban university told the story of his experience after he presented a paper on microeconomic issues in his home town. "A rural fellow came up to me and said: 'What you value is not what I value. What you see when you look at the land or forest is much different than what I see. So what's all this talk about universal values?'"

At the end of the third day, the workshop organizer reminded us of that evening's cocktail party, urging participants to meet World Bank loan managers who worked in their home regions. This is your big opportunity, he advised us: "They're looking to hire consultants to work on their projects." Although by week's end, many of the participants were already disappointed with the U.S.-centric and doctrinaire style of the presentations, the lack of time for discussion, and the absence of case studies from Africa, they certainly understood the rewards. As one Zimbabwean development consultant said contentedly, "With this training certificate, I'll be getting plenty of jobs back home with the international organizations." A less sanguine participant, the department chair of economics at a prominent East African university, remarked, "Under the Bank's structural adjustment [program], the university tenure system has been abolished. We have been forced to take on other jobs, private tutoring, anything we can get. To get a Bank consultancy," he said, "well, that helps. We teach with books that are twenty years old; the libraries are empty. The best things about this workshop are the materials." A third participant concurred, "We can sure use these materials. And we can use them how we choose." On a walk after a long day trapped in the seminar room, an Ethiopian trained in Marxist economics—the dominant science of his day—explained to me in a resigned tone: "A consultant for the [World] Bank in Addis makes the equivalent of thirty times what an equally qualified economist makes. In the army, you get a bullet for deserting, but with the World Bank, you lose your astronomical salary. It is much easier dodging bullets from the army for desertion than [saying 'no' to] the World Bank."

African professionals selected by the World Bank to carry out its mission enact their roles in diverse ways that defy simple categories. The only commonality is that they are rarely docile in their relationship with the Bank. People work for the Bank for many reasons, some very different from what the Bank might hope for. They may translate their assignment and improvise in ways that do not follow the Bank's credo. Nonetheless, less than six years after this workshop, one of the Bank's earliest on "environmentally sustainable development," the World Bank and its European-based aid partners have established more than fifty policy and training institutes throughout Africa, where many of the Bank's training programs are being taught by African professionals on themes ranging from environmental economics to water-sector privatization to "making the WTO work in developing countries." The coveted training materials handed out at these workshops are not just required reading in economics courses in underfunded universities; they have become background resources for African policymakers who, as preconditions for World Bank loans, are being compelled to act expeditiously to redraft national constitutions and land laws, liberalize forestry and water sectors, and restructure state agencies and regulatory authorities. The guiding discourse of the Bank's outreach and training programs, development projects, and national policy programs reflects a confluence of tensions that come from what one observer calls the "finance ministry agenda" of neoliberalism and the "civil-society agenda" of social justice and environmentally sustainable development (Wade 2002). How these two seemingly divergent worldviews have emerged and converged to form the Bank's most recent and most powerful framework for intervention in the global South and Eastern Europe—green neoliberalism—is the subject of this book.

In the chapters that follow, I argue that the World Bank and professionals from the North and the South are busily constructing such a global agenda. It is a dance of inordinate consequence, one that is laden with power and meaning and is highly contentious and yet contingent. It is infused with strategies, desires, constraints, and possibilities—all with world-altering significance. In this book I try to capture and explain the ways in which the World Bank and its partners have worked to create a representation, analysis, and mode of action for the project of development that have become naturalized, legitimate, and durable. I show through ethnographic research how, in response to the effective organizing efforts of its critics, the Bank has successfully worked to reinvent itself, tame its critics, and intervene in an ever-growing number of institutions, terrains, and social bodies located across the postcolonial map. These interventions take shape in highly diverse forms, generating a "very particular, historically specific, and temporary 'moment,'" a hegemonic set of practices, with a "multi-dimensional and multi-arena character" (Hall 1996, p. 424).

Over the past twenty years, enormous external pressures have arisen to force the World Bank to either "green" its global project of development or to retreat from its work. This greening is neither simply window dressing nor mere public relations, as many critics argue. It is rather the Bank's latest and most profound discursive framework, producing a power/knowledge regime of green neoliberalism. Green neoliberalism has become influential the world over and has enabled the Bank to expand into more places and insinuate its worldview into more lifeworlds than ever before. In the following chapters, I describe a number of linked sites where these transformations are taking place: inside World Bank headquarters, along a dam site on the Mekong River in Laos, inside the state agencies of debtor countries, and among members of transnational water policy networks. At each of these sites a wide array of professionals from the World Bank, national and transnational development agencies, governments, multinational firms, chambers of commerce, and nongovernmental organizations (NGOs) participate in the production and circulation of this new set of knowledge/ power practices. Each of these organizations helps to embed the Bank's green-neoliberal regime into the architecture of local governing institutions.

As the Bank has become more active in the management of borrowers' political concerns, it brings new worlds and expectations into its range of operation. The Bank no longer meets just with capital-goods contractors who supply the turbines and concrete or with financial executives who supply the capital and buy the Bank's global bonds; Bank officials are now expected to engage groups of irrigation users in Pakistan, international anti-dam activists, lawyers and marine biologists from environmental NGOs, and judges from remote Chinese municipalities. Conversely, underpaid provincial judges and low-level bureaucrats are now required to engage in the world of the World Bank and to work closely with Northern conservationists and civil-society advocates who are always seeking funding for their own projects.

That a specific ideology of development has become the dominant lens through which South-North relations are understood is a testament to the immense power of the World Bank over the past sixty years. That few development practices, beliefs, and truths can be expressed today outside the parameters of environmentally sustainable development, on the one hand, and neoliberalism, on the other, is a testament to the efficacy of the Bank's latest power/knowledge regime. As Italian political theorist Antonio Gramsci noted years ago, the moment of hegemony is revealed when the dominant bloc "also pos[es] the questions around which the struggle rages" (Gramsci, Hoare, and Nowell-Smith 1971, p. 182; Hall 1996, p. 423). Because so many people—including promoters, interpreters, and even critics—now accept as fact that there is no alternative to development and that the only question is how to make it more sustainable, that Gramscian moment may have arrived.

## The Rise of Green Hegemony, World Bank Style

The most recent development regime of the World Bank, green neoliberalism, rose to prominence in the early 1990s when widespread popular protests against the World Bank forced it to come to terms with the environmentally and socially deleterious effects of its projects. Activists never anticipated, however, that the Bank's response would be to reinvent and expand its neoliberal economic agenda to include new social and environmental dimensions, helping it to intervene into more geographical territories and lifeworlds and in ways that its earlier work never permitted. This process ushered in a new regime of environmental practices that involved civil-society actors from development organizations, environmental groups, academic institutes, and state agencies. It fundamentally altered the defining features of the Bank's neoliberal agenda by adding as a goal the restructuring and capitalization of nature-society relations that exist as uncommodified or underutilized by capital markets.

Originally conceived of and portrayed as a macroeconomic policy initiative to make troubled third world states and
economies more accommodating to global economic actors—
especially large transnational corporations—neoliberalism has
become a social, cultural, and ecological project of enormous
significance. Strictly speaking, neoliberalism is an audacious
political agenda dating from the Thatcher-Reagan era that
promotes an "economic growth first" approach, presents the
view that "the market" is naturally efficient and impartial, and
pushes for downsized governments, privatization of public
goods and services, and deregulation of capital in order to nurture the "self-regulating" capabilities of transnational markets
(Peck and Tickell 2002). At first, neoliberal advocates vigor-
ously pushed to reduce barriers to international trade and currency flows; next, they succeeded in privatizing public transport systems and power companies, and then, social security,
prisons, garbage, and health services. Neoliberalism has now
become a frame of mind, a cultural dynamic, an entrepreneurial personality type, and a rule of law that penetrates the
most intimate relations people have with each other, state apparatuses, and their natural environments.

Traveling beyond the advanced capitalist states of the
North, neoliberalism reflects a set of aggressive interventions
into the less capitalized territories of the South where "undervalued" and "undervalorized" human and natural resources
are hypothesized to exist, and where "backward" social institutions are said to rule. Indeed, as this book will demonstrate,
the current, neoliberal political-economic agenda did not start
in the West and then spread to "the rest" but was constituted in
postcolonial capitalist North-South relations from the start. It
built upon the power relations embedded and embodied in
former colonial capitalist relations; wove its way through the

World Bank's development regimes of poverty alleviation, debt management, and structural adjustment; and now thrives in the Bank's version of environmentally sustainable development, expanding the neoliberal project and new avenues for capital accumulation worldwide.

In the name of both export-led capitalist growth and ecological sustainability, the World Bank has forged national political agendas that have sparked the expansion of commercial land markets in regions where land-deprived people have demanded progressive land redistribution. The Bank has pushed states to auction off publicly owned natural resources and resource-based industries to transnational corporations in conjunction with international conservation groups instituting new global sanctions for biodiversity protection. In remarkable synchronicity, the sustainability crowd and the neoliberal development crowd have united to remake nature in the South, transforming vast areas of community-managed uncapitalized lands into transnationally regulated zones for commercial logging, pharmaceutical bioprospecting, export-oriented cash cropping, megafauna preservation, and elite eco-tourism (Greenough and Tsing 2003; Moore 2003; Neumann 1998). Aggressive transboundary conservation politics and neoliberal economics have coevolved and spread around the world in large part because of the lucrative and muscular financial support of the World Bank's project of development.

This process has unfolded since the 1980s, when concerted pressure by disparate campaigns around the world conjointly forced the World Bank to "reform or die." Significantly, the Bank was able to reform itself by both "mainstreaming the environment" into its everyday activities and mainstreaming its activities into the work of transnational environmental actors (World Bank Environment Department 1995). As it refined its position through consultation with senior environmental organization leaders in Washington, D.C., and environmentally minded faculty at the North's major universities, the Bank began to argue that "sustainable development" could not occur without proper economic valuation of the environment (World Bank 1992; World Bank 2003). But for that to happen, social institutions that regulate the use of environments according to noncapitalist principles needed to be transformed. According to the World Bank, under existing social institutions in the global South, the valuation of land, forests, minerals, and water has been highly distorted and thus natural resources have been poorly utilized. This is the World Bank's main explanation for why water is supplied at below-cost prices and is thus "wasted" by the poor majority, why tropical forest species are unsustainably harvested, and why valuable land is dedicated to "low-value" subsistence crops (Environment Department 1995; IUCN 1993; IUCN 1997; Pearce 1994; World Bank 1992). Under such "underdeveloped" institutional conditions, elite sustainable-development scholars and World Bank staff argue, local environments will continue to be destroyed, and "irrational" collective behavior will continue to contribute to the global environmental crises that have become the major barriers to sustainable development and globally shared prosperity. Throughout the 1990s, this new, green-neoliberal development logic was not merely the preoccupation of internal reports or rhetorical debates; it was the basis for major policy shifts and preconditions to World Bank loans to borrowing countries, especially the most indebted, where so much of the world's natural resources and biological diversity exists.

When the World Bank lends large sums of capital for the lofty goal of environmentally sustainable development, it requires borrowing countries to do much more than repeat the mantra of sustainability in its official texts. To qualify for loans, borrowers are often required to restructure state agencies, to write national legislation that creates new commercial land and resource markets, and to adopt new scientific protocols that result in the shaping of knowledge and expertise on the causes and solutions of ecological destruction and halted development. Under this development regime of green neoliberalism, borrowers are compelled to thoroughly reform their national budgets and tax systems, open their banking and insurance sectors to new foreign bidders, and subordinate national laws to WTO standards and regulations. In other words, the greening and neoliberalizing of the development agenda is not merely a rhetorical move but is profoundly material—and world-altering. Moreover, these World Bank interventions have been highly profitable for a very particular set of World Bank constituencies that critics often ignore or take for granted, that is, the Northern capital goods, finance, and service sectors, especially from the "Big Five" countries (U.S., UK, Germany, Japan, and France) that control the majority of the vote in the World Bank and in other global institutions competing to manage the global political economy (George and Sabelli 1994).

Although many observers have sought to show either how the Bank's foray into environmentalism has failed miserably or how neoliberalism is strictly a disabling force, I see these two phenomena not as appendages or wrong turns in an otherwise apolitical or technical process. Indeed, I see neoliberalism and green development as fundamentally constitutive of two dimensions of development—development as a post–World War II project of recovery from war and colonialism in the global South, or what Gillian Hart calls "development with a big D," and development as a set of capitalist processes with uneven and contradictory effects ("development with a small d") (Hart 2001; Hart 2003; Hart 2004). The argument that their histories have unfolded together is central to this book and helps demonstrate the basis of World Bank power.

My thesis is that the World Bank is much more than a single global entity with a singular agenda and easily ascribed "impacts." It is much more than twenty buildings across the road from the White House and the U.S. Department of Treasury. Instead, it should be understood as a productive agent maintained through its interactions in multiple sites (from MIT's economics department to Wall Street investment firms and Cargill's agro-industrial goods division in the United States, to rural research institutes, fertile fields, and the agro-industry sector in India), enabling a diverse set of elite projects, with deeply exploitative effects. The argument is not that the world is run by the World Bank president, but rather that the global political economy has at its core a set of elite power networks in whose reproduction the World Bank is deeply embedded. Understanding the World Bank offers us a glimpse into the workings of the global political economy and the hegemonic powers that maintain it. Whereas others have documented well the gross violations of development projects, I emphasize the more mundane forms of violence perpetuated in the name of development—not the corporeal abuse, but the everyday forms of building up hegemony that influence and pressure people to participate in the formation and stabilization of the World Bank's green-neoliberal agenda, even if such participation may not be in their own best interest (Bond 2003; Caufield 1996; George and Sabelli 1994; Rich 1994). Of course, all these forms of violence are deeply connected and hang over people's heads as they try to survive the onslaught of neoliberal capitalist development.[1]

## Tensions in Development Scholarship

In thinking about development, scholars of all political stripes have become obsessed with the question: "Why does development fail?" This route has led scholars off some rather steep precipices as they have sought to "improve" the process by promoting what they think are the right management solutions and social-behavioral modifications. In pursuit of improvement, however, they also legitimate and expand the project of development, writ large, justifying it as a necessary if flawed uniform project of modernity and progress for the South. The development literature is enormous and diverse, but it has a few common threads. In this and the next section, I highlight the problems with many of these approaches and suggest an alternative perspective on the role of the World Bank in development as well as the role of development in the world system. Simply put, there is a dichotomous split in the development debates: the "pro-development" scholarship, with its roots in modernization theory, and the "post-development" scholarship, with its critique of modernization. Yet, as I argue below, they converge in unexpected ways.

### THE MODERNIZATION MODEL OF DEVELOPMENT

In their view of development, modernization scholars start from the assumption that there is no alternative to Western-style capitalist development, that development unfolds naturally based on a set of laws of capital, or what they call and reify as "the market" (Dasgupta 1998; Dollar 2002; Easterly 2001; Germani 1971; Gilman 2003; Hoselitz 1960; Hoselitz and Moore 1963; McClelland 1961; Meier 1995; Ray 1998; Rostow 1971). These scholars believe that development falters in third world countries because indigenous institutions are poorly equipped to take full advantage of the benefits of capitalism. The problem lies not within the world capitalist economy and the power dynamics of the world system, but in those elements of the South that are unable to adapt to and accommodate the infusions of capital, technology, and know-how offered to them by the West. Institutional immaturity and lack of moral restraint are two attributes ascribed to countries that are seen as development failures. For these scholars and practitioners, the techno-scientific question thus becomes "What is the best model of development?" and the answer is invariably a managerial-disciplinary one, "Learn from the developed West," as if the West has been some isolatable or unchanging organism that can teach the non-West the how-to of economic growth and prosperity, as well as the social norms and behaviors necessary to become "civilized," "developed," and "rich."

In the 1950s, early development policies at the World Bank were framed by such a modernization model, albeit one with a Keynesian economic worldview, which emphasized government intervention into arenas of the economy where private capitalists are reticent to invest. Hence, the job of the Keynesian "developmental state" was to actively step in, with World Bank help, and stimulate job creation and economic growth. From the Bank's perspective, there was much work for states to do under the flag of development, and Bank loans kept states busy borrowing in (relatively expensive) dollars to purchase power plants, transmission grids, and other capital-intensive goods from Northern firms. The World Bank inched forward in its plans to lend prudently in the name of development.

This conservative agenda rapidly disappeared when a tidal wave of events hit the global economy in the early 1970s.

With the rising surplus of Eurodollars and OPEC petrodollars (from high oil price hikes) coupled with a mounting U.S. deficit and an American economy mired in military expenses, President Nixon and his advisor Paul Volcker declared the end of the longstanding Bretton Woods system. That system had tied the values of all currencies to a gold standard linked to the U.S. dollar (Block 1977; Gowan 1999; Kapstein 1994; McMichael 2004). This move represented the beginning of a U.S.-led mandate to deregulate flows of international finance capital in ways that would ultimately benefit the U.S. economy. As I show in chapter 2, the new World Bank president, Robert McNamara, tapped this surfeit of capital to expand the Bank's project lending and transform the institution into a global player.

By the early 1980s, the chickens came home to roost as overspending helped spur the Southern debt crisis, which led the International Monetary Fund (IMF), World Bank, and U.S. Treasury to articulate a strikingly different policy for borrowing countries. The new version of the modernization model emphasized state fiscal austerity, market liberalization, and public-sector privatization for the South, the three pillars of what came to be called the "Washington Consensus" (WC).[2] Within the World Bank, the shift from a development economics that promoted "growth with distribution" to a "market-only" fundamentalist perspective was cemented with the hiring of the orthodox Anne Krueger as chief economist and the purging of the growth-with-distribution economists. In the wake of Krueger's appointment, Washington Consensus neoliberals inside and outside of the Bank convincingly persuaded others that the World Bank and other multilateral development institutions were simply prolonging the South's woes by carelessly lending to "irresponsible" leaders for "nonproductive" public investments. In their view, this "profligate" development lending served only to encourage irrational economic behavior, or what Krueger famously called "rent-seeking" (Krueger 1974).

When this neoliberal development agenda took root, it was highly draconian. In strict economic terms, for most of the global South, the 1980–2000 period marked a sharp reversal of the economic gains of the previous two decades (1960–1980) (Easterly 2001; Wade 2001; Weisbrot 2001). While there were some exceptions to this rule—most notably, China, India, and South Korea—these were also the countries that had rejected the strict neoliberal prescriptions of currency devaluation; elimination of trade barriers and capital regulations; state fiscal austerity; and the privatization of public goods, services, and infrastructure. Those countries that did follow the Bank/ IMF prescriptions most closely, often with little choice, suffered far more.

By the mid-1990s, social and economic conditions in many Southern and Eastern European countries had become so terrible that a core group of Northern policy makers publicly denounced the Washington Consensus for destroying the Russian, Mexican, and East African economies and for precipitating the economic crises of the 1990s in East Asia and Latin America. After more than a decade of WC ideological dominance, the post-Washington Consensus crowd concluded that the Bank's and IMF's neoliberal orthodoxy had created a series of colossal disasters around the world (Easterly 2001; Meltzer 2000; Sachs 1993; Stiglitz 2002). At the forefront of this new view were the new institutional economists, with a disillusioned Joseph Stiglitz at the helm (Hart 2001). A former chief economic advisor for the Bank, Stiglitz argued that these particular modernization policies had become "ends in themselves, rather than means to more equitable and sustainable growth. In so doing, these policies were pushed too far, too fast, and to the exclusion of other policies that were needed."[3]

More recently, the post–Washington Consensus policy crowd has traveled down two divergent roads to reshape the modernization model. One group argues that the World Bank and IMF need to set up many more safety-net and social welfare institutions to blunt the impact of neoliberal policies, that is, selectively revisit and expand Keynesian social buffers. In the view of these economists (and development practitioners), the Bank and IMF need to dispense with their "shock therapy" approach to change and instead prepare countries for global integration on a more gradual schedule, with a greater sensitivity toward local differences, needs, and capabilities (Fine 2001). They fear that a world in which the poor live without hope for jobs or clean water is a world ready to go up in revolutionary—or fundamentalist—flames.

Others demand that the World Bank and IMF return to their original mission, when the Bank, they believe, was small and effective and its loans were highly discriminating (Finnemore 1997; Pincus and Winters 2002; Wade 1996a).[4] Today, these "development has gone astray" analysts see the octopuslike Bank and arrogant IMF fueling corruption and undermining these institutions' mandate for democracy by politicizing development. These observers assume that by becoming leaner and more discerning, the Bank and IMF can return to what they imagine these institutions once were: shrewd catalysts for economic development in the third world.

## HAS DEVELOPMENT GONE ASTRAY?

As a leading scholar on the World Bank, Robert Wade of the London School of Economics makes a strong case for a particular cause of the recent demise of development: U.S. hegemony over the World Bank (Wade 1996b; Wade 2002). The argument Wade puts forth in a 2002 article starts with the observation that U.S. foreign and national security policies during the cold war were defined by a tension between the United States' desire to open the world's markets to U.S. capital, goods, and services and its policy of containing and excluding communist-influenced states and populations. But after 1989, the U.S. replaced its doctrine of containment with one of enlargement. As U.S. national security advisor Anthony Lake argued in a 1993 speech: "During the Cold War, even children understood America's security mission: as they looked at those maps on their schoolroom walls, they knew we were trying to contain the creeping expansion of that big, red blob. Today . . . we might visualize our security mission as promoting the enlargement of the 'blue areas' of market democracies" (Wade 2002).

According to Wade, the World Bank and IMF have become the primary vehicles for the United States' enlargement strategy. "Powerful segments of [U.S.] national elites" realize that Southern and former communist markets could be transformed into U.S.-influenced "blue areas" more cheaply through multilateral arm-twisting by the Bretton Woods institutions than through direct coercion by the U.S. state and its military. As a result, the United States has created a dilemma of its own hegemonic power: by forcing the World Bank to become subservient to its political interests, the United States undermines the multilateral character and personality of the Bank, which the Bank needs in order to maintain its legitimacy and spread its agenda worldwide. Yet without control over the Bank and IMF, the United States' brand of market fundamentalism would lose sway, as not only its borrowers but even European and Japanese states find this ideology offensive, and the United States might then consider pulling its support from these institutions. Without U.S. support, the World Bank and IMF could disappear into the dustbin of history. In sum, Wade argues, "the Bank would be a better development agency if the U.S.—both the federal government and American-based NGOs—had less control over it" (Wade 2001).

Throughout his recent writings on the Bank, Wade emphasizes what other critics have also demonstrated: the Bank is an extremely arrogant institution that commits more egregious mistakes the more it expands its scope and aim in response to criticism (Finnemore 1997; Pincus and Winters 2002). Wade and others call for a trimmed-down development bank driven by sharp and flexible development models that come from "successful" polities besides the United States, such as South Korea, Taiwan, Japan, and countries in Western Europe. The Bank could learn from these recent success stories to modernize its own development agenda.

Whereas Wade's strength is his ability to demonstrate the hubris of the Bank's U.S.-centered policies, he falls short in explaining the political economy of the Bank's work. He understands hegemony as the intricate power plays inside and between Bank headquarters and the corridors of power in Washington. But the World Bank as a global institution can thrive only if its hegemonic power can be maintained through practices outside of Washington as well, in a wide variety of social arenas and borrowing state agencies. Moreover, the Bank's most important clients are not residents of Washington, even if their lobbyists might work there. They are multinational firms located around the world, firms that depend on the Bank to mobilize resources for, and generate laws to promote, capital accumulation in the "undervalued" South. When Wade dismisses the "governance, participation, environment" agenda of the Bank as conjured by a narrow constellation of U.S.-based NGOs that ignore the value of economics and economic growth as the catalyst for poverty alleviation in the South

(Wade 2001), he misses the important role of the Bank's "civil-society agenda" in creating political consent and ensuring that civil-society actors gain ground, albeit only within the parameters set by this institution. Moreover, by ignoring the central role the World Bank plays in enlarging the scope for global capital accumulation, Wade underplays the significance of the World Bank in the making of the highly inequitable global economy.

Indeed, Wade and other development advocates do not seriously consider the connection between relatively stable growth rates in the North and the lack of growth in the South, except in terms of "good" models of development that capital-poor countries should emulate. But how can Zimbabwe emulate South Korea, for example, when the latter's postwar growth was predicated on the tremendously privileged status afforded it by the United States, with its massive flow of capital for geopolitical reasons (the war against communism in Asia) and the subsequent inflow of Japanese capital for Japan's regional expansion (Amsden 1994; Hart-Landsberg 1993; Lie 1998)? By contrast, Zimbabwe, like many other no-growth states, has played a much different role in the global political economy based on its historical location in the world system. While Korea's economy was blossoming, Zimbabwe was pushing Europe out of southern Africa and fighting U.S.-backed counter-insurgents, as well as supporting the struggle against apartheid in South Africa (Bond 1998; Moore 2000). These political and military efforts did not endear Zimbabwe to Western European countries or the United States. For us to reduce our analysis of different trajectories to good or bad development models completely elides these and other historically distinct reasons behind differences.

In general, it is naive for development scholars and specialists to speak of the gains of global economic integration from one side of their mouths, and then speak of national economies as being the product of domestic models constructed by national actors on the other. Such a position denies the ongoing dialectic of localized and transnationalized politics, as well as the realities of a global political economy characterized by vast power inequities. Markets, by this thinking, are national in character and are most successful when they are left alone or gently prodded by entrepreneurially oriented but noninterventionist states. In this modernization worldview, each country becomes an isolated case, hardly rubbing shoulders with others except in trade or war. What fanciful world is this? As I will show in this book, fundamental links between countries within the North-South world system are made invisible through the everyday discursive practices of development, such that today development is still interpreted as a gift of the North and any specific failures are attributed to the shortcomings of leaders or cultures of the South, reductively assumed to be mired in corruption and irrationality. The occasional failure emanating from the North—disastrous projects of the World Bank, Enron-like corporate corruption, and U.S. abuses of power—are reduced to institutional idiosyncrasies and discrete irrationalities. This double standard has deep colonial roots, and it profoundly affects our capacity to analyze the project of development and locate it within the larger political economy. As long as we perpetuate the claims that there is no connection between increased poverty in the South and increased wealth accumulation in the North, and that such global institutions as the World Bank are composed of mere technocratic experts offering transhistorical truths to those who lack know-how, experience, and skills, we are merely retelling imperial-modernization myths.

## POSTDEVELOPMENT SCHOLARSHIP

Not all development scholars share the assumptions and world-view of the modernization model; indeed, there are many alternative analytic frameworks. In recent years, one set of development observers has produced a highly influential canon that can be called the "postdevelopment" literature.[5] Led by such Southern and Northern intellectuals as Arturo Escobar, Majid Rahnema, Gustavo Esteva, Vandana Shiva, and Wolfgang Sachs, the postdevelopment view makes a persuasive argument that since World War II and the creation of the Bretton Woods accords, development has emerged as a singular, top-down project of institutionalization, professionalization, and domination by Northern states, Northern capital, and professional experts (Escobar 1995; Sachs 1992).

Starting from an anticolonial perspective on the history of colonialism and successive regimes, postdevelopment scholars suggest that the World Bank's sixty-year history reflects a seamless and self-expanding venture that started in the West and spread throughout "the rest." Whereas the Washington Consensus/modernization scholars interpret this perpetual expansion of development as (imperfectly) paving the road for Southern progress and improvement, postdevelopment scholars argue that the project of development is linked to large structural forces within the world system that produce wealth and poverty. These social inequities become masked and/or legitimized through "development talk," a series of discursive strategies that explain development failures as the result of cultural, psychological, and biological traits of Southern populations. Consequently, some of the most powerful actors in development are the experts who invent and disseminate new idioms and knowledge that enable forms of domination to become normalized within civil society. Development, therefore, becomes interpreted as both a set of institutions (e.g., capitalist markets, global organizations) and discourses (i.e., fighting poverty through capital investment) that combine to engender and legitimatize the highly exploitative social relations between the world's wealthy and the poor.

As a sweeping critique of Western-imposed institutions of modernity, development, and progress, the postdevelopment scholarship is enormously effective. Indeed, no one who has read these writings should ever be so naive again as to think of development as some gift of charity or neutral act of technology transfer. From Esteva to Escobar, these scholars stress the power dynamics and assumptions that permeate this apparent "gift" from the West. In emphasizing how the North imposes its will on the South, exercising power from top to bottom and from core to periphery, these scholars construct a historical narrative of inevitable and unidirectional expansion. In this highly deterministic history, we lose the sense of a variegated landscape with diverse sites of production, resistance, instability, and political opportunity. With such an imposing history, it is hard to see spatial and temporal unevenness, historical ruptures and structural crisis, or alternative politics and social change. Simply put, the postdevelopment literature makes the imposition of domination sound so simple; it is like a steamroller running roughshod over the third world with no one in the driver's seat and nothing to stop it. In this sense, the postdevelopment literature shares a certain metanarrative reading of history with that of the development boosters even as the former demands that development itself be discarded. To the question "from where will radical social change arise?" they give a truncated answer: new social movements composed of people excluded by the modernization project of development. But is it really possible to speak of alternatives that arise from people who stand outside North-South development relations, and who, they suggest, reject all aspects of development? After all, as we shall see, development as a discourse has been rallied for very different political projects, from taming the rebels of colonial rule to supporting independence movements throughout the South. Understanding development within its uneven historical and cultural contexts is essential for a critical analysis of it and its alternatives.

## A Third Way: An Analytics of the "Terrain of the Conjunctural"

Missing from these perspectives is a narrative of the actual production of development hegemony, the contested sites and the tussle over specific policies and interventions that would give us a clearer sense of the historical conjunctures and political volatilities of hegemony making. For a more complete picture, we need to develop an approach that enables us to see these sites of encounter in the South and the North as being filled with diverse groups of conflicted people (Cooper and Packard 1997; Crush 1995; Moore 2003; Peet and Watts 2004; Young 2003). People do not simply agree or consent, or fully stand with or against universal notions of progress, development, and modernization. They do not build up the scientific case for a tropical forest highway or pour the concrete for a megadam without some reflection, reservation, or fight. If we always assume its success or failure without first looking at how hegemony gets constituted, we lose all sense of why people offer their consent without force, and why they do not. We lose the ability to discern where the political openings are, the sites and spaces where dominant structures get constituted, how people try to subvert them, and from where alternatives arise. It is only within the specific interstices of hegemony's production that we can observe concrete organic struggles over power. In fact, we find these terrains of struggle within the space of development only if we understand the project of development as embedded within the uneven and contradictory history of capitalist development. By offering a few observations on the history of the World Bank, I seek to show the value of a critical ethnographic approach that emphasizes historical conjunctures and the analysis of specific production processes (of commodities, knowledge, environments, capital, and subjects) in order to reveal vulnerabilities and contingencies (Hall 1996; Hart 2003). In sum, what is missing from most scholarship on development is an explanation of the processes by which its hegemony and counterhegemony are constituted, producing the whole spectrum of political and cultural closures and opportunities—from the extremes of societywide approval to major resistance—with full understanding that most social activity occurs in the spaces in between.

## REREADING DEVELOPMENT HISTORY

To many scholars who study the World Bank and development, Harry Truman's 1949 inaugural speech was a critical moment in the invention of the contemporary development project, for in it the newly elected Truman appealed to the American public to solve the problems of the "underdeveloped areas" of the postwar world (Escobar 1995; Sachs 1992; Saldana-Portillo 2003). "Greater production is the key to prosperity and peace," Truman declared. Hence, "we should make available to the peace-loving peoples the benefits of our store of technical knowledge" (Escobar 1995, p. 4). Supposedly, the Truman doctrine sparked a new era of North-South relations via the project of development. But in designating this speech as a sign of a dramatic shift in global politics, development scholars typically ignore the terrains development had traversed up to that point, such that these words could ring true. By taking seriously development as a colonial and capitalist project, steeped in conflict and convulsions, we can see that development practices were always changing and always volatile and that development as an ideology was produced by different actors for different reasons amidst historically specific political projects. In other words, most approaches to development (with the World Bank as its global trailblazer) fail to explain development as shaped as much by historical and geographic contingencies and ruptures as by continuities and inevitabilities. It is from an understanding of these shifts that we begin to see how and why development power proliferates and gets subverted. By emphasizing the historical conjunctures, we can begin to understand—and imagine—possible alternatives.

One place to start is with the observation that development under colonialism was never simply an enlightened proposition but rather a set of strategic tools designed to quell heightened political tensions and uprisings in the colonies by bringing in new forms of colonial rule that bridged new economic liberal policies with—in some cases—the colonial cultural politics of trusteeship. For example, in the mid-1800s, the British were forced to contend with an unruly and rebellious Indian subcontinent. John Stuart Mill, an employee and ideologue of the East India Company, argued that India needed to be ruled by an "incorruptible" imperial corps exercising trusteeship in order to create the conditions under which development (e.g., prosperity, progress, civilization) could occur (Cowen and Shenton 1996). After a steady stream of rebellions against colonial officers, factory owners, and landlords, peaking during the 1857 Indian Mutiny, in which the East India Company had no choice but to transfer control to the British crown and military (with brutal consequences for Indians), Mill's principle of trusteeship through development became the basis for the new administration.

Yet it should not be forgotten that rapid capitalist industrialization in the mid-1800s also squeezed European peasants and small producers, igniting widespread resistance and sabotage throughout Western Europe. In England, this strife produced the Luddites, radicals, trade unionists, Chartists, democrats, and utopian socialists (Cowen and Shenton 1996; Shenton 1995). These incendiary times also generated some of the core tenets and development institutions of the day, namely, economic liberalism and social welfarism. In England, the death of the Speenhamland period (1795–1834) and the Poor Law reform of 1834 coincided with an industrial working-class movement from which came a flurry of demands for protective factory laws and social legislation (Burawoy 2003; Burawoy 2000). The minds of "Bentham and Burke, Godwin and Malthus, Ricardo and Marx, Robert Owen and John Stuart Mill, Darwin and Spencer" (Polanyi 1957) turned to a new anguish of concern about the "great transformation" that was occurring. This anguish provoked what Karl Polanyi called the "birth of society," the social space that required active intervention and development by government in order to survive the violent tumult of industrial capitalist development (Polanyi 1957). Development by government unfolded differently over space and time, but it always invoked new management roles for imperial state institutions in both the metropole and the colonies. In short, regimes of development (Ludden 1992) were constantly being reshaped though political struggle. Moreover, that which surfaced in the colonies cannot be understood in isolation from those regimes that emerged in the core—such as economic liberalism and social protection laws—as they resulted from overlapping imperial-colonial tensions.

The predecessor to the current development policies of economic neoliberalism, safety-net welfarism, good governance, free trade, global integration, and investments in "civil society" can be found within the context of highly explosive and violent colonial-metropole relations. New idioms did not come "from the brow of the colonial officer" but from the crossfire of mass rebellions and violent state responses (Cooper 1997). That the ideologues of the World Bank and the Washington Consensus mobilize similar types of arguments and rationales as the East India Company did one hundred and fifty years earlier should give us pause. It should strengthen our resolve to understand both the particular historical violence and the au currant common sense in which development gets enacted and proliferates.

In contrast to this colonial context, during the twentieth century and entangled with World War II, development looked very different. At certain moments and places, it was both a device for weakened imperial powers to extricate themselves from the colonies and a tool for anticolonial liberatory politics among the movements pushing the imperial powers out. In India, development planning continued to be the primary political discourse in the years following independence (Bose 1997), but instead of merely playing out existing British-fueled discourses, the political field became more diverse, with anticolonial, autarkic-Gandhian, nationalist-socialist, and other political positions filling the void. In many African countries at the time of independence, "the notion that seemed to envelop every ambition, practice, and discourse was unquestionably that of development." According to Mamadou Diouf, the term "was synonymous with modernization, cultural reconquest and renewal, economic progress, and the achievement of social equity; development implied the construction of nation and citizen as much as the reconstruction of the economy" (Diouf 1997, p. 291).

Liberation movements produced their own powerful development discourses as they sought to hold Europe accountable to its broad claims of universal rights, making these rights the basis for extracting certain types of independence and justice from the modern world system (Cooper and Packard 1997; James 1963).

These and other historical insights into the changing regimes of development should eclipse the facile view of development as either an obvious and rational technocratic plan or, in contrast, as the subjugation of "docile" third world subjects by unchanging Northern organizations like the East India Company or the World Bank. Indeed, the political space of development generated through relations with the Bank also become key sites of counterhegemonic mobilization, even if, as has been the case of some revolutionary movements, they may embrace Western-inspired ideas of development in ways that may undermine radical social-justice agendas (Saldana-Portillo 2003).

REINTERPRETING THE ROLE
OF THE WORLD BANK

We need not repeatedly invoke the colonial past when inquiring about the World Bank of the present. Rather, critical readings of colonial history suggest that when we consider from where World Bank power erupts and wanes, we need to pay close attention to the "terrain of the conjunctural" (Gramsci,

Hoare, and Nowell-Smith 1971) and consider the actual practices that make certain development regimes hegemonic while
subjugating and silencing others (Hart 2004). From this perspective, we can see that typical approaches to the World Bank
are only partially correct. It is true that one of the biggest
changes in recent development history occurred through the
creation of the Bretton Woods institutions (the World Bank
and IMF) in 1944, but at that time, the World Bank was not primarily engaged in what many assume to be the "bread and
butter" work of the contemporary world of development, that
is, investing in poverty reduction and supporting the "basic
needs" of the world's poor. Contrary to conventional wisdom,
in its beginning, the World Bank principally lent money to
Northern countries to rebuild their war-torn infrastructure
at home and abroad, in their former or existing colonies (see
chapter 2).

When the U.S. government introduced interest-free
loans and grants to Europe through its Marshall Plan, the
World Bank was forced to switch gears and start lending to rebuild infrastructure in Europe's (ex-)colonies. Typically, the
Bank channeled its capital through the same European-based
colonial banks, using Western currencies and hiring European
and U.S. firms to rebuild the railways, ports, and mines. Hence,
in the post–World War II era, the World Bank played a pivotal
role in the global economy by introducing new actors—the
U.S. Treasury Department, U.S. investment firms and banks,
and U.S. contractors—into the center of existing inequitable
trade and production relations between Europe and the third
world. Not coincidentally, in the first decade after the war, the
United States controlled the highest proportion of the vote in
the World Bank as well as the highest percentage of foreign
procurement from the Bank's loans (i.e., U.S. firms received

the contracts for projects in borrowing countries). After all, this so-called global institution did most if its business transactions with clients working just a stone's throw from its Washington, D.C., headquarters. By agreement between the United States and European leaders, the World Bank's president would always be a U.S. citizen, usually a power broker from Wall Street, while the IMF's president would always be West European. At the start, the original Bank staff was composed mostly of colonial officers from Europe's overseas offices who were reanointed as the midcentury's transnational experts on North-South trade, capital investments, and rule.

In spite of these particular details of history, the literature on the World Bank emphasizes one theme when highlighting the Bank's origins: poverty alleviation (Caufield 1996; Kapur, Webb, and Lewis 1997; Pincus and Winters 2002; Rich 1994). During the Bank's early history, however, poverty was never on the agenda. It never presented development as a process of working with the rural poor or directing its capital investments to social upliftment. In the 1950s, that would have been a highly suspect claim and an "irrational" endeavor. The early World Bank invested in capital projects to rebuild old colonial infrastructure for its main clients and constituents, which were New York and London banks and investment firms and the West's capital good sectors. In those days, few expected the World Bank, based in Washington and run by Wall Street bankers, to be concerned with the downtrodden and impoverished. So, then, from where did such expectations arise?

The idea of fighting poverty with large capital interventions came from the historical conjuncture of a number of related events: the bloody and costly U.S. war in Indochina; the crash of the U.S. economy; the yearning of capital-flush Western Europe, Japan, and OPEC nations to find investment opportunities outside of the U.S. economy; a revolutionary spirit spreading through the global South; and a world crisis in the "international food order" spurred not by food shortages but by a flood of cheap U.S. food exports (Friedmann 1982). This momentous conjuncture became a great opportunity for Robert McNamara, the new World Bank president, to harness the North's capital surpluses and the South's economic woes into a new development regime that helped transform the World Bank into a global "defender of the world's poor." As I will show in chapter 2, a completely different set of historical circumstances would precipitate the rise (and fall) of subsequent development regimes, that is, structural adjustment and green neoliberalism.

## THE ROLE OF KNOWLEDGE PRODUCTION

Although by the end of this book it will become abundantly clear that the Bank wields enormous political-economic power in borrowing countries, my emphasis is actually less on pure economic power than on the complementary power of its knowledge-producing activities. I think that the way the Bank exerts its power through lending is fairly straightforward. Much less understandable is how such power and authority becomes strengthened and normalized over time. To grapple with this question requires a thorough interrogation of the ways in which common sense is produced and how the terrain of ideas on which the "practical consciousness" of people is actually formed. "Common sense is not rigid and immobile," Gramsci once wrote, "but is continually transforming itself, enriching itself with scientific ideas and with philosophical opinions which have entered ordinary life. Common sense creates the folklore of the future, that is as a relatively rigid phase of popular knowledge at a given place and time" (Gramsci 1971, p. 362n5). We should not take for granted popular beliefs and scientific ideas because they merely exist in the life of the mind; on the contrary, they are themselves material forces that have a direct impact on the world in which we live and which we struggle to change.

So we need to ask: how do new society-wide projects, such as the projects of modernization, development, or neoliberal capitalism, emerge and become common sense? Although these society-wide projects may reflect the interests of specific elite social classes, they are made dominant and sensible through processes of what Gramsci called "civil hegemony," or the dispersal of power through civil society, such as through schooling; religious life; scientific, cultural and voluntary organizations; and popular forms of communication and media. These knowledge- and idea-producing processes do not, however, occur simply to legitimate or make more palatable the sour-tasting effects of, say, neoliberal capitalism. On the contrary, the realms of knowledge production and political economics are mutually constitutive and codependent. The World Bank's latest regime of green neoliberalism did not arise from a corporate or bankers' plot, but through a series of events and practices centered on professionals working in government, firms, NGOs, and the scientific community.

Therefore, we need to focus on the particular sites where these ideas, concepts, policies, and loans get debated, crafted, and challenged. These production sites exist where these diverse and dispersed professionals meet, and they together generate the world of development without which the World Bank could not exist. Hence, a highly volatile and tense dynamic has emerged between the Bank and its offspring, and the Bank today has become much more dependent on its knowledge-production capacities than its ability to raise capital. The Bank has never had trouble raising money; its trouble has always been in lending it. To drum up continuous business in a circumspect world, the Bank depends on its capacity to generate the ideas of new global problems as well as on its own global expertise, new mechanisms for intervention as well as new reasons for countries to borrow, new development subjects and subjectivities as well as new forms of its own legitimation. The Bank works hard to create its own demand through the production of new transnationalized institutions, networks, norms, beliefs, and professionals (who have become a class in itself). In this odd space of "transnational society," some government agencies and civil servants can participate in a potentially lucrative neoliberal agenda even while their peers in government and society do not. The future of the World Bank lies in the balance between these countervailing positions on the ground, between those benefiting from and those losing out to neoliberal activities. In these places where the Bank plies its trade, knowledge production has become a highly important and yet fragile affair, one that matters much more to the Bank than it would like to acknowledge.

How did neoliberalism become so convincing, so quickly, worldwide? One cannot assume that a sea change in philosophy conjured up by a handful of leaders in Washington would so simply become the rule of law around the world. On the contrary, the World Bank's sponsorship of a neoliberal agenda occurred because it was able to mobilize a well-financed institutional architecture that was already in place, with people and agencies well situated to participate. The evolution of the Bank's knowledge-production machinery occurred in fits and starts; in the 1950s and 1960s, the Bank focused primarily on training a small group of elites, some of whom became prime ministers, ministry heads, and senior Bank and IMF staff. During the early period when infrastructural investment was central, the Bank helped nurture national-level development banks and quasi-state electricity and power boards, often training their directors. Under Robert McNamara (1968–81), the Bank's efforts expanded rapidly into the agricultural and industrial sectors and generated a whole new cadre of state bureaucrats (Kapur, Webb, and Lewis 1997). McNamara's Bank funded a new scientific-bureaucratic infrastructure in borrowing countries to produce the knowledge necessary to support its loans; these investments fueled the growth of national agencies, institutes, universities, and a burgeoning class of professionals whose budgets and livelihoods depended on development agency funding. As development institutions grew in size and stature, so did the roles of the knowledge being produced, the knowledge producers, and the "underdeveloped" social groups that were being scrutinized in development's name.

## DEVELOPMENT'S CONTRADICTIONS

After a decade of the "McNamara revolution," the contradictions inherent in large-scale development lending and policy making became manifest. The World Bank's program of capital-intensive development forced large populations off the land, out of the forests, and away from their fisheries, alienating them from the ecological conditions of production (Caufield 1996; Kapur, Webb, and Lewis 1997; O'Connor 1998; O'Connor 1994; Pincus and Winters 2002; Rich 1994). In Indonesia, the Bank-sponsored Transmigration Project forcibly dispossessed hundreds of thousands of ethnic minorities and destroyed huge areas of wetlands and tropical forest. In the Brazilian Amazon, Bank-financed highways and timber, mining, and agricultural

colonization schemes sped up deforestation, river contamination, and the death of forest-dwelling indigenous peoples. Large
dams, power projects, and industrial agriculture had similar
effects in the Philippines, India, Thailand, and elsewhere. If
one could find a silver lining in these disastrous clouds, it was
that these projects helped stimulate the formation of mass opposition movements critical of Bank-style development. In
countries (such as Indonesia and the Philippines) where protest against the state was met with murder and torture, protestors targeted supranational "external" actors, such as the World
Bank and the U.S. government. In places where the state was
less brutal to dissenters, communities organized themselves
into an array of activist networks, leading to the flowering of
what has been called the "public sphere" or "civil society." In
sum, on the coattails of highly destructive World Bank interventions a flurry of political activity has emerged, which the
Bank did not intend and could not effectively control.

Meanwhile, capital-poor states were becoming seriously
overextended. They had borrowed dollar-based development
capital in the hopes of producing export-quality commodities,
the income from which could be used to pay back the debt and
reinvest in society. But the glut of World Bank capital pushing
for the export of a handful of commodities—sugars, cooking
oils, grains, cotton, rubber, coffee—helped spark a dramatic
fall in commodity prices (George and Sabelli 1994; McMichael
2004). The millions of people displaced by these projects began
making demands on the state for reparations, protection, jobs,
land, housing, water, and food. Cities swelled with a steady
stream of dispossessed rural producers. The common nomen-
clature describing the ill effects of this period of development—
an accumulating "debt crisis" of national-level finances—does
not adequately capture the magnitude of the devastation
wrought upon large segments of society.

After the explosion of capital investments during Mc-Namara's "Basic Needs" era, the World Bank's job became overwhelming. Its work became heavily criticized around the world, leading to a temporary legitimation crisis. And yet, even while the Bank was at the center of disapproval, development remained a vibrant if disputatious discourse and industry. A creative effervescence sprouted from development's "failures," helping to generate new actors and networks, from influential aid agencies to NGOs. Whereas in 1970, less than .2 percent of overseas development assistance was channeled through development NGOs, by 1995, the U.S. government alone was channeling 30 percent of its aid funds through NGOs (Donini 1995). The World Bank learned to work with, and even cultivate, NGOs, hiring them as consultants to conduct project-related research or to help implement and improve World Bank projects (Nelson 1995). These new opportunities for NGOs and academics enabled them to get off the sidelines and become involved in expanding the business of development.

As it became more commonplace for the international development institutions to hire NGOs as consultants and contractors and as some NGO staff began to feel less adversarial toward the Bank, these trends became highly divisive. Those NGOs that worked with the Bank prospered appreciably, while many of the most vocal NGOs either refused to take on this role or, if they remained critical, were rarely rehired. Most of the scholarly literature explains this proliferating world of NGOs within a static analytical frame in which NGOs are situated within a middle space of "civil society," separated by the imagined walls of the "state," on the one side, and the "market" and corporate actors, on the other (Florini 2000; Fox and Brown 1998; Frey et al. 1984). Yet as I show in chapters 5 and 6, the world of development is one where individuals often wear multiple hats and move across agencies and structural loca-

tions. Indeed, in the early 2000s, the Bank created an employee
exchange program with firms, NGOs, and its own staff, so that
one now finds staff from Monsanto and Cargill in the Bank's
agricultural division and NGO staff sharing projects and review board assignments with Bank staff.[6]

## THE BIRTH OF THE ENVIRONMENTAL STATE

In sum, the Bank's achievements in the world of transnational
networking have been truly remarkable but hardly remarked
upon. When a wide range of actors, such as World Bank lawyers,
U.S. management firm staff, and NGO scientists, contribute to
rewriting property rights laws, redesigning state agencies and
retraining their staff, and reconfiguring local production relations in borrowing countries, it seems obvious that we need to
rethink our old assumptions about the nation-state and its
"public" employees. Focusing on the development practices
emerging from a "greened" World Bank, we find the proliferation of hybridized state actors who have become responsible for
the fundamental activities of natural resource management,
and yet who are often employed by agents outside the borrowing state, such as U.S. AID, the World Bank, the World Conservation Union (IUCN), and even PricewaterhouseCoopers.

These hybrid state actors are incorporating a set of green
neoliberal practices that circulate through transnational pro-
fessional-class networks and help produce ways of valuing nature as well as ways of valuing rights of access to environments
and natural resources. They also staff newly formed agencies
within national boundaries and in the world system. Hence, as
I argue in chapter 5, the World Bank's practices are facilitating
the birth of environmental states in the global South, marked
by new roles for state actors and new forms of legality and eco-

rationality that have fragmented, stratified, and unevenly trans-nationalized Southern states, state actors, and state power. Environmental states are characterized by government agencies that are no longer run solely by nation-based citizens who have risen through the civil-servant ranks. Some are employees of PricewaterhouseCoopers or of a British engineering firm; others may be paid from a particular development project rather than from the typically small pot for bureaucratic salaries. Some government employees work alongside Europeans in air-conditioned computerized offices whereas others remain at their old typewriters trying to find a second job to supplement their shrinking (neoliberalized) government salaries. Some receive overseas training in neoliberal practices of state management while their job security becomes linked to the longevity of a particular eco-development project, thus encouraging consent on controversial projects receiving World Bank or bilateral financing.

The idea of the environment has risen in official discourse but the meaning may be completely foreign and may reflect better the wishes and paradigms emerging from the wave of privatization policies sweeping through governments, especially those highly indebted to the World Bank, IMF, and private Northern banks. Environmental states are defining such public goods as river basins, forests, wetlands, and aquifers as undervalued in an effort to use natural resources as the catalyst to integrate countries into the global economy and to move out of debt. In the process, the ideological and practical differences between finance and environmental ministries have narrowed appreciably. By successfully restructuring environmental agencies in its borrowing countries, the World Bank has implemented a decade-long plan of the "EPA-ization" of ministries of the environment, forests, agriculture, mining,

land management, and water. This has become a perversely
top-down undemocratic reorganization that reflects an unrealistic image of the origins of the U.S. Environmental Protection Agency (EPA), an agency born from sustained social-
movement activism of the 1960s and 1970s. (Ironically, this
EPA-ization process has occurred at the same time the EPA in
the United States has been completely gutted by domestic neoliberal forces of a different ilk, leaving it as a faint shadow of its
former self.)

One result of these sweeping changes has been the rise in
a new global water initiative, the "Water for All" policy. As a response to the horrible reality that 40 percent of the world's
population has no access to clean water, over the past decade,
seemingly arising from nowhere, water privatization has become the singular solution of choice by most global institutions. In chapter 6 I focus on this phenomenon, asking the
question: how did so many leaders in governments, global
agencies, NGOs, and the scientific community so quickly embrace this particular water policy, using the same language and
arguments in major policy forums in Kyoto, The Hague, Johannesburg, Casablanca, and elsewhere?

This new water policy has temporarily transformed the
way water is supplied in the global South. State responsibilities
are being downgraded from a provider of an essential public
good to a mere regulator of a privatized commodity. The poor
majority is being asked to become a "good customer" and yet
is unable to afford the newly commodified goods, which is ag-
gravating public health and sanitation problems. At its worst,
the state becomes an absentee landlord and the poor become
temporary tenants in their own countries—a global phenomenon that exemplifies David Harvey's notion of "accumulation
by dispossession" (Harvey 2003). The new overseers of land,

water, energy, and other basic public goods have moved off-shore, far from the civil-society spaces that the green neoliberal regime of development in rhetoric promotes. Not coincidentally, from 2000 to 2003, most World Bank and IMF loans to countries on the African continent were conditional on the agreement by borrowing governments to have a privatization water policy on tap (Grusky 2002; Hall, Bayliss, and Lobina 2002). Today, a highly indebted country cannot get a loan from a foreign bank or multilateral institution without first proposing a national privatization plan for the sale of public goods, such as water, medical care, and electricity to large Western corporations, such as Bechtel, Vivendi, and Suez.

## A Fragile Hegemony

Privatizing water has become one of the most inflammatory and controversial neoliberal policies yet, with mass mobilizations rising up against it in South Africa, Ghana, Bolivia, Argentina, the Philippines, and even France (headquarters to the two largest global water firms). From a Gramscian perspective, hegemony is a concept that points to exercises of power made up of both force and consent, the latter of which reflects a "negotiated compromise [that] replaces irreconcilable interests" (Burawoy 2003, p. 225). The central questions of hegemony—how is it constituted? whose interests does it represent? how does it mask power?—help us think about how green neoliberalism becomes palatable even to those who might otherwise be opposed to it, such as environmentally or socially oriented nongovernmental organizations and social movements. Hegemony can occur within the realm of production, as it did in the case of the mid-twentieth-century U.S. "Fordist" factory regime in which higher wages and a new consumer culture brokered the destruction of trade unionism. It can also emerge within such civil-society institutions as public education, mass communications, and religious and civic organizations. Gramsci understood the expansion of civil society and its layered interweavings of popular organizations and networks as an arena in which modern class formation becomes articulated and class struggle becomes contained and absorbed, especially in its close connections to the mediating "expansive state" (Burawoy 2003). It is within civil society that dominant classes often make their values and interests those of the larger society, such that popular consent becomes constituted through everyday practices of social interaction. Gramsci's idea of hegemony pushes us both to think seriously about the motives behind the current "rise of civil society" in the agendas of such disparate actors as chambers of commerce, development NGOs, and multilateral development banks and to interrogate the new realms that have become common sense in the world of development, and which have overtaken or redefined local-regional political agendas.

For the moment, the World Bank has successfully made nonnegotiable certain demands for global normative standards on questions of state restructuring, good governance, an activated civil society, and environmental sustainability—standards that are constituted within the parameters of a highly authoritative, hydra-headed, and capital-driven World Bank. Yet because we find so many other social actors far from the Bank's payroll ascribing to the same truths and tenets, we need to understand the World Bank's hegemonic power within a context of numerous other social institutions and political-economic projects, as I seek to do here.

At the same time that World Bank hegemony reflects a successful degree of mastery of popular and elite consent that inculcates a moral and social authority worldwide, it remains fragile. As I will show in chapter 2, many times in its sixty-year history the Bank has almost disappeared into obscurity due to disinterest from investors and borrowers, trenchant protest from social activists, and a mountain of bad and unrepayable loans—all of which have threatened the World Bank's ability to raise capital and its political authority to lend. Although the Bank is not a private capital-accumulating firm, its main source of capital since the early 1970s (besides loan interest repayment from its Southern borrowers) has been the global bonds market, not Western taxpayers. And bond investors are notoriously squeamish and never loyal when it comes to a threat to the rate of return on their investments. There is no reason to think that investors could not retreat in a flash from World Bank bonds if they felt that their profits were being threatened. Confidence is the Achilles' heel for firms that depend on publicly traded stocks and bonds, and the same is true for the bond-dependent World Bank. If a cluster of African or Latin American leaders were to refuse to repay what many Southern country citizens consider odious and unfair World Bank and IMF debts, market confidence in what are now "AAA" World Bank bonds would plummet and access to capital (and therefore power) for the Bank could easily vanish.[7]

Nor is such pressure purely hypothetical. As many borrowing countries are forced to pay back to the World Bank and IMF in interest alone more than they invest in public health, welfare, and education, some national election campaigns in the South are focusing on debt repayment as a threat to national sovereignty. Joblessness, deep social spending cuts, privatization of public utilities and goods, landlessness and the failure of land distribution programs, and a newly liberalized capitalist landscape dominated by foreign corporations are all being attributed, rightly or wrongly, to the power of the World Bank. Indeed, many political elites in the global South invoke the World Bank as "an enemy of the nation" as a way to unify the country against an external adversary, even as these same state elites continue to tap into the Bank's bountiful credit accounts and buy public industries sold on the auction block at bargain-basement prices.

At the nonelite grassroots, millions of people have mobilized to challenge the status quo and produce alternative political agendas, as I discuss in this book's conclusion. Even before the sleeping giant Western media awoke to the antiglobalization politics at the WTO meetings in Seattle in late 1999, social movements in the global South were hitting the streets en masse to protest a series of deprivations imposed on them by the neoliberal policies of the World Bank, IMF, and WTO. While media in the West presented the "battle of Seattle" as a major event, yet often dismissing protestors as the misguided middle class wanting to deny development to the poor, mass movements were energetically taking to the streets in Ecuador, Thailand, Bolivia, Argentina, Haiti, South Korea, South Africa, India, Brazil, and Mexico. At great personal risk, people have organized against water privatization, job loss and wage cuts, police crackdowns, and the loss of national sovereignty due to government commitments to the World Bank and IMF. Twenty million Indians walked off the job one day and half of South Africa's workforce went out on strike on another, demanding that their governments repudiate their subordinate position with the World Bank and IMF (Bond 2000).

These movements represent a cross section of people challenging development authorities on issues of right-to-livelihood, military repression, environmental destruction, and the privatization of natural resources and public goods.

Broad-based coalitions of various shapes and sentiments have formed over the past decade, bringing together people from the Annamite Mountains to the Mekong Delta, from Cochabamba to Buenos Aires. They get tremendous support from transnational networks, fighting on multiple fronts against megadams, human rights abuses, genetically modified food imports, corruption and cronyism, and development-led indebtedness. In sum, just as certain arenas of national civil societies have become dominated by neoliberal hopes and desires, other arenas have become hothouses for transformational politics with limitless potential. They are engaged in a series of "wars of position," to use Gramsci's phrase, which are "not so much a matter of creating movements outside the hegemonic order but rather on its terrain, radicalizing the meaning of democracy, appropriating the market, democratizing sovereignty, and expanding human rights" (Burawoy 2000).

In the face of seemingly intractable global hegemony, the World Bank remains extremely vulnerable, which might explain why the institution currently spends more on public relations than it does on research (Finnemore 1997; Kapur and Culpeper 2000; Kapur 2002; Pincus and Winters 2002; Rich 2002; Standing 2000). Although the World Bank does not exist as an independent actor, but only as one that is deeply embedded in many institutions located across the global political economy, it could crash as quickly as the Iron Curtain or the Southeast Asian and Latin American currencies did. If it does, it may become a world-historical event for which there are few parallels. I hope that my ethnographic exploration of World Bank power reveals not only how this powerful global institution has constructed fragile hegemony, but also the possibilities for emerging counterhegemonic forces and political opportunities for profound social change.

# II

# The Rise of the Bank

*The New World had to be yoked, and kept yoked, to the Old*
*World, if the latter were to enjoy durable peace and prosperity.*
—*John Maynard Keynes, 1946, personal correspondence*
*(Skidelsky 2002)*

As World Bank/IMF officials gathered in Washington, D.C., for the 1995 annual meetings in the face of an ailing global economy the mood was anything but grim. The meetings marked the fifty-first anniversary of the Bretton Woods conference, which led to the establishment of these institutions and the Bank's stewardship of the global development project. But the party had its gate-crashers—an energetic global activist network that stormed downtown Washington with an impressive "50 Years Is Enough" campaign. The protesters successfully undermined the anniversary celebration and shocked the complacent Bank and IMF leadership. Over time they have played a major role in the reforming of the World Bank and giving shape to its next development regime. Inside and outside this oppositional campaign, a broad range of observers identified Bank policies as the catalyst for the collapse of economies throughout Latin America, Africa, and Asia, and for the two "lost decades" during which whole regions of the world suffered from substantial backsliding in per capita income, GDP, and health and social indicators. Representatives of the displaced, aggrieved, and angry stakeholders of Bank/IMF projects had crossed oceans to come speak out at street protests, teach-ins, and workshops scattered throughout the city. From their perspective, we should have all been wearing black. Few officials and delegates at the Bank/IMF annual meetings, however, seemed to agree.

The majority of those attending the annual meetings were not members of the development community one learns about in development studies courses or through the media. They were not associated with church-based charities or food aid NGOs. None spoke the language of charity or of desperately poor third worlders. There was no discourse of resuscitation or emergency aid to avert catastrophe. In fact, they spoke only of business. Packing Washington during the week of the Bank/IMF meetings were the world's central bankers and finance ministers, and they were obviously on a shopping spree. At one hotel, they met with Henry Kissinger, Bill Gates, and the CEOs of Westinghouse, Bechtel, Citicorp, and major banking, insurance, finance, defense and armaments, telecommunications, energy and power, and computer companies. At the main hotel, they had breakfast courtesy of Bear Stearns, Baring Securities International, the Istanbul Stock Exchange, ING Capital, Banco Portugal, and Standard Chartered Bank. Lunch was hosted by Chemical Bank, Creditanstalt-Bankverein, and ABN-AMRO in the Corcoran Gallery of Art and the National Museum of Women in the Arts. In the late afternoon, the official program brought all delegates and guests back to the Sheraton Hotel to listen to the Bank president and IMF managing director officially convene the annual meetings. But by 5 p.m., the early round of cocktail receptions commenced, courtesy of the Bank of Tokyo, Brown Brothers Harriman & Company, Unico Banking Group, Citicorp/Citibank, Arab Banking Corporation, and Bank of America, among others. First Chicago Bank hosted a dinner party at the Meridian House, Morgan Stanley at the Phillips Collection, Chase Manhattan Bank at the Decatur House, and ChinaTrust Commercial Bank at the Twin Oaks. An elite group of high rollers attended a black-tie dinner with J. P. Morgan executives. Later, guests were invited to after-dinner parties, which included the 10 p.m. live show, "Broadway Meets Berlin," hosted by Bankgesellschaft Berlin. Delegates looked exhausted after the first day of the meetings, but there was little to suggest they were anything more than weary revelers.

Running concurrently for the scientific community was a conference sponsored by the National Academy of Sciences (NAS) and World Bank that included Vice President Al Gore; UN Secretary General Boutros Boutros-Ghali (by video); World Bank President James Wolfensohn; Jacques-Yves Cousteau; Harvard Professor E. O. Wilson; Worldwatch Institute President Lester Brown; the director general of World Wildlife Fund, Claude Martin; Mali Prime Minister Ibrahim Boubacar Keita; the administrator of China's National Environmental Protection Agency, Xie Zhenhua; and CEO and chair of Enron Corporation, Rebecca Mark. For three days, in panels and plenaries, scientists and officials from the World Bank, governments, NGOs, universities, research institutes, and private corporations discussed "Effective Financing of Environmentally Sustainable Development" at the prestigious National Academy of Sciences. In his welcome address, the academy's president, Bruce Alberts, announced his gratitude to the World Bank for helping the academy incorporate the concept of *environmentally sustainable development* into its scientific work. The conference was glamorous and upbeat in ways uncommon to the tweedy world of science and academics.

The business of development is a profitable and inclusive one, and the topics discussed at these and other World Bank meetings are not typically hunger or poverty. Whereas most writings on the World Bank claim that some combination of the "poor" borrowing states, Northern aid agencies, and development NGOs are the main constituents and partners of the World Bank, my observations of the Bank's annual meetings lead me to suggest that the actors in the world of development are much more diverse, with powerful ties to familiar for-profit interests. Moreover, there is nothing intrinsic or inevitable about the specific discourses of development the Bank has pursued or its role in the global political economy during its sixty-year history. Most authors assume as inevitable the Bank's rise to prominence as the world's premier global institution, and they take for granted the authority of global institutions in general. By contrast, in this chapter I will explain the political-economic contexts and discursive strategies that helped the Bank to become a globally hegemonic institution by emphasizing the historical conjunctures that others have glossed over —in particular, the phenomenal way that Robert McNamara inserted the World Bank into the global economy as a powerful institutional force. Although historians of the World Bank note the Bank's growth under McNamara, they do not examine the key historic shifts in the global political economy and how the technologies of power/knowledge (Foucault 1990) established under McNamara enabled the Bank to grow and prosper even during difficult times. These technologies have become crucial for the Bank as it tries to maintain its reputation in a world where anti-Bank social movements have gained considerable legitimacy.

Four distinct periods mark the history of the World Bank: the "reluctant Banker" period of 1944–68; the Bank's "rise to power" in the period of 1968–80 during which the calls for "poverty alleviation" and meeting "basic needs" for the "absolute poor" reflected a new rhetorical turn in development; the "debt and adjustment" period of 1980–89; and the "green neoliberal" period from 1989 to the present. This first period was shaped by the absolute control over the Bank by the U.S. Treasury, the State Department, and Wall Street bankers, who were the Bank's main constituents during its early years.[1] These actors were primarily interested in having the Bank lend for bricks-and-mortar types of projects. They kept tight control over Bank expenditures based on conservative banker ethics, except when the State Department insisted that providing support for its cold war allies was more important. Under these constraints and conflicting rationalities, the Bank remained small and ineffectual. During its first two decades, the Bank was unable to articulate a universal project of liberal capitalist development, and as a consequence, it played a very minor role in the realms of development and political economy during its first twenty years.

It was only during the McNamara era (1968-81) that the World Bank emerged as a powerful organization, spurring the creation of a new transnational space that the Bank helped fill with professional networks and discursive regimes of rule, truth, and government. During his thirteen-year reign as World Bank president, Robert McNamara, a former U.S. secretary of defense, converted the Bank into a major transnational institution as well as the world's foremost authority on development. Ironically, the engines of growth for the twin Bretton Woods institutions fired up only after the longstanding Bretton Woods agreement on currency and capital controls failed. As no single institution had before, the World Bank under McNamara facilitated an explosion of financial capital investment in the global South as well as a surfeit of development knowledge, which repositioned development as a global project. By bringing together the ideas of economic growth, social upliftment, and global security, and making it into a "science" backed by World Bank finances, McNamara created a power/knowledge leviathan of a completely new sort. Not a state, not an international agency, not a finance bank, the World Bank became something quite unique in the world—a one-of-a-kind supranational development institution.

After a decade of growth in the 1970s, the Bank's capital, ideas, and institutions set root and flowered in many different forms around the world: national development banks, national development institutes, national centers for agricultural (or green revolution) research, large dams, highways, power plants, mines, and national forestry projects. A major learning initiative sparked by the World Bank, United Nations agencies, and universities in the North fueled studies in development economics, poverty, and the green revolution. This research became meaningful when it was supported by Northern foundations, used by major agro-industrial corporations, and situated in Bank-financed research institutes in borrowing countries. In short time, the Bank's large capital flows into the South were explained in terms of the financing of poverty alleviation, basic needs, and the green revolution. As a consequence of the Bank's well-financed knowledge production machinery, one could find middle-class people almost anywhere with an opinion about how to help poor peasants in India, Brazil, or Kenya.

In no small part because of the World Bank's metamorphosis during the 1970s and early 1980s, development power/knowledge writ large became common sense. The Bank's role as global economic and political manager became more entrenched during the 1980s, when the Third World debt crisis it helped to create further reduced the political autonomy of borrowing countries while increasing its own. The Bank's phenomenal rise to power, however, also induced the conditions for its own legitimation challenges. The Bank could no longer pretend to be the dispassionate technical expert offering advice from an apolitical distance when it was also making the daily decisions for finance ministers and central bankers in its client countries (i.e., Mexico, sub-Saharan African countries). As a consequence, at the height of the World Bank's hegemony, the Bank became a target of a growing worldwide movement with street riots, parliamentary demands, and mass mobilizations to try to close it down. Forced to "reform or die," the World Bank experienced yet another transformation in the 1990s, an equally profound shift, to *green neoliberalism.*

## An Auspicious Start

In the beginning, the World Bank was just an afterthought. In May 1944, the U.S. government invited forty-four countries to participate in a conference at Bretton Woods, New Hampshire, to consider creating an international monetary fund to rebuild international currencies sunk by the war (George and Sabelli

1994; Mason and Asher 1973). The invitation included the idea of "possibly a Bank for reconstruction and development," but John Maynard Keynes and the British were against it. Of the fourteen days spent in Bretton Woods, one participant estimated that no more than a day and a half was dedicated to discussing this possibility (Kapur, Webb, and Lewis 1997, p. 58). Keynes did see the sense in some international coordination over the rebuilding effort, but "international" clearly meant Europe, which in turn translated only to the imperial West. He argued that with "proper" economic management, governments could "have a boom that would raise the standard of living of all Europe to the levels of America today." When Keynes was asked, "Does this apply to India and the rest of the (British) Empire?" he replied, reflecting the colonial view of the day, "That must wait until the reconstruction of Europe is much further advanced" (Kapur, Webb, and Lewis 1997, p. 61). In the mid-1940s, much of the South, with Latin American exceptions, was still colonized, and Western leaders still had empire on their minds, even as the war was destroying European economies and attenuating their colonial power. Consequently, although some delegations from the South were invited to attend, they knew enough to articulate their needs in ways that emphasized imperial self-interest.

Indeed, as one observer noted, "at Bretton Woods, the developing countries tended to view (or at least present) themselves more as new, raw-material-producing nations and less as countries with general development problems" (Bauer, Meier, and Seers 1984, p. 9). Brazil, Colombia, Cuba, and Bolivia had their own proposals on how to steer the global postwar economy: recalibrate prices for raw-material goods from the South and manufactured goods from the North, which were "notoriously far out of proportion" before the war. To Southern delegates, the price gap was the fundamental reason their economies were imperiled. At Bretton Woods, Southern delegates tried to put this issue on the table. A Mexican delegate tactfully argued that Europe could not be reconstructed without the raw materials and the markets of the South: wouldn't capital be best spent in the colonies to help reconstruct Europe (Kapur, Webb, and Lewis 1997, p. 69)? In the end, it did not matter much what these delegates argued; proposals from the South were not taken seriously by the organizers from the United States and the United Kingdom.

Keynes, in fact, anticipated such arguments. He preferred a completely different meeting format: a one-on-one meeting between the British and the United States. In private, Keynes remarked that with "twenty-two countries which clearly have nothing to contribute . . . [the meeting will be] the most monstrous monkey-house assembled for years" (Kapur, Webb, and Lewis 1997, p. 69). But Harry White, assistant to U.S. Treasury Secretary Henry Morgenthau, was much more sanguine and strategic: "There's nothing that will serve to drive these countries into some kind of—ism—communism or something else—faster than having inadequate capital" (Kapur, Webb, and Lewis 1997, p. 61).

Just as the British perspective on the Bretton Woods conference was starkly summarized by Keynes in this chapter's opening epigraph, the U.S. position is outlined in the following State Department press release from the first day of the (July) 1944 conference:

> The purpose of the Conference is . . . wholly within the American tradition, and completely outside political consideration. The United States wants, after this war, full utilization of its industries, its factories and its farms; full and steady employment for

its citizens, particularly its ex-servicemen; and full prosperity and peace. It can have them only if currencies are stable, if money they receive on the due date will have the value contracted for—hence the first proposal, the Stabilization Fund [i.e., the IMF]. With values secured and held stable, it is next desirable to promote world-wide reconstruction, revive normal trade, and make funds available for sound enterprises, all of which will in turn call for American products hence the second proposal for the Bank for Reconstruction and Development [i.e., the World Bank]. (U.S. Department of State 1948, p. 1148, as cited in Peet 2003, p. 47)

From these "monkey house" histrionics emerged the International Bank for Reconstruction and Development (IBRD), or the World Bank, and the International Monetary Fund.[2] Beginning without much direction or trust in it by the leading Western powers, the World Bank began to find its personality under its second president, one of the most powerful men in the "American Establishment," Wall Street veteran John McCloy (Bird 1992).[3] McCloy's initial measures clearly reflected the type of institutional character he sought to create. For example, when the first three loan applications came in to the Bank from France, Poland, and Chile, McCloy worked quickly to select only France as a recipient, sending a strong tough love message to the watching world. As his biographer notes:

By April 1947, . . . McCloy decided that the first loan would go to the French. . . . The terms would be tough: The Bank would lend only half of the requested $500 million, Bank officers would monitor end use of the funds, and the French government would have to pledge that the repayment of the Bank's loans would have absolute priority over any other foreign debt. Furthermore, the Bank would closely supervise the French economy to ensure that the government took steps to balance its budget, increase taxes, and cut consumption of certain luxury imports. The French protested that such conditions infringed on their sovereignty. But when McCloy refused to budge, they reluctantly agreed to his terms. Simultaneously, the [U.S.] State Department bluntly informed the French that they would have to "correct the present situation" by removing any communist representatives in the Cabinet. The Communist Party was pushed out of the coalition government in early May 1947, and within hours, as if to underscore the linkage, McCloy announced that the loan would go through. Even then, he warned that the French would not receive the loan until the Bank successfully floated $250 million worth of bonds on the New York market. . . . This was exactly the message McCloy intended to convey to Wall Street. For the next two years, he planned to run the Bank as if its clients were private Wall Street investors and not the forty countries that had joined in the hope of receiving development aid. (Bird 1992, pp. 288, 290–91)

Selectivity, caution, and Wall Street respectability were the mantras of the early World Bank and the signal sent to potential borrowers as to what lay in store for them. These ideals, however, rapidly gave way to the reality that the Bank's potential client base in Europe and Japan had been erased by the U.S. government's Marshall Plan. In direct competition with the

Bretton Woods institutions, the Marshall Plan, a multibillion-dollar giveaway by comparison, was the antithesis of the World Bank's mandate: it was indiscriminate, massive, and seemingly free (Kolko and Kolko 1972; Wood 1986). The Marshall Plan was a social welfarist project deployed to jumpstart Europe's capitalist economy through a large infusion of capital. Indeed, because of the Marshall Plan, the Bank had to reinvent itself as a bank for the non-European world, albeit one guided by strict (colonial) rules and regulations that stood in stark contrast to the ones catering to postwar Europe. As highly inequitable colonial-imperial relations had been the norm, the different approaches to Europe and the colonies easily passed as legitimate, dispassionate, and rational for leaders and constituents from the United States and Western Europe.[4] In this fashion, a major postcolonial discourse of development was launched.

Wall Street had a clear revulsion for anything but the most "sound" financial investment, as defined by Wall Street and its officials employed by the Bank.[5] For example, as the Bank's treasurer from 1947 to 1959, Robert Cavanaugh understood that his main priority was to allay Wall Street's fears of financing risky investments in the colonies. For Cavanaugh, the Bank was constrained in the early years by Wall Street's refusal to allow the Bank to invest in what later became its staple development areas, namely, public education, health, and housing: "If we got into the social field . . . then the bond market would definitely feel that we were not acting prudently from a financial standpoint . . . if you start financing schools and hospitals and water works, and so forth, these things don't normally, and directly increase the ability of a country to repay a borrowing" (Cavanaugh 1961).[6] During the Bank's first twenty years, only the most direct investments in "productive capital" (i.e., roads, ports, power plants) were promoted.[7] Interviews with the managerial elite who served the World Bank in its first few decades demonstrate that every decision regarding the fundamental architecture of the World Bank, and its potential stability and growth, hinged on pleasing the five nations with the largest vote in the Bank—the "Big Five" countries (the United States, Japan, Germany, the UK, and France) and their firms.[8] Every project was negotiated in terms of which of these countries' currencies would be used and whose financial intermediaries and capital goods would be purchased.[9] Only in hindsight might this seem abnormal: foreign currency and investment were extremely scarce and precious, and for the rebuilding economies of France and Japan, every yen and franc counted. In discussions of the third world, there was no reason to bring up such concerns as poverty alleviation or local needs. That this should surprise us today precisely reflects the hegemonic effect of just a few decades of contemporary World Bank developmentalism. At the start, the role of the Bank was unambiguous and its beneficiaries so few that they were all on a first name basis.

Meanwhile, U.S. political leaders demanded something quite different from the World Bank. While senior Bank management strove to persuade economists, including some of its own, that the non-European world was more predictable, visible, and attractive than they might believe (Kapur, Webb, and Lewis 1997, p. 129), the U.S. government pushed the Bank to act for U.S. strategic purposes. Whereas McCloy's Bank preferred strict and unforgiving loan policies based on "economic" criteria, the U.S. government insisted that the Bank work only with countries identified as friends of the United States. The Bank could not lend to Guatemala and Ceylon, for example, because of the political position of the parties in power (Kapur, Webb, and Lewis 1997, p. 135). When conservatives within the Bank and on Wall Street objected to the idea of generous or "soft" loans with low interest and long repayment schedules—now the Bank's modus operandi—Secretary of State Dulles argued: "It might be good banking to put South America through the wringer, but it will come out red," that is, communist (Kapur, Webb, and Lewis 1997, p. 136). Because of U.S. political power, Turkey, Egypt, and brutal authoritarian regimes in Latin America received generous and unscrutinized loans that were matched by substantial U.S. military and foreign aid (Payer 1982, p. 42), while more "economically worthy" countries received none.[10]

Clearly, in this first period of its history, the Bank was heavily constrained both by the conviction it shared with Wall Street that "loose lending" had precipitated the pre–World War II financial collapse and by political pressure from the United States . Each loan was a painstaking process marked for its ability to ruffle the fewest feathers in Washington, New York, and London. It quickly became clear to Bank presidents and staff that the Bank was doomed to stagnate. Indeed, the first president, Eugene Meyer, stayed on only from June to December 1946, saying after his abrupt resignation, "I could stay and fight these bastards, and probably win in the end, but I'm too old for that" (Kraske 1996, p. 31). John McCloy lasted for two arduous years before he had enough.

To navigate out of these political straits, the Bank had to prove it could provide steady profits to its bondholders while sustaining the confidence of political elites—two different but related constituencies. Postcolonial "public" banking was new to the world; it had to be invented in a form agreeable to the Bank's Western founders and constituents before it could take root. As one of the Bank's first senior officials noted, people at the Bank "didn't know much about the developing world except as colonies. They didn't know much about development lending, didn't know much about development economics."[11] In fact, these ideas of economy had to be invented, and Keynes and his colleagues were the early inventors (Mitchell 2002). This suggested that the World Bank had to invent more than just "safe" loans. Rather, it needed to construct a whole new way of thinking about its role in the world and the institutional infrastructure to cultivate and reproduce that new vision.

In sum, after its inception, the Bank's mission shifted from *reconstruction* of Europe to *development* of Europe's remaining and former colonies, and from intervention not as bilateral representatives of eroding empires but as a multilateral apolitical doyen of the new global economy. The odds of success were not good. Northern political and financial institutions insisted that these worldly endeavors were irrational, wasteful, and counterproductive, as this type of development lending looked to them like preferential "subsidies" to the former colonies. Under such overwhelming skepticism and criticism, it was slow going for the Bank in its first two decades. In fact, the World Bank remained a rather minor player until Robert McNamara, the man who ran the ignominious war in Indochina, took over.

## The McNamara Era

In addition to devastating Vietnam, Laos, and Cambodia, the U.S. war in Indochina undermined the United States' dominant position in the global economy. It also had a profound and generative effect on the World Bank. As the United States' share of the world's gross domestic product (GDP) fell precipitously, from a high of 35 percent in the early 1950s to a low of 26 percent by the early 1970s (Gwin 1997), so too did its ability to dominate the Bank and its capital flow. With the decline of

U.S. hegemony in the international political economy arose new opportunities for the Bank to assert its own limited power. President Johnson, mired in a war he was losing badly, had no choice but to fire Secretary of Defense McNamara, but he wanted to do it in a face-saving way. So he gave McNamara the less-than-glamorous job of running the World Bank. Upon receiving the position, and amidst worldwide acrimony towards him and "his war," McNamara, in his characteristically obsessive manner, sequestered himself in his office, immersed himself in numbers, charts, and tables, and two weeks later resurfaced with two main goals for reorganization. As he wrote in his personal notes, his strategies were, first, to "develop new sources of financing: try to increase the holdings of the Bank's securities by the central Banks. Break into the European pension trust market. . . . Obtain approximately $50 million per year from Kuwait, the head of the Kuwaiti Fund is young, educated at California and HBS [Harvard Business School]" (May 25, 1968, cited in Kapur, Webb, and Lewis 1997, p. 953).[12] His second strategy was to develop new mechanisms to protect the Bank against funding risks: "In the event the U.S. Government refuses permission for large borrowing for FY 69, develop a plan for standby credit with commercial banks."

Realizing from the start that the Bank he inherited was weak and ineffectual, McNamara wanted to increase its power base by finding—or creating—new sources of finance. Indeed, he riled everyone when he announced with a frankness uncharacteristic of the staid Bank, that the project of development he had inherited had failed abysmally. Poverty increased and lending was sluggish; populations were growing and the Bank's resources were shrinking. Something had to be done, and quickly. Institutionally, the Bank had little autonomous power to expand and innovate upon the project of development; it had become a supplicant to the old-boys' network that McNamara himself, as a former Harvard Business School professor, Ford Motor Company CEO, Ford Foundation board member, and secretary of defense, knew so intimately. Nonetheless, as the newly anointed World Bank president, he sought to wrench control of the Bank from these Northern elite networks while tapping into their capital and power: have them work for the Bank rather than the other way around. In 1968, the Bank was stagnating under the weight of the U.S. and European bond markets, which were demanding fiscal prudence and high returns; the U.S. government was continuing to support loans in its political interest; and the U.S. Treasury and key corporate lobbies wanted American firms to benefit from (or certainly not be hurt by) World Bank loans. The World Bank was financially solid but, despite its grandiose name, it was weak and severely underutilized. McNamara made two bold moves.

First, he turned to his staff and board. Apparently at his inaugural senior staff meeting, he listened to senior staff boast about the successes of their organizational turfs—a longstanding tradition of optimistic spinning for one's superiors (George and Sabelli 1994; Wade 1997)—until he had no more patience. He abruptly ended the meeting with a pointed request: "I am going to ask you all to give me very shortly a list of all the projects or programs that you would wish to see the Bank carry out if there were no financial constraints" (George and Sabelli 1994, p. 42). He made his conservative staff extremely uncomfortable by suggesting that the Bank needed to unleash its potential. He demanded from them a development plan for every borrowing country with a list of top priority projects and persuasive explanations as to their worthiness. His next move was at his first board meeting, where he told his cautious directors that he planned to double the Bank's lending (Kapur, Webb, and Lewis 1997, p. 216). He then expanded his personnel by 120 percent and started a new staff promotion policy, in which productivity would be measured by the size and turnover rate of a loan officer's loan portfolio. Consequently, in his first five-year term, the Bank financed more projects (760 versus 708) and loaned more money ($13.4 billion versus $10.7 billion) than it had during the previous twenty-two years combined (George and Sabelli 1994, p. 43).

McNamara then turned to Wall Street to promote his idea of what the Bank *could* be if it changed its modus operandi. Surprising all, five months into McNamara's tenure, the Bank had borrowed more funds on capital markets than in any calendar year of its history. The Bank was rolling under the new chief; miraculously, he was able to finance virtually all of the Bank's increased lending without soliciting any new paid-in capital from the Big Five countries. In short time, he had effectively nullified past controls on the Bank's access to capital. "The Bank's capacity to lend is now based almost entirely on its capacity to borrow," claimed the Bank's new treasurer, Eugene Rotberg (Rotberg 1994, p. 199). It was Rotberg who realized how to unleash the Bank's borrowing potential by utilizing the nascent market for global bonds—and to do it profitably. With this remarkable growth in the Bank's capacity to borrow and lend, the "McNamara era" began.

## THE FALL OF THE BRETTON WOODS DOLLAR-GOLD AGREEMENT, THE RISE OF THE WORLD BANK

The backdrop to political change inside Bank headquarters was some substantial structural shifts in the global political economy and a series of momentous decisions made by the U.S. president, just a few strides from McNamara's new office. Still within the loop of decision making in Washington, McNamara was able to quickly insert his Bank into the middle of new U.S.-centered plans and help the Bank to grow in tandem with U.S. power. As a result of the tumultuous period of 1968 to 1973, when a wave of events hit the global economy, the conservative banking agenda of the pre-McNamara Bank disappeared in a flash (Block 1977; Helleiner 1994; Kapstein 1994).

In spite of money managers looking for good investments to absorb the worldwide glut of Eurodollars, OPEC petrodollars, and Japanese yen, a floundering U.S. economy did not attract foreign investors to its currency, government bonds, real estate, and firms. In a brilliant move aimed at stemming the free-falling U.S. economy, on the recommendation of his economic advisor Paul Volcker, President Nixon pulled out of the postwar Bretton Woods system of fixed currency that tied all world currencies to a gold value through the U.S. dollar. By forcing the gold-dollar standard to collapse and then by liberalizing international financial relations against the will of Western Europe and Japan, the United States skillfully placed the burden of its huge deficit upon other states and investors. When foreign investors purchased U.S. assets and dollars in order to participate more actively in global markets, they were also assuming the U.S. deficit risks as well as buoying the U.S. economy. This move to deregulate international finance capital also shifted the balance of power away from state-managed financial institutions (and national development projects) to private financial institutions and capital investors. Nixon's bold decision sparked an incredible rise in speculative capital activity that would, by the 1990s, shift hundreds of billions of dollars across national borders and national currencies with the bat of an eye and beyond the control of national governments. But more immediately, holders of the abundant financial capital were enticed by McNamara to invest in World Bank "global bonds," which would help finance large productive capital investments in undercapitalized markets in the third world. By promising a range of risk guarantees to these investors, McNamara tapped into their surplus capital assets, dramatically expanded the Bank's lending base, and began to finance his vision of large projects in the highly volatile postcolonial world. But Rome was not built in a day, and McNamara had much work to do before he could take full advantage of this momentous historical conjuncture.

### FIRST REVOLUTION: GLOBAL BONDING

Within weeks of assuming the Bank's presidency, McNamara asked his newly hired treasurer, Eugene Rotberg, whether and how the Bank could increase its access to capital. "Do you think we can raise one billion dollars a year?" McNamara queried Rotberg. "Sure, why not?" was Rotberg's reply. In a 1983 interview, Rotberg explained that fifteen years later, the Bank was easily borrowing $10 billion a year (Institutional Investor 1988, p. 242). "I think I helped create an environment," Rotberg claimed, "where my [Bank] colleagues could raise $100 billion for poor people and where we could attract those funds from institutions that do not ordinarily lend, directly or indirectly, to that constituency."

Rotberg opened a trading floor in Bank offices and traded assets at highly competitive yields. By the end of the 1970s, the "pit," as it came to be called, was earning 8.8 percent, or $835 million, a year on liquid assets of $9.5 billion (Shapley 1993, p. 528). These profits not only funded the Bank's new palatial headquarters and staff expansion; they enhanced its independence from its Big Five executive directors. This was a major break from the past, when each currency transaction had to be approved by the central bank in the country whose currency was being sold—a disciplinary device imposed by Western bankers and ministers to prevent the World Bank from spiraling out of their control.

Rotberg searched the world for underutilized capital. He approached the Japanese for a few billion dollars even though, at the time, their international bond market was relatively small. But he knew they had a high savings rate, and so he tapped into their growing interest in the global financial market (Institutional Investor 1988, p. 245). German markets, then the coffers of the capital-flush, oil-producing OPEC members, were equally alluring. Rotberg summarized his strategy in this way: "What one must focus on is who has the wealth, how fast it is accumulating and what kind of instrument do the controllers of wealth want in order for you to take it. Do they want equity? Do they want to be liquid? Long? Short? Leveraged or not leveraged? Fixed or floating? That is essentially what every government, private corporation and quasi-public institution has to figure out worldwide. And once you know that, creation of the instrument is child's play" (Institutional Investor 1988, p. 244).

By the 1980s, the Bank was successfully borrowing from countries as diverse as Kuwait, Japan, Libya, and India and was working with large pension funds and multiple brokerage firms, not just the U.S. undersecretaries of treasury. The Bank also diverged from its traditional source of currency, the U.S. dollar, borrowing in franc, Turkish lira, yen, Kroner, bolivares, and rupees.

The McNamara-Rotberg revolution was as transformative for the World Bank as it was for the world of international finance.[13] Because of the Bank's new ability to borrow globally, it gradually ceased to rely on Northern governments and their paid-in capital. Whereas in 1968 the Bank received $2 billion worth of paid-in capital from twenty Western countries and borrowed $3.5 billion from financial markets, by 1994, it collected $4.7 billion in paid-in capital and a whopping $99 billion from the global bond market (Rotberg 1994). Its power allegiances became much more dispersed because it never borrowed too much in one place or currency and it worked to create new markets and investment tools in new locations around the world.

As remarkable as these feats were for the new World Bank, it paradoxically suffered from an inability to stimulate—of all things—*demand* for its capital. After twenty years, the Bank was still short of borrowers and loan packages that could satisfy its rigorous approval requirements. Borrowing countries, soured by political and institutional constraints on the loan-approval process, had difficulty agreeing with Bank staff on projects. To utilize effectively this huge influx of "development capital" required a few more revolutions from above.

## A NEW AGENDA

The World Bank's first twenty-five years were marked by a cautious approach to investment. Most Bank loans went into areas of infrastructure deemed necessary to stimulate economic growth, but not to actually grow the Bank, which would have been frowned on by the U.S. Treasury and Wall Street. To assure secure results, the Bank also loaned only to the more affluent countries. From 1946 to 1968, the Bank loaned approximately $13 billion, most of which went to high- and middle-income borrowers, including Japan, Italy, France, and the Netherlands.[14] When McNamara assumed control, he made public his astonishment about how little the Bank actually loaned in the name of "equity" and "poverty alleviation" and about the failure of its development model in general. In his early speeches and in private, he argued emphatically that most Bank loans completely bypassed the "poorest 40 percent" (McNamara 1973; McNamara 1981).

McNamara, by contrast, wanted to lend to the poorest countries and for concerns that had been consciously avoided by the Bank's economically prudent managers. In his first public speech as Bank president, McNamara noted that since 1960, in the developing world "the average annual growth thus far has been 4.8%. . . . And yet . . . you know and I know that these cheerful statistics are cosmetics, which conceal a far less cheerful picture. . . . [M]uch of the growth is concentrated in the industrial areas, while the peasant remains stuck in his immemorial poverty, living on the bare margin of subsistence" (McNamara 1981, pp. 3–5, as cited in Kapur, Webb, and Lewis 1997, p. 217).

In a dramatic shift, he began to use the language and political strategy of "development" rather than "investment banking," borrowing liberally from old and new political discourses. Whereas today this new development discourse may seem formulaic and predictable, for the time, and the institution, it was disconcertingly novel and risky. From the beginning of his presidency, McNamara wanted to put Bank money into the hands of the "absolute poor," a radical concept to his banking clients. Loan composition also greatly changed as McNamara insisted on shifting the focus to agriculture and rural development, a sector universally shunned for being much too dicey and unproductive for capital. Yet, McNamara argued boldly that no amount of investment in coal production or port development would directly help the poor, since their lack of access to new technologies, capital, and know-how—and their absolute numbers—were the primary reason the investment banking model of development had failed.

According to McNamara, the Bank needed to turn its full attention to third world rural peasants if it wanted to solve the problems of poverty and underdevelopment. From his vantage point, the key question became: what was the most efficient vehicle for reaching the peasantry so that their lives could be transformed? This, of course, was precisely the concern of elite policy circles in the nascent U.S. Agency for International Development, the Council on Foreign Relations, the CIA, and the Defense and State departments, and it reflected the fears of many who believed that the war in Indochina was making it harder to win the hearts and minds of third world peasants, whose participation in rebellions and revolutions around the world seemed to be growing. Perhaps he understood better than most from his experience in Vietnam that instabilities around the world would not be ameliorated by private capital investment but required public funding and a more comprehensive approach.[15] Hence, over time, the McNamara Bank, with its virtually unlimited access to capital, blanketed whole regions with new kinds of projects, shifting from individual loans in specific types of infrastructure to society-wide interventions.

In one of his earliest speeches, to the annual meeting of the board of governors of the World Bank in September 1968, he spoke at length on how deep he expected Bank interventions to go in "poor" countries: "to help them rise out of the pit of poverty in which they had been engulfed for centuries past. . . . Our aim here will be to provide assistance where it will contribute most to economic development. This will mean emphasis on educational planning, the starting point for the whole process of educational improvement. It will mean expansion of our support for a variety of other educational activities, including the training of managers, entrepreneurs, and of course, agriculturalists. . . . To carry out this program we hope over the next five years to increase our lending for educational development at least threefold."[16]

But the most significant expansion was in agriculture, which McNamara defined as the "stepchild of development." "Here again there has never been any doubt about [agriculture's] importance. Two-thirds of the people of the developing world live on the soil, yet these countries have to import annually $4 billion of food from the industrialized nations. Even their diet is so inadequate, in many cases, that they cannot do an effective day's work and, more ominous still, there is growing scientific evidence that the dietary deficiencies of the parent are passed on as mental deficiencies to the children" (McNamara 1973, p. 24).

To resolve the problem, McNamara proposed to bring to Asia, Africa, and Latin America the green revolution, an integrated project of high-yield-variety seeds, fertilizer, irrigation, capital, and technical support. "In the past," he noted:

Investment in agricultural improvement produced but a modest yield; the traditional seeds and plants did better with irrigation and fertilizer. But the increase in yield was not dramatic. In the past twenty years, however, research had resulted in a breakthrough in the production of new strains of wheat and rice and other plants that can improve yields by three to five times. What is more, these new strains are particularly sensitive to the input of water and fertilizer. Badly managed, they will produce little more than traditional yields, but with correct management they will give the peasant an unprecedented crop.

Here is an opportunity for irrigation, fertilizer, and peasant education to produce near miracles. The farmer himself in one short season can see the beneficial results of that scientific agriculture that has seemed so often in the past to be a will-o'-the-wisp, tempting him to innovation without benefit. Our task now is to enable the peasant to make the most of this opportunity. (McNamara 1973, pp. 23-25)

Although McNamara's idea for poverty alleviation focused heavily on the rural sector and the undercapitalized "small farmer," his ambitious plans for the developing world did not end there. Whereas in the pre-McNamara era, the Bank loaned no money for primary school education and very little for nonformal education, by the end of his tenure, lending for education increased substantially, almost half of which went to primary and nonformal education to attack the problem of low literacy rates. McNamara also pushed for nutrition, population control, and health components to rural projects, which represented a marked shift for the Bank; he also increased lending for urban poverty concerns, starting projects for low-cost housing and slum rehabilitation. At first, these investments dismayed the dominant powers in development financing. His staff lacked the resources to fend off critics from the banking sector and to demonstrate how Bank projects would contribute to productive capital expansion and overall economic growth. By the 1980s, however, these types of poverty alleviation investments became standard for the Bank, the transnational development agency network (bilateral aid agencies, NGOs, and charities), and borrowing-state bureaucracies.

## OVERCOMING RESISTANCE

Despite the availability of megaplans and money, McNamara learned that it was not going to be easy to embrace his new agenda without losing the confidence of the Bank's main constituents, namely, Wall Street, the U.S. Treasury, and the Big Five political elites. In fact, it required an intensive lobbying effort as well as a whole new discursive approach: the capacity to produce a social imagery to rationalize the lending and borrowing of large sums of capital for things other than roads, mines, and power plants, the bread and butter of the old investment regime. To convince institutional investors that the Bank would remain financially strong as it expanded its portfolio to include many more capital-poor countries and investments in such intangibles as poverty alleviation, the McNamara Bank needed to generate a major shift in perceptions and the institutional means to put theory into practice. Even within the Bank, McNamara's new vision was met with considerable resistance. To win support for his interventionist and expansive development agenda, McNamara needed to sell it as *rational, politically and economically necessary,* and *profitable.* The effort required a new organizational culture and a much grander development science.

For inspiration and support, McNamara looked outside the Bank's traditional intellectual and financial networks to new ideas and approaches that were emerging in U.S. and Western European academic and policy circles. If the postwar era from 1945 to 1965 was the "development as growth" era, as economic historian H. W. Arndt has suggested (Arndt 1987), then the 1965 to 1975 period was the "social objectives" era. Amidst worldwide social protest, such influential development scholars as Dudley Seers of the Institute for Development Studies in Sussex and H. W. Singer of the United Nations were officially dethroning the hegemony of GNP (gross national product) as a determining marker of development. Since substantial poverty and inequality could clearly be generated in the midst of high GNP growth rates, Seers and others argued, it was time to discard an approach that was exclusively concerned with economic growth (Arndt 1987).

The larger political-economic context helped McNamara convince skeptics that his Bank expansion plans were not only sound, but also necessary. Growth rates in high- and middle-income countries were falling, unemployment and poverty rates were rising, and the war in Indochina had substantially weakened the U.S.-dominated world economy. The late 1960s and early 1970s were also a period of street protests and revolutionary challenges to colonial and imperial orders around the world, the effects of which were to unsettle Northern political elites, economists, and McNamara himself. Even as secretary of defense, he began to borrow liberally from such enlightened policy makers as Barbara Ward, Mahbub ul Haq, and David Morse (head of the International Labor Organization), and ideas from the decade-old war against poverty in the United States. Moreover, as Bank president, McNamara proselytized alongside powerful third world leaders, such as Indira Gandhi (who called for a "new international economic order" or a radical re-balancing of power between North and South), to address the poverty question in terms of North-South inequities. If development experts continued to "concentrate on the modern sector in the hope that its high rate of growth would filter down to the rural poor," McNamara declared in numerous high-profile venues, "disparities in income will simply widen" (McNamara 1981, as cited in Caufield 1996, p. 99). Further, he asked, how will the world's nearly 800 million people, whom he called "the absolute poor," continue to survive on 30 cents a day? Rich countries had the *responsibility* to redistribute their wealth to the poorer countries, for moral and ethical reasons, as well as the more pragmatic reason of stemming the tide of revolution. Vietnam, of course, was the elephant on the table.

## REORGANIZING THE BANK

Once McNamara reinvented the Bank's mission, he had to refashion the Bank. Robert Strange McNamara had entered the Bank riding on his reputation of having modernized the auto industry at Ford Motor Company and streamlined the Pentagon as secretary of defense (Shapley 1993). Described as "an IBM machine with legs" by Senator Barry Goldwater, McNamara was one of the business world's whiz kids who transformed corporate managerialism through a completely rationalized and numbers-based systems analysis. He then went on to be part of the Kennedy and Johnson administrations' "best and brightest," the elite Ivy League boys who navigated the country through the tumultuous 1960s and 1970s, albeit not without some very serious miscalculations. To many observers, taking over the World Bank was to be a salve on his tormented conscience (Clark 1986; Shapley 1993). As defense secretary, his public speeches claiming "there can't be security without wealth redistribution to the poor" fell on deaf ears (McNamara 1973); from the pulpit of the Bank presidency, they sounded like prophetic activism. He believed in a frontal assault on poverty, but he found the potency of the World Bank lacking. At the Defense Department, McNamara worked with an annual budget of more than $70 billion, and he was taken aback that the Bank lent less than $1 billion a year. According to one of his senior managers, "He kept talking in billions and then he would correct himself and say 'I mean millions'" (Shapley 1993).

McNamara had a well-known history of instilling, for the times, a unique managerial culture onto the organizations he ran. David Halberstam, author of *The Best and the Brightest*, explained it as a pathology that allowed him and his colleagues in the White House to rationalize the devastating war they were supporting. McNamara's quantifications may have helped numb the public with numbers that the U.S. press by and large accepted as a legitimate language for describing the carnage, but they belied pictures on the evening news as well as the stories from journalists and soldiers. As McNamara's biographer noted: "He searched out the enemy, poverty, and quantified it. He and his staff at the Bank were trying to identify the 700 million absolute poor in the fall of 1974. 'We do not now have all the information we need to identify the different groups in individual countries,' he said. But they were building a database with 'present and potential levels of productivity of individuals in each category.' Some in the Bank objected that counting and classifying people as absolutely or relatively poor was a poor exercise, so to speak. 'We did a lot of body counting in those days,' remarks a staffer, not without irony" (Shapley 1993, p. 519).[17]

Moreover, the Bank of the early 1970s seemed an "unlikely vehicle to fix the slums of Calcutta. . . . The 767 staff members were overwhelmingly Anglo-American . . . men from the former colonies [who] were overwhelmingly anglicized. . . . Meetings of the Oxford-Cambridge Society were announced in the Bank's newsletter. The place had the air of a boarding school such as Eton" (Shapley 1993, p. 477). The culture of the old Bank was simply not conducive to the McNamara regime. As one Bank staffer recalled: "[In those days,] we made a loan to Ghana and then waited for years to see how it came out before making another." At this rate, progress in the third world would be snail-like at best, a pace McNamara found intolerable. He told his closest aide that this was "an inefficient way to run a planet" (Clark 1986, p. 31, as cited in Shapley 1993, p. 477).

Upon taking over, McNamara infused the Bank with the same highly hierarchical and numbers-based managerial style that made him famous at Ford and the Defense Department. He started by changing the organizational structure from one that was fastidious, plodding, and risk-averse, to one that was fast growing, risk-taking, and reached in many different directions. He insisted that staff members not only increase their loan portfolios to include new types of investments to reach the absolute poor, but also that they provide empirical data to justify the risk. In other words, within an ever-shrinking time frame as staff promotions became linked to the turnover time of loans, Bank staff had to simultaneously invent and design new projects, drum up demand for them, and justify through data that these projects were necessary for economic growth and poverty alleviation in borrowing countries and financially rewarding for the Bank's investors.

McNamara was convinced from early on that academia was incapable of supplying the theories and tools that could help explain and solve the problems he perceived as essential (Stern and Ferreira 1997, p. 604). Both the Bank he had inherited and the academic professions at large had no good understanding of, for example, how to get economies to transition from protectionist ones to ones that used price mechanisms and competitive markets as vehicles for luring foreign direct investment. They had no model or formula for measuring and explaining poverty and its rise or fall in connection to specific interventions, such as low-interest credit to small farmers or primary school education to illiterate youth. McNamara had no confidence in the trickle-down theory of growth; he insisted economists and development specialists had no idea—certainly not one based on hard, quantifiable facts—how to solve the problems of poverty, malnutrition, ill health, and rapid population growth. His strategy was therefore to create a new paradigm in development thinking: to measure, analyze, and overcome.

In the prevailing culture at the Bank and in the world where Bank staff worked, it had been the *self-evidentiary* aspect of their carefully packaged productivity-oriented loans that had kept Wall Street and the Treasury Department content. An institutional support system existed that affirmed and reproduced the Bank's claims that large-scale infrastructural investments were the way to generate growth and development in places incapable of achieving them on their own. But no internal institutional support system existed to make McNamara's audacious claims ring true that "investing in the poor" was the most efficient route to growth with equity in the third world. Nor was anyone in the larger community of constituents, development officials, or economists prepared to accept the financial soundness of such investments. That was a perception that McNamara's team had to create. The World Bank thus became central headquarters for research, economic modeling, data collection, report writing, and dissemination of information on the so-called less developed world.

The impetus to develop an institutional capacity to justify the Bank's dramatic expansion and its involvement in new types of work and new experiments in the field of development rapidly took on a life of its own. The job required data, greater involvement in borrower countries, and the establishment of a transnational division of labor that included, over time, the adoption, adaptation, and the indigenization of data collection and project design responsibilities. Following McNamara's mandate, teams of professional staff and consultants traveled on extended "missions" to conduct economic research. They collected data on standards of living, consumption, production, and poverty; they also generated analyses of barriers to change, the workings of societal institutions, and the status of natural resources. Staff began to focus their energies on these economic missions as in-country economic analysis and formal policy discussions with borrowers and other key development agencies became part of their regular mission activity.

## GAUGING CHANGE

To see how much the Bank changed under McNamara, it is useful to compare the pre-McNamara Bank with the Bank that emerged after he took control. In the 1961–62 World Bank annual report, the greatest problem cited for the Bank in its early years was a lack of demand: "The principal limitation on the Bank's rate of lending has been the limited number of projects or programs presented to it, which were ready for financing and execution. The studies and analyses needed to prepare a project or program are often beyond the capacity of many less developed countries because of the local shortage of experience and of trained personnel" (World Bank 1962, p. 6).

To resolve this problem, the Bank's third president, Eugene Black (whose term ran from July 1949 to January 1963), established a Development Services Department and Development Advisory Service that offered advice and technical services in the preparation of loan applications (World Bank 1962). In 1961, the Bank loaned $882.3 million. Electric power accounted for more than half of the total, with Argentina, Australia, and Mexico receiving the largest loans. Transport, mainly highway construction (an obsession of U.S. industry), comprised the second largest category, with loans going to Japan, Costa Rica, Mexico, Peru, and Venezuela; a smaller portion was invested in railways in South Africa and India; and the smallest portion was lent for port projects in India and the Philippines. The only loan for agriculture, for $8.4 million, went to Kenya, for land settlement costs.

Most of the technical assistance in 1961 was directed toward very specific pre-loan project assessments, such as a study for a bridge over the Hooghly River in Calcutta, a study of feeder roads in northeast Nigeria, and a mineral survey in Surinam. A Bank mission helped Spain set up a development program, and two-man advisory teams were posted in Chile, one in Nigeria, and a few were assisting Thailand and Pakistan on development investment strategies. One hundred and forty-three government officials attended the Bank's Economic Development Institute (EDI) ten-week courses in project development and management. The courses were held in English, with an experimental course introduced in French, and one under consideration in Spanish. Four hundred book libraries were dispatched to ninety-three different sites in developing countries.

In 1961, a typical Bank loan was described in this way:

*South Africa/Railway Loan*
($11 million, 10-year 5¾% loan)
This loan will help to meet the current investment requirements of a large program of railway expansion and modernization of the South African railway and harbours. Administration has been carrying out since 1947. Earlier Bank loans totaling $136.8 million assisted the program, and the new loan will cover part of the foreign exchange requirements for 1961–63. About 80% of the mining and industrial freight of South Africa goes by rail

and further investment in the railways is essential to economic growth. The current expansion program involves an increase in capacity, the elimination of traffic bottlenecks and progressive dieselization.

*Participations:* The New York Agency of Barclays Bank D.C.O; Girard Trust Corn Exchange Bank, Philadelphia; Morgan Guaranty Trust Company of New York; Bank of America, San Francisco; the New York Agency of The Bank of Montreal; Fidelity-Philadelphia Trust Company; the First Pennsylvania Banking and Trust Company, Philadelphia; and The Riggs National Bank of Washington, D.C., were among the banks participating in the loan for a total of $1,966,000. (World Bank 1962, p. 18)

For technical assistance, the following description was quite common:

*British Guiana:* The Bank is acting as executing agency for the UN Special Fund project to survey the bar siltation and erosion problems at the port of Georgetown. The field study has been completed and the consultants' report is in preparation. (World Bank 1962, p. 28)[18]

Whereas in 1961, the Bank committed just under $900 million in new loans for 29 projects in 19 countries (World Bank 1962), twenty years later, it was committing $8.8 billion in support of 140 projects in 50 countries (World Bank 1981b). By 1981, when McNamara retired, projects, and the language to describe them, had changed completely. The Bank was no longer simply providing its clients with money for large-scale infrastructure; it was now training staff, supporting local research facilities, and doing "integrated rural development" as part of its mission, as the following project descriptions indicate:

> *Brazil: Bank—$60 million.* To assist the country's national agricultural research agency in expanding its current research programs and to support several new programs, funds will be provided to train scientific manpower and upgrade existing research facilities. Technical assistance is included. Total cost: $150.1 million. (World Bank 1981b, p. 99)

> *Brazil: Bank—$56 million.* About 60,000 farm families and more than 1,000 small-scale entrepreneurs will benefit from a second rural development project in the northeastern state of Ceara that includes agricultural extension services, development of cooperatives, assistance to small enterprises, construction of feeder roads, marketing facilities, and irrigation systems, and education, health, and sanitation services. Co-financing ($25 million) is being provided by IFADS. Total cost: $163.2 million. (World Bank 1981b, pp. 99–100)

> *Cameroon: Bank—$25 million; IDA—$12.5 million.* The incomes of 163,000 farm families living in a Northern province will be increased through improved rural infrastructure, effective extension and credit services, training, and research. In addition, financial and technical assistance will be extended to local agencies to plan, monitor, and evaluate a wide range of rural development activities. Total cost: $66 million. (World Bank 1981b, p. 100).

The definition of development's beneficiaries also changed substantially as the Bank's annual reports became a discursive tool intended for a broader—and more public—audience. Rather than emphasizing the economic benefits that would flow to Northern firms and investment banks as these entities supplied hardware, technical support, and financial services for projects through the procurement process, the focus shifted to the various civil-society "beneficiaries" of the development process: for example, the "163,000 farm families" who would be affected by a loan to Cameroon; the local officials, agronomists, and researchers who would receive "scientific

Senior government officials participating in an early World Bank training seminar, Washington, D.C., 1960. Courtesy World Bank Archives.

manpower" training through various Bank projects; and the research facilities that would be established or upgraded with World Bank capital (World Bank 1981b). In the McNamara years, it became inappropriate to highlight the Northern beneficiaries (that is, Northern finance capital) in the loan description itself; in their place were development's new clients—the third world poor. Overall, these were not mere rhetorical changes, designed to satisfy a discerning left-Keynesian political elite in the North. Rather, they were changes with deep meaningful and material consequences.

Men working the railways, Nigeria, 1961. Both this and the facing photograph come from the World Bank annual report of 1961, a time when such juxtapositions were not perceived as politically awkward. Courtesy World Bank Archives.

## Sowing the Seeds of Bank Power

World Bank power grew remarkably during the McNamara years in ways that have now become commonplace to the world of development and, more generally, North-South relations. Few today would think twice of calling upon U.S. experts to offer their know-how to African or Indian farmers after a bad harvest. The ease with which such information can be transferred reflects the Bank's success during the 1970s in creating both the worldwide institutional structure and the discursive formations to make such ideas realistic and workable. Part of that institutional structure included the facilities erected to assist the transfer of green revolution seeds and technologies to major borrowing countries. The World Bank helped bring the green revolution to the South by offering substantial institutional support to state ministries, credit banks, and research centers, and loans for heavy infrastructure, such as dams, power plants, irrigation systems, and agro-industrial factories.[19]

To boosters like Lester Brown (currently director of the Worldwatch Institute), the green revolution bore "witness to the fact that careful evaluation, sound scientific and economic planning, and sustained effort can overcome the *pathology of chronic under-production.* . . . A formula for success can be designed for any area that has available the new adapted plant varieties and the other inputs and accelerators that must be applied in logical fashion" (Escobar 1995, p. 159). In practice, the poor's pathologies were defined in relation to the technological innovations occurring at international agricultural research institutes and agro-industrial corporations.[20] Development planners, meanwhile, began to intuitively "'know' that villagers have certain habits, goals, motivations and beliefs," according to Stacey Pigg, an anthropologist working in Nepal. To the development expert, "the 'ignorance' of villagers is not an absence of knowledge . . . [but] the presence of too much locally-instilled belief" (Pigg 1992, pp. 17, 20). By the 1980s, "miracle seeds" were followed into the third world village by an entire power/knowledge complex based on a specific type of elite knowledge production. This became the terra firma on which the World Bank's hegemony was constructed. The idea of a green revolution became world-significant primarily because of the size of the World Bank's financial support, and the new breadth of its development assistance network.

As McNamara sent his staff into the field demanding that they come back with both solid data and projects in hand, the Bank generated its own transnational demand for information about the conditions of the rural poor, transforming the previously imperceptible millions into visible objects of development. McNamara was dissatisfied with the pace of collecting information. He wanted data collection to match the fast-paced cycle of the Bank's loan approval process (Kapur, Webb, and Lewis 1997). To expedite and legitimate new loans, McNamara created his own knowledge-generating machinery by adopting two Rockefeller Foundation-funded research centers in Mexico and the Philippines, from which he created the multisited research network called the Consultative Group on International Agricultural Research (CGIAR). With a growing number of Bank-supported research campuses around the world, the CGIAR quickly became "one of the greatest successes in the annals of development promotion" (Kapur, Webb, and Lewis 1997, p. 401).[21] Eventually, there were sixteen institutes comprising the CGIAR system. Through them, green revolution technologies swept the South. In 1965, innovative semi-dwarf varieties of wheat covered less than one-tenth of

1 percent of the total area planted in wheat in developing countries. By 1983, 50 percent was planted with CGIAR-promoted green revolution wheat, with 80 percent of the total area for wheat in Latin America and India under CGIAR varieties. For rice, by 1983, almost 58 percent of total area in developing countries was planted with semi-dwarf varieties, with China planting 95 percent, India, 54 percent, and the rest of Asia, 40 percent (Baum 1986, pp. 283–4).

Over the first twenty-five years of its existence, the Bank's CGIARs trained approximately 50,000 scientists, many of whom subsequently took up prominent positions as ministers of state, agriculture, and finance (Baum 1986), as well as CEOs and research directors for major multinational firms (World Bank 1999). This global research enterprise represented a marked change from the early World Bank, which in 1961 had only twelve professionals working on agriculture, most of whom were experts in drainage and irrigation (Kapur, Webb, and Lewis 1997). During the McNamara years, the Bank's agriculture divisions could not hire staff fast enough (Kapur, Webb, and Lewis 1997).

As the Bank reinvented the professional landscape in which the international agricultural scientist worked into one flush with financial and political rewards, this science-industry-government network enabled the Bank to overcome the historic skepticism of capital markets to invest in rural production. With its huge spillover effects on industry (e.g., energy, fertilizer, chemical pesticides, synthetic seed, farm machinery), the Bank's green revolution became extremely lucrative for its Northern clients. The Bank and its bilateral aid partners created agricultural universities and research and policy centers throughout the South to direct the trajectory of this development (Anderson, Levy, and Morrison 1991; Anderson et al.

1982; Stakman 1967; Wright 1990). These prominent national institutes attracted development dollars and university exchanges with American land-grant institutions (e.g., the Universities of Illinois and Iowa) and economic and law departments (e.g., University of Chicago), helping to "Americanize" agro-food systems, property-right traditions and statutes, and trade and investment laws in the Bank's borrowing countries (Dezalay and Garth 2002).

Overall, the Bank under McNamara took Norman Borlaug's miracle seeds and used them to expand its lending portfolio in many different directions: large dams to electrify and irrigate industry and agriculture, mining and factories for farm-based capital goods, transportation, the development of market towns, and basic education and primary health in the countryside to facilitate the green revolution. But the rapid growth of the Bank's loan portfolio, associated with this and its other endeavors, eventually led to crippling effects in the South: high external debt, loss of diverse food production, land enclosures that displaced millions of peasants, the dollarization and Americanization of food production, and plummeting food prices due to a worldwide glut in agricultural commodities, for example, U.S. wheat dumped on the world market (Bonanno 1994; Friedmann 1982; Wright 1990). Because of highly imbalanced terms of trade, McNamara's "end poverty" decade ended with a highly indebted South and a highly stratified farming system.[22] With the devastation of local systems of food production and the triumph of export-oriented production, the South became a net importer of foods from the United States and Europe. None of these changes solved the problems of development or significantly reduced absolute poverty. Instead, poverty grew as a result of the Bank's development industry.[23]

Although highly profitable for foreign investors, the new development regime was too costly for borrowers who did not have the resources to repay the large Bank loans. Combined with the collapse of world food prices and the spike in oil prices, trouble loomed. While the Bank's newfound large capital assets allowed it to expand beyond its wildest dreams, it also fueled a mounting debt crisis amongst its borrowers.

## Debt and Structural Adjustment

The Bank's long string of loans helped fuel a dramatic increase in the South's foreign debt, which grew at an average annual rate of 20 percent between 1976 and 1980 (McMichael 2004; Mosley, Harrigan, and Toye 1991; Toussaint 1999). By the 1980s, much of what the World Bank was lending did not go for bricks and mortar, seeds and tractors, or even research and training; most went to pay the interest on national budget deficits (Mosley, Harrigan, and Toye 1991; World Bank 1986). The twin effects of massive borrowing for rural industrialization and the linking of Southern food and agricultural sectors to the consumption of Northern-based capital goods and farm inputs, contributed heavily to the net flow of capital out of the South and into the North.

Although the impending debt crisis could have toppled the World Bank's stance in the world, the opposite occurred. Because of the vulnerable position of its borrowers and its unique role as development master, the Bank positioned itself as one of the major transnational institutions that could manage the process of debt restructuring. Despite its deep-seated entanglement in the roots of the debt crisis, the Bank emerged from the era, quite unexpectedly, as the newly anointed global arbiter of debt relations between the North and the South (Gowan 1999; Helleiner 1994; Kapstein 1994).[24]

Ideally, countries could have repaid their development loans from revenues generated from the commodities produced from dams, power plants, and seeds, but the world-market prices of many of the goods produced with Bank financing had plummeted (George and Sabelli 1994). Many key commodities that the Bank assiduously promoted for production across the South were being replaced by commodities produced in the North, such as corn syrup for sugar, glass fiber for copper, soy oils for tropical oils, and synthetic alternatives to rubber, cotton, jute, and timber (McMichael 2004). By 1986, third world debt had risen to $1 trillion and countries were borrowing large amounts from the Bank and IMF just to service the interest on their old loans. Many African countries were forced to use all their export earnings to service their ballooning debts.

One of the most significant effects of the debt crisis was the dramatic shift in power that took place between borrowing states and the World Bank and IMF. As soon as these sibling institutions assumed control of countries' foreign debts, they required governments to reorganize and reorient their economies. In particular, they pushed them to produce for export rather than to produce for domestic needs, to reduce trade barriers and tariffs, and to open up key public sectors for international competition (i.e., telecommunications, electricity and mining, manufacturing, insurance, banking, and transport). As private lending dried up, governments succumbed to these pressures and dramatically cut their spending on health, education, and welfare in order to comply with the new conditions placed on World Bank and IMF loans.

The ensuing era of structural adjustment was supposed to have been a short-lived "shock" that would help countries adjust to the oil price hike and ride out a two-to-three-year period of economic restructuring, after which liberalized trade relations between North and South would kick in to draw capital to structurally adjusted countries (Dasgupta 1998). Instead, shock therapy became a never-ending cycle of large debt-servicing loans and additional policy requirements that further destabilized borrowers. By 1987, rather than having a net *outflow* of capital, the Bank had a net *inflow* and received far more from its borrowers in the form of loan repayments than it was lending (Dasgupta 1998; Mosley, Harrigan, and Toye 1991). By the late 1980s, UNICEF reported that World Bank adjustment programs were responsible for the "reduced health, nutritional, and educational levels for tens of millions of children in Asia, Latin America, and Africa," resulting in a "lost decade" for many of the Bank's borrowers (Cornia 1987).

This lost decade for many countries affected Northern interests as well, which only served to deepen the Bank's involvement and commitment to resolving the crisis. For instance, in 1982, U.S. banks had almost half their capital in Mexican loans at a time when Mexico built up $80 billion worth of debt and became unable to pay off its loans (McMichael 2004). To avert a catastrophe, the World Bank and IMF bailed out overextended Northern banks and investors while forcing a much more interventionist structural adjustment regime on Mexico. In only ten years, Mexico took out thirteen adjustment loans from the Bank and six adjustment agreements with the IMF that completely revamped the Mexican state and economy, eliminating food subsidies, rural public agencies, national food security systems, and state-owned food monopolies (McMichael 2004). Yet commercial banks made windfall profits in Mexico ($500 million) and, under similar circumstances, in Brazil ($1 billion) (Peet 2003, p. 76). By 1989, most new loans across the global South were adjustment loans and a debt-ridden post-Soviet empire had joined the ranks of the borrowers. The Bank's adjustment regime had definitively become global.

With the debt and structural adjustment crises, the Bank reformulated the post-1989 question of democratization and governance, and the green-revolution era concerns with redistribution and equity, into the neoliberal question of the *freedom and sovereignty of capital.* The World Bank, IMF, and WTO provoked a global managerial state of mind that eclipsed alternative regional and national politics. If the green revolution transformed North-South relations at the point of production, giving rise to a new global agro-food system, then the structural adjustment era affected relations at the point of social reproduction, reconfiguring the way in which states and citizens interact, in what can be called the "government of the social" (Polanyi 1957). Spearheaded by the Bank, these overlapping regimes of development—poverty alleviation and structural adjustment—only deepened and expanded World Bank power in borrowing countries, intensifying McNamara's mission beyond his wildest dreams.

These overlapping regimes also reflected a major shift at the Bank and in Washington, as part of the Reagan-Thatcher neoliberal revolution, as well as multiple shifts in many other countries where neoliberal agendas have hatched. Soon after President Reagan selected A. W. Clausen (president of Bank of America) as the World Bank president, Clausen cleaned house of the Bank's "redistribution with growth" advocates. First he fired McNamara's chief economist, Hollis Chenery, a world-renowned innovator, and replaced him with Anne Krueger, the Milton Friedman neoliberal. Krueger's intellectual contribution to the field of development economics was the argument of the "rent-seeking" state as a significant drag on economic growth in the third world (Dezalay and Garth 2002; Kapur,

Webb, and Lewis 1997; Krueger 1974); she seemed to be an odd
choice because she was not an enthusiastic supporter of the
idea of development lending. By the end of the Bank's 1987
reorganization, many of Chenery's supporters were fired and
nearly 800 orthodox macroeconomists were hired. This was
the final stage of what one Bank official called "economic geno-
cide" for the older generation of development economists (Dezalay and Garth 2002; George and Sabelli 1994).

Although structural adjustment became, for the World
Bank and the IMF, the primary program for all countries with
troubled economies, the blueprints for change were based on
ascending neoliberal tenets. Known as the ideological foundation of the Washington Consensus, the neoliberal agenda did
not necessarily originate or evolve in Washington alone. Instead, the specifics of the agenda were generated through political struggles and compromises unfolding through North-
South, as well as World Bank-borrower, relations. This global
debt crisis, derived from volatile flows of finance capital in and
out of the South, catapulted the neoliberal agenda into the
global arena. In many countries, the neoliberal mandate of
lowering trade barriers, opening up markets to foreign imports, reducing the role of the state in production and social
service provision, and eliminating restrictions on foreign capital has led to the destruction of domestic productive sectors.
In the 1980s, for example, Michael Manley, then president of
Jamaica, described as a "Faustian bargain" the series of structural adjustment policies he was forced to accept, an arrange-
ment that subsequently killed off Jamaica's domestic agriculture, dairy, and poultry industries as a result of a flood of cheap
imports from the United States (Black and Kincaid 2001).
Moreover, dispossessed rural families had little choice but to
work in the new, highly exploitative tax-free enterprise zones

that obliged them to compete with the world's lowest wages (McMichael 2004).

The Bank's neoliberal turn was supported by a whole network of policy elites based in Washington, as well as professional lawyers, economists, business leaders, and technocrats in capital cities like Santiago and Mexico City, working in a variety of state and nonstate institutions (e.g., universities, the legal system, the private sector, even human rights agencies) and pursuing their own national agendas (Babb 2001). As a consequence, the neoliberalism that evolved in Venezuela looked markedly different than that which emerged in Chile, and both had little resemblance to the prototypes mapped out in Washington. As Yves Dezalay and Bryant Garth brilliantly document, the roots of the idea of the "neoliberal revolution" can be traced through these traveling elites and their institutions of training and work, constituting a North-South institutional network of neoliberal "technopols" (Dezalay and Garth 2002). The production of actually existing neoliberalism was (and remains) a transnational dialectical process, a product of tension, struggle, and negotiated compromise among the World Bank, IMF, powerful bankers and political elites, and scores of actors working in corporations, governments, and professional societies around the world. Under the leadership of the World Bank, one significant strand that has emerged from these transnational institutional practices is green neoliberalism.

## Tensions between the Green and the Neoliberal

After decades of being ignored and dismissed, and after working diligently to create a milieu in which there would be few alternatives to its rules, the World Bank of the 1980s found itself firmly at the helm of the world of development. Yet the two transnational institutions in charge of the debt crisis, the World Bank and the IMF, did not have much time to celebrate. As economies crashed and people took to the streets, both institutions became the focus of scorn, anger, and frustration. No longer was the World Bank seen as a dispassionate expert offering technical advice at a distance. Instead, it was blamed for reduced public spending; mass unemployment; currency collapse; rising prices for food, fuel, and other goods; and falling wages and export prices. At the precise moment that the Bank belted itself into the driver's seat, many of its client governments were on the verge of collapse.

Adding to these pressures was a series of high-profile activist campaigns directed at revealing and reversing the negative social and environmental effects of Bank projects. The image in the North of the happy recipients of Bank aid—the "objects of development"—was sabotaged as rural peasants and urban laborers began a series of bread riots and project protests, including mass marches and fasts to dramatize their discontent with the World Bank and its policies. In the mid-1980s, activists "beyond borders" began to organize to increase the effectiveness of their protests (Fox and Brown 1998; Fox and Thorne 1997; Keck and Sikkink 1998; Smith, Chatfield, and Pagnucco 1997), such that the Bank's policies and practices in the most remote areas of India, Brazil, and Indonesia became front page news in the North and were the topic of significant parliamentarian and congressional debates in Bonn, London, Tokyo, and Washington (Fox and Brown 1998). They were also the source of high-anxiety political conflict in the streets of Manila, Jakarta, and New Delhi. The global master of development was on trial in the world's court of public opinion.

In Thailand, activists protested dozens of destructive dam, mining, and forestry projects in support of the hundreds of thousands of people, especially ethnic minorities, who had been forcibly displaced by Bank projects with little compensation (Parnwell and Bryant 1996; Rich 1994). The list of grievances included gross human rights violations and the impoverishment of large rural populations through projects that mostly benefited a narrow set of state-class, urban, and industrial interests.[25] In Indonesia, protests erupted against the World Bank's extensive support of General Suharto's Transmigration Project, a military-cum-development scheme that forcibly resettled more than two million ethnic minorities from the inner islands of Java and Bali to the outer islands between the mid-1970s and mid-1980s.[26]

Campaigns were also launched against the World Bank's support of the Narmada Dam project in India, and the Polonoroeste highway project in Brazil. Ironically, the Bank publicly promoted its Polonoroeste project in the Brazilian Amazon as a leading example of sustainable development, suggesting that its five successive loans to Brazil would be the key lever to force a reluctant Brazilian government to take seriously the needs of the indigenous peoples who lived in this region. Others, by contrast, saw this massive highway project as the death knell for the rain forest and its indigenous population, as it would invite millions of colonizers into a region without sufficient state authority to prevent clear-felling the forest and harassing its dwellers—which is precisely what happened. As scholars and activists documented the destruction, this campaign became a catalyst for a type of transnational advocacy networking that has become remarkably common today (Keck and Sikkink 1998).

The anti-Polonoroeste campaign became a significant threat to more than just the Bank's work in the Amazon. The exposure of Bank practices evoked strong criticisms on the part of key Northern policymakers. After sitting through more than twenty hearings before the U.S. Congress, in which passionate and media-genic speakers from Amazonian indigenous groups, clad in their traditional clothing, testified to the project's destructive effects on their communities, some members of Congress threatened to cut support to the multilateral development banks, while others became determined to discipline the World Bank and impose upon it some form of accountability. As conservative Republican Senator Robert Kasten noted in 1986, "When people find out what's been going on, you're going to see people out in the street saying, 'My God, did you read this information? Why are our dollars being used to fund this kind of destruction?'" An official in the Treasury Department agreed: "I think it's a disaster, it's a mistake, and it's been going on for years" (Wade 1997, p. 671). The fact that this campaign coincided with Bank efforts to request additional commitments from European governments and the United States to replenish the International Development Assistance (IDA) fund placed the Bank in an extremely vulnerable position.

To survive this onslaught of criticism that shook the confidence of Northern policy makers, the Bank responded with stubborn denial and then, when that backfired, with substantial organizational change. Through the efforts of a handful of reform-minded actors within the Bank, the environment became the Bank's chief area of concern. New theories, idioms, images, slogans, departments, priorities, and data were generated at breakneck speed. New World Bank reports determined that there could be no sustained economic growth without a

sustainable environment and just treatment of the ethnic minorities and indigenous peoples living on fragile ecosystems.
Money and other institutional resources were thrown at the
problem. As late as 1985, the Bank had only five staff people officially working on the environment; by 1995 it had more than
three hundred. In 1985, the Bank loaned less than $15 million in
the name of the environment; a decade later, it was lending almost a billion dollars. Between 1985 and 1995, budgetary resources for environmental policy, research, and loans grew by
more than 90 percent a year.[27] The small Office of Environmental Affairs ballooned into an Environment Department, with a
significant body of staff. In 1992, the Bank established a new vice
presidency for environmentally sustainable development.

By the mid-1990s, environmental issues had become so
central to the Bank's identity and work that its clients could
not borrow until they had signed off on a National Environmental Action Plan (NEAP), which committed them to "mainstream" their environmental concerns in national development policies. Large-scale projects were no longer approved by
the Bank's executive directors without rigorous environmental
and social assessments based on a scientific protocol that the
World Bank, meanwhile, was busy inventing. The Bank imposed on its borrowers "environmental adjustment" policies
throughout the 1990s (often in concert with its fiscal structural
adjustment policies), which pressed governments into creating
cookie-cutter-like environmental protection agencies; redraft-
ing forestry, land, and water laws; establishing national environmental policy and research institutes; and training a cadre
of professionals to carry out environmental reforms. These interventions attempted to make national standards more compatible with a set of "global" standards that the Bank and its
partners were working hard to create at the same time.[28]

## Conclusion

Although its birth in the mid-1940s reflected a noteworthy event in postcolonial history, the World Bank became a powerful organization only two decades later, under Robert McNamara's leadership. McNamara seized the opportunity to expand the Bank's role in the global economy at a pivotal moment when U.S. hegemony was being challenged by Europe, Japan, and the oil-producing OPEC nations, on the one hand, and by anti-colonial insurgents throughout the South, on the other. Under McNamara's stewardship, the Bank instigated new transnational spheres of political and economic influence in which it and Southern professional supporters worked together to produce a new regime of development. McNamara's remarkable system of knowledge production and dissemination enabled the Bank to lend substantial amounts of capital and influence decision making within borrowing-country institutions as it never had been able to before. Even after McNamara's retirement and major changes within the Bank, McNamara's mark on the Bank helped it to overcome threats to its authority and legitimacy and to grow stronger and more powerful, as it had after the debt crisis and the anti-Bank street riots and mass protests of the 1980s.

In the late 1980s, the environment became a category of broad significance in the world of development in part because of the widespread ecological and social devastation that resulted from Bank projects and policies. To survive the onslaught of criticism that made the Bank into an institution non grata and attracted the critical eye of Northern policymakers, the Bank was forced to engage in major organizational reform. Remarkably, by the late 1990s, the World Bank was setting new global standards for environmental management and regulation such that by the early twenty-first century, no inter-national organization could afford to stake a position without working through the parameters set by the Bank on issues that range widely from biodiversity and sustainable forestry, to poverty and public health, to fundamental rights for indige-nous peoples to access environmental resources, to society-wide rights to access safe water. The Bank responded to its crit-ics with renewed vigor, increases in finance capital, and global expansion.

The greening of the World Bank has successfully engaged numerous governments and development and environmental activists, as well as Bank investors and borrowers, proving to many skeptical observers, including those within the organiza-tion, that it could lead on the environmental front without compromising its "AAA" bond ratings. But transforming this massive technocratic hulk from culprit to vanguard would not be an easy job.

# III

# Producing Green Science
# inside Headquarters

*Lending capital is no longer the World Bank's
greatest asset on the global market; knowledge is.
Knowledge is its greatest source of power.*
*—Senior Bank official, author interview,*
*January 1995*

*The dominant internal view at the Bank on how to
best deal with the Board [of Executive Directors]
is often summed up as the Mushroom Principle:
"Feed them shit and keep them in the dark."*
*—George and Sabelli 1994, p. 208*

As a data collector, the World Bank is unrivaled, sending missions abroad to study everything from government budgets to ownership records for village lands. Much of this information is not actually published by the Bank, largely because governments consider such disclosures to be national security risks, but the Bank's published reports do not hesitate to draw conclusions from this exclusive information. The Bank, therefore, is doubly well situated as the largest "research" organization in the world with such remarkable access, yet one that is unable (and unwilling) to release its coveted data, imbuing its reports, conclusions, and policy statements with especially high value. This exclusive cache of information puts non-Bank scientists at a comparative disadvantage, not just because of their more limited data-gathering capacities, but because they cannot replicate, elaborate upon, or refute the Bank's research methods and conclusions without it.[1]

As a producer of scientific knowledge, the Bank is also peerless: not only does its professional staff have access to rare data, but they have been trained at top universities. According to one report, 80 percent received degrees from the same top U.S. or British Ph.D. programs (Frey et al. 1984; Wade 1997). At more than $30 million, the Bank's annual research budget is one of the largest among global institutions.[2] As one senior Bank official exclaimed, "I never had such access or support in all my years working for a major U.S. university."[3] Moreover, most Bank officials comfortably embrace the dominant epistemological paradigm in their work, which on the surface presents a scientific esprit de corps that is rare among research institutions. For this reason, and because of its consensus-eliciting institutional norms, Bank publications rarely contradict or challenge the latest policy line coming from the top echelons of Bank hierarchy.

When it comes to dissemination of research findings, the Bank, again, is tops in the field. In the academic world, university courses in development economics rely heavily upon Bank publications (Stern and Ferreira 1997).[4] World Bank publications are cited considerably more often than the average economics or business journal article in the Social Science Citation Index, another indication of the centrality of Bank ideas, data, and analysis in the production of academic thought. Its latest publications (and well-timed press releases) are regularly featured in major newspapers around the world. On certain topics—for example, structural adjustment; debt; and the economies of most African countries, the former Soviet Union (since 1989), and China (since the early 1980s)—the world media depend almost exclusively on World Bank data and interpretations.[5] It not only has the respect of the media, it has the ear of the world's most important policy makers, from prime ministers and presidents, to national academies of sciences, to chambers of commerce. In remote rural research institutes of the Indian desert or southern African bush, researchers have come to depend on free, regularly posted Bank reports for their daily staple of information. Its flagship publication, the *World Development Report* (*WDR*), is the most cited economic development publication the world over. With an annual press run of more than 120,000 in six languages, *WDR* is required reading at development research institutes around the globe as well as at the international desk at the *New York Times.*[6]

In sum, Bank knowledge circulates widely and has become an important tool in policy making and debate; more specifically, it lays the groundwork for Bank innovations, new political rationalities, and new ambitions. Over time, we have taken it for granted and it has become widely accepted worldwide. Knowledge is indeed power for the World Bank. Although scholars, activists, and the occasional journalist have written about the "quality" of Bank information, especially in criticisms of particular projects or policies, few have written about the actual production process. In this chapter, by contrast, I will focus precisely on the assembly line of knowledge production inside Bank headquarters and, more specifically, on the production of green knowledge.

In searching for an explanation as to why the Bank never seems to improve or take environmental concerns seriously, many have pointed to the Bank's intensely hierarchical and punitive organizational culture (Caufield 1996; Pincus and Winters 2002; Rich 1994; Wade 1997). Famous stories circulate about fierce and humiliating temper tantrums by senior managers, including President Wolfensohn, that serve the purpose of reminding Bank employees never to step out of line. In this chapter I will describe elements of this organizational form of social control because it helps to explain what staff members have to watch out for when they participate in the production of knowledge on the environment, which is still a controversial issue within Bank headquarters. Controversy surrounding environmentalism looms large within the Bank, not because Bank employees are anti-environmentalism, but because the organizational incentive system for promotion pressures staff to make their loans big and move on them quickly. Safeguarding projects against environmental problems is an expensive and time-consuming process that works against an individual's desire to rise among the ranks. This is the common explanation for what is seen as the Bank's failure to create a robust environmental program, but it does not account for the fact that Bank environmental assessments, policies, reforms, and projects can be found in every country where the Bank works—indeed, Bank-style environmentalism is state-of-the-art in many governmental and development agencies. This is not the sign of failure.

Hence, I describe the way the Bank works inside headquarters in order to elucidate these characteristics of Bank organizational culture as symptoms of the Bank's roles as an institutional wedge for Northern capital expansionism and the major harbinger of development. As I argue in later chapters, these practices inside headquarters have enabled the Bank to become a leader both in the global economy and in global cultural production, insofar as it fabricates a powerful green agenda, political rationality, and tools to institutionalize its approach in the workings of states, organizations, and transnational policy networks. I describe the organizational culture and constraints at World Bank headquarters in Washington, D.C., in order to portray the pressures and incentives that dominate the workplace for Bank staff. But the organization does not exist in a vacuum, and the institutional culture is not merely the result of obstinate managers. Instead, we need to understand this culture as reflective of the larger role the Bank plays in the world. Therefore, in this chapter I will explore the following questions: How does the Bank construct its own version of environmentalism, based on what criteria, internal and external influences, and for what purposes? And on what basis does this version of environmentalism become persuasive outside of headquarters? Indeed, because of the Bank's dominant role in the global economy and in the global production of knowledge, what it produces is very powerful. Its role in the global economy shapes the ways in which knowledge is produced. Note that the Bank entered into the business of the environment only in the early 1990s, yet today, its interpretation of environmentally sustainable development rules.

On our tour of the assembly line of knowledge production, we start with a typical research project within the Bank's main research unit, the Policy Research Department (in what is called "the Center"), to find out where the policy research professionals get their funding, how they craft their research questions, and how research gets defined by the organization. Next, we travel from *policy* research to *project* research (in what is called "Operations") and learn about knowledge production intended specifically for project design and assessment. From there we move into the arena of environmental assessment and analysis, where we meet the environmental science watchdogs for project loan management. Further down the line, we hear how Bank reports are produced and examine their content, arguments, and bibliographic notes. Finally, our travels take us down the dark corridors of decision making, from staff hiring to career management. Here we hear about deep-seated staff frustration and observe some of the microtechnologies of Bank power that rely on intellectual strong-arm tactics to carve out a unified front on green development that can circulate through the Bank's transnational professional networks.

## Institutional Constraints on the Framing of Research Questions

In the World Bank's Policy Research Department (PRD), the main aim is to develop scientific knowledge on questions that emerge from policy debates.[7] In any given year, the Bank publishes approximately 450 official publications, more than 150 journal articles and more than 200 working papers, a few of its own journals (including *World Bank Economic Review* and

*World Bank Research Observer*), numerous departmental magazines, and hundreds of in-house "confidential" reports (such as Staff Appraisal Reports and Country Assistance Strategy reports). Approximately $25 million, or 3 percent of the Bank's administrative budget, is formally allocated for research, but this figure does not include loan-related research or environmental assessments (which perhaps adds another $23 million per year). An additional $10–15 million is spent on economic analyses of projects, sectors, and policies from PRD, the country departments, and technical assistance offices.

Despite their large research budget, researchers in the PRD are fairly limited as to what questions they can pursue. "This is not like a university," explained one PRD analyst.[8] "I have no research assistants I can call upon. Consultants cost $600 per day just to work in D.C.; to have them do research in the field, with travel costs, field assistants, jeeps, fuel, per diems, well, the money's just not there."

More precisely, the money is there, but it is allocated elsewhere. This analyst specializes in research on energy pricing, an attractive topic at the Bank since it is one of the key environmental components of structural adjustment policies (Reed 1992). He studies the impact of government-initiated energy price increases on different income groups. The Bank promotes energy price increases, or subsidy reductions, to minimize market distortions and reduce wasteful consumption, believing that current wasteful energy practices in the South can be changed if national energy prices more accurately reflected real energy costs ("getting the price right"). Although governments typically subsidize the costs of fuels so households and industries can afford them, these state subsidies are said to have lasting market- and behavior- distorting effects. These days, the Bank also argues that energy subsidies lead to wasteful energy consumption that unnecessarily harms the environment.

There are many questions that arise from such a policy: How do price increases affect the behavior of different groups of consumers? Should there be a multi-tiered subsidy system or a special "social fund" to help the lowest-income groups that would suffer under increased fuel prices? Which energy resources should be included (e.g., oil, cow dung, forest cover)? What are the secondary effects of reducing energy subsidies— would communities switch to more polluting or more ecologically fragile resources? These are the hard-to-answer questions that could shed light on the wisdom of standardized policy recommendations, research that could show how these policies work in particular contexts and what the implications for the environment are.

Indeed, this is the role that some Bank researchers envision for themselves, but there are institutional constraints that limit their opportunities for carrying out such in-depth studies. For example, testing these hypotheses requires elaborate household and community-based data on different types of fuel consumption—a formidable task when your research site is a country as large as India, much less the world. Aggregate data sets on fuel consumption are generally insufficient for such questions; what is required are disaggregated, local-level data that can describe why some resources are preferred over others and what price levels would get consumers to reduce or switch, and to what fuels they would turn. For the closest approximations, one would need to know the physical, economic, and cultural terrain; however, the national data sets Bank analysts use cannot begin to reveal such specificity and nuances.

Although PRD and the Environment Department (also in the Center) are both uniquely positioned to answer this question in that they have the best-trained staff, some money to hire consultants in the field, contacts in all the right ministries, and access to hard-to-get data, there are plenty of obstacles and disincentives to doing so. One major barrier is that demand (and money) for such assignments comes from Operations, and the professionals in Operations (i.e., loan managers) want reports quickly in order to support their policies or projects. "But to do household studies—to find out why different households choose certain fuels for certain uses—requires time, money, and lots of field research," one analyst explained. "How can I do a medium-term study if they always want the results in the short term? That's why [that] type of research is not done here. It's just not realistic when the loan managers are the ones funding us."

Another serious problem is finding a unit within the Bank to fund the research. "I wanted to do a study on energy pricing impact on the poor," said this Policy Research Department analyst, "because we can't know the impact of our policy until we actually test the idea. The problem is that it's hard to get anyone to fund it." Like his colleagues, approximately half of his salary and research budget comes from project managers who work in Operations; they submit requests, or bid, for his time to do research for them.[9] Although many loan managers are sympathetic to his research concerns and would love to have a comprehensive study that confirms their beliefs about the effects of their energy loans, none is interested in spending the $500,000 or more to perform the study.

Other constraints shape the research that is done as well. As this policy analyst explained:

> I got one manager to agree [to fund my study], since he needed data in a few states [in that country]. But we disagreed as to which states. I was planning a medium-term study over a few years, comparing a few states picked based on a comparative method with a decent-sized sample. But he only wanted to

fund research in states where he was working. So, in spite of my hesitations, I accommodated him. But by the time I designed the study, the state ministers weren't interested in his projects, so he had to switch to other states. This happens all the time; if one project doesn't fly, they try another one, elsewhere. Well, it's not so easy for us to switch research sites in the middle of a study. Yet, they expect us to do the background work for their projects.

In a recent interview on intellectual innovation at the World Bank, former president Robert McNamara referred to a number of "pathbreaking" ideas that emanated from the Bank, often despite vehement protests from U.S. administrations: his 1973 Nairobi speech on the centrality of the issue of poverty, his invitation to China to enter the World Bank in the late 1970s, his 1980 speech on structural adjustment. McNamara argued that in many of the significant international policy shifts of the 1970s and 1980s, political leadership in the North *followed* the lead of the World Bank. In the early 1980s, McNamara planned to establish a semi-autonomous research subsidiary of the Bank to formally institutionalize the Bank's global intellectual leadership. He hoped to raise an annual budget of $50 million, with $100,000 research grants distributed to each of his best and brightest 500 World Bank "brains"—McNamara's vision for solving the world's problems in the most expeditious, technomanagerialist fashion.[10] His plans never came to fruition. Instead, as the previous examples indicate, Bank researchers depend heavily on loan managers to fund their brain power. When project loan managers are paying the bill for research—whether they are shepherding a small and simple road project or a massive and complex structural adjustment package—they tend not to be interested in findings that complicate or throw a shadow upon their project objectives. This basic tension is endemic to the production of knowledge at the World Bank.

Although McNamara failed to produce the institutional mechanisms to finance the Bank's brain power in the way he wanted, his dream of producing a unified voice within the Bank to lead the world was, to a certain degree, realized. That is, one learns from Bank staff that Bank researchers and analysts receive unambiguously clear messages to pursue their science in such a way that leads to a unified policy voice. This is one reason the Bank was able to quickly build a cache of expertise in environmentally sustainable development and to utilize it in its many borrowing countries.

## Environmental Research and the Project Cycle

From the Policy Research Department in the Center, we travel across the World Bank complex to Operations, where loan projects are conceived. Here, we gain some insights into the production of scientific research that is utilized for project design and assessment. Research—green or otherwise—is just one component of the Bank's objective to design and sell "quality" loans. For the Bank to exist it must sell loans; the success of an individual's career, too, is contingent on his or her ability to sell loans. As other critiques of the Bank's organizational culture have shown, this staff incentive—indeed, imperative—has created serious problems for the Bank's capacity to design quality loans (Pincus and Winters 2002; Wade 1997). Yet this is not the only factor that shapes outcomes here.

To understand the relation between research and project loans, it is useful first to discuss where research fits into the project cycle. Picture a line diagram of the typical World Bank project cycle: stage 1 starts with project design, cost-benefit analysis, and (often) environmental assessment. Then loan managers must package the loan for approval by Bank upper management and executive directors, and after that, the loan must be negotiated with the borrowers. The loan cannot pass through these steps without a complete plan for procurement of goods and services and the creation of the legal contracts for the loan. Once approved by lender and borrower, which might take a couple of rounds, the next step (stage 2) is the actual implementation of the project, which typically takes several years. At the end of the project cycle, there is follow-up, aimed at ensuring that all is well years after the loan agreement has been signed (stage 3).

According to Bank documents and interviews with Bank staff, more than half of project-related staff time is devoted to just two tasks of stage 1: *procurement,* or the contracting for all project-related goods and services, and *legal affairs* (e.g., the drawing up of the loan contract between lender and borrower) (Wapenhans 1992, p. iii). Despite years of environmental reforms, less than 1 percent of a project's budget (and an average of only four weeks of a task manager's time) is dedicated to environmental assessment, conducted during the project's design phase.[11] Compared with stage 1, the staff time and money allocated for project implementation, supervision, evaluation, and follow-up (stages 2 and 3) is minuscule, despite the fact that these parts of the project take longer to execute than stage 1 (7.5 years versus 1.5 years, on average).[12] To conduct increased research and additional scrutiny based on new green criteria adds costs and tension to the already long time frame of the project.

Moreover, less than 40 percent of Bank projects actually keep the same staff for more than two years, even though a project life cycle averages nine years (Wapenhans 1992, annex A, p. 19). That means that few project managers and their support staffs actually see a project through beyond stage 1; in fact, their careers depend on their success rate in packaging and selling loans, not on following them up in the field. Indeed, across the Bank, loan managers are leaving their loans before they even begin disbursing funds, but usually after they are approved.

A look at the project cycle shows that the opportunities for data collection, research, environmental assessment, and project evaluation are small. At the start, much staff time and money is focused on legal and procurement matters. Then the main task is to sell the project to the Bank's executive directors and government officials, which is obviously not the moment for squeamish loan managers to divulge controversial facts and analysis. By stage 2, when the project is actually being implemented, most loan managers have moved on to the next set of loan preparations. None of my interviewees could come up with an institutional incentive that encourages them to allocate resources to research the project while it evolves: the institutional disincentives far outweigh the incentives to collect environmental data, observe problems with the project, and make adjustments throughout the project's tenure, when the real environmental and social externalities unfold. In this highly routinized project cycle, in which every staff-hour is accounted for in the budget, loan managers are not rewarded if they add months to their budget for careful research in stage 1 or tack salaries for a team of data collectors and analysts onto stages 2 and 3. This would be stepping way beyond the norms and culture of the World Bank.

## Staff Training on Environmental Assessment

Conducting environmental assessments (EAs) for the Bank's largest projects is no easy task. As official Operational Directive (OD) guidelines state: "[Through an EA,] all environmental consequences should be recognized early in the project cycle and taken into account in project-selection, siting, planning, and design. EAs identify ways of improving projects environmentally, by preventing, minimizing, mitigating, or compensating for adverse impacts."[13] Comprehensive EAs are required for investments that are certain to have "significant adverse impacts that may be sensitive, irreversible, diverse, comprehensive, broad, or precedent-setting."[14] These types of investments are categorized as "A" projects. If investments will lead to environmental impacts that are only "site-specific in nature and do not significantly affect human populations or alter environmentally important areas," partial EAs are required for the particular issues in question (World Bank Environment Department 1995, p. 2). These are categorized as "B" projects. Investments that do not require an EA fall into the "C" category; they are typically in the fields of health, education, and welfare, and structural adjustment loans, which comprise more than 30 percent of the Bank's annual lending portfolio.[15] Interestingly, the total amount of Bank loan money invested in category A projects has risen significantly between 1991 and 1995, from 11 percent of the Bank's nonadjustment loan portfolio to 24 percent.[16] Eighty percent of category A projects comes from the Bank's three main sectors: energy and power, agriculture, and transport. With an increase in category A project investments has come a demand for more complex EAs. Environmental assessment has become a veritable growth industry in and outside of the Bank.

To transmit the basic concepts, norms, and procedural rules of EAs to loan managers, the World Bank Institute (WBI) and the Environment Department have teamed up to offer regular day-long training seminars for Bank staff. At the staff training seminar I attended as a participant-observer in 1995, the Environment Department official running the workshop spent the morning presenting the Bank's approach to environmental assessment; in the afternoon, he invited two Washington-based consultants to walk through case studies of "strong" and "weak" EAs. Throughout the day, staff received straightforward explanations as to what an environmental assessment is, its significance for Bank projects, and the strengths and weaknesses of the Bank's past EA performance. From this exposition, we received a boiled-down version of the concepts considered important by the Center's Environment Department, as transmitted to Operations' loan managers.

According to EA specialists, environmental assessment is an opportunity for loan managers to conduct a study of possible future environmental problems—"[to] create a risk scenario," our staff trainer explained—before the project gets approved, so that funds can be allocated and project components redesigned to reduce these risks. If a dam is being built, for example, it is important to estimate the probability that a glacier lake will burst and create havoc for the project (as well as for the project manager).[17] The staff manual on EAs lists the full range of what is meant by the environment: water, air, noise, biodiversity, flora and fauna, and even human health. By the end of the day, Bank staff were quite clear on what concepts and definitions were considered important and appropriate to use and which were not.

In the morning session, the trainer reviewed findings from the Environment Department's recent evaluative study of World Bank EAs, suggesting that current EAs are a vast improvement over those from the old days. There is less reluctance among staff to follow procedures, and in many cases EAs have helped both borrowers and Bank staff to agree on the critical environmental issues. Although EAs rarely stop a project dead in the water, they do add an important dimension to project design: they force the Bank and its borrowers to collect baseline data that, it is argued, can translate into better-designed projects (World Bank Environment Department 1996; World Bank Environment Department 1994). Yet there are some basic shortfalls in the Bank's EA work, according to the report and the trainer. One of the most obvious is the number of EAs that fail to provide an analysis of alternatives. Although it is required, only half of project EAs actually look into the question of alternatives—that is, study the option of *not* building another power plant (a supply-driven project) and consider replacing it with a plan to reduce energy consumption (a demand-driven project).[18] A second shortcoming is in the area of public consultation, which most EAs avoid. For example, it was only through a public meeting for a Caribbean landfill and waste disposal project, our trainer noted, that one Bank project manager learned of an endangered species making its home at the proposed site. Since the project had not yet been implemented, it was moved to another site and the problem was averted. (Seminar participants gave a collective moan, signaling their sympathy toward their colleague who had to start over because of a rare grasshopper.) "Remember," the trainer instructed, "the public can be a great source for data." A third weakness is in the area of supervision. Fewer than 40 percent of Bank A projects are supervised.[19] Of the unsupervised A projects, the trainer admitted, "We really don't know what the environmental impacts are."

These EA problem spots can be overcome through careful planning, he suggested, which will lead to fewer hassles for managers downstream. To illustrate his point, the trainer offered a case study of an EA that "handled 90 percent of the issues well, but missed a few." The participants were asked to find its weaknesses and suggest ways to overcome them. A Washington-based consultant helped run the exercise. The following discussion illustrates some of the institutional incentives for Bank staff to conduct "good" EAs and some of the conceptions of nature and environmental management that are deemed relevant.

The trainer introduced a project of a Ghana gold mine expansion, assessed as a category A project, which requires an extensive environmental and social assessment because of the potential high risks. The gold mine, active throughout the past century, is failing; it is owned and operated by the Ghana government (55 percent) and by a British company (45 percent). Its gold production represents one-fifth of Ghana's foreign exchange, making it a project of "national concern." The Bank's investment is supposed to increase the life of the mine by only a decade and increase production to 33 tons. For mine expansion and processing, the Bank developed a $555-million project to improve infrastructure for power and water supplies, underground and open pit mining, and ore processing. To safeguard against future liability, the trainer and a visiting consultant explained, the project needed a baseline study; therefore an EA was essential. According to the trainer, category A environmental assessments safeguard loan managers from any problems, environmental or legal, in the future. "The Bank has to document where it started to get involved, so it cannot be held responsible for what has occurred before." At a cost of $1 million, this particular EA covered four main concerns: hazardous and toxic materials, involuntary resettlements, occupational health and safety, and watershed preservation.

The baseline study conducted by the Bank's British consultants showed that poisonous emissions from previous years of gold mining had denuded the surrounding hills, filled the air with high concentrations of toxic chemicals, and contaminated the rivers and groundwater. Sulfur, cyanide, and arsenic are some of the chemicals that are used either for processing or get extracted along with the gold in "gold roasting." Out of concern for these toxins, the EA recommended scrubbers for air quality but found no reason, or legal obligation, to mitigate future effects—or remediate previous damage—on flora or fauna, water supplies, or human health. "Since no flora or fauna remains in the micro-area," the consultant stated, "this new project has no effect on them." Hence there would be no obligation to spend additional funds. In the case of water pollution, he added: "Although arsenic emissions would be high for this project, river levels are already much higher than WHO standards for drinking water." That is, even with expensive technological alterations, future emissions would have no appreciable effect on water quality since the river will always be undrinkable. Moreover, the community has long ago become accepting of the poisoned river. For example, he said: "The children even swim in it."

To get local feedback, a concept that was heavily promoted throughout this staff seminar, the consultant explained that public information sheets were distributed and public discussions were held at local schools and at the royal palace. When a seminar participant asked why the information sheets were not printed in the local language, the consultant replied that because only 10 percent of the locals were literate, local teachers and leaders were given the task of disseminating the information. Someone else asked how likely it was that locals would question elements of a project if the meeting was held at the royal residence. The consultant said that the community always held important meetings there, and no one, he surmised, seemed to mind.

As the session wound down, the trainer asked the Bank

staff what was missing from the project's EA. When no one answered to his satisfaction, he replied that what was missing was an overall plan delineating who was responsible for specific environmental externalities—local groups, state agencies, or the mining company. The EA study, he pointed out, never defined a role for the government and its new environmental agency, which is important for the purpose of delineating ownership, responsibility, and, of course, liability. Everyone nodded. When there were no more questions, we broke for lunch.

So what did we learn from this staff training? For one, we learned that the "environment" refers only to that which the specific project will affect, and that measurement is actually quite important and is open to interpretation. Hence, deciding the exact parameters of the temporal and spatial dimensions of a project is a significant outcome of a World Bank environmental assessment. It helps define, with an apparent aura of precision, the question of liability and responsibility of a project's impact on, for this mine project, flora, soils, air, water, and human health. Questions about the range of impact for which project backers are responsible are very important to determine at the outset and is the job, in part, of a good EA. Is it hundreds of yards or hundreds of miles? How can we determine what the downstream and upstream responsibilities are? Is the project responsible for subsoil and underground aquifer conditions? At what point in time or on the terrain can we stop worrying about project impact and responsibility? These are complex questions that could have any number of legitimate answers, especially in front of a claims court or in public opinion.

On the one hand, we learned that EAs can serve as a prod to challenge engineers and planners to design a project that mitigates negative effects for human and nonhuman populations and environments at great distances from the site, over great time periods, down to the most minute WHO health and safety specifications. On the other hand, EAs can precisely delineate the parameters of a project, its measurable impact, and the backers' liability. The difference between measuring downstream effects as 100 yards *or* 100 miles from a project site can translate into millions of dollars in compensation, land and water cleansing, or population resettlement. The incentive, hence, becomes to minimize project risk through the process of constructing environmental assessments and its components, such as the baseline (i.e., was the area *already* poor and degraded?), the definition of what counts as a natural asset (i.e., the river and the surrounding flora were already dead and hence not the project's responsibility), human health (i.e., people's health was already contaminated), and what counts as an impact (i.e., how much additional damage could arsenic and mercury inflict if existing conditions were already of low value?).

The science and art of constructing EAs, therefore, becomes much more than a smokescreen of good intentions or a mindless bureaucratic exercise; EAs can serve as a very important legal, scientific, and economic tool to help mitigate the potentially high costs of future claims against the project and its owners. They can have a lasting impact on how environmental costs and risks are measured and defined. The stamp that the World Bank puts on the making of environmental assessments—a process with a very particular U.S.-based litigious history (Espeland 1998; Porter 1995; Scott 1998)—is the pressure to conjoin discourses of the environmental, legal, proprietary, and economic into one tool. As we will see, the science and art of environmental assessments is being sculpted under the auspices of the World Bank, as it is the main source of so much of the demand, and supply, of EAs worldwide.

Since the Bank is also financing the restructuring and retooling of the national environmental ministries of its borrowers, Bank-style EAs are being used around the world by state agencies to assess the value of nature, natural resources, and human health under the influence of large capital-intensive projects.

We also learned that a Bank-style environmental analysis uses as its yardstick an economic cost-benefit analysis that weighs "national" benefits, such as gold earnings, against "local" costs, such as community and environmental poisoning. To Bank staff, a multimillion-dollar investment in a poor and environmentally degraded area is usually considered a good idea, even if such investments historically have led to further site contamination and a limited number of years of income generation. In this case, for instance, the project's goal was to extend the life of the gold mine for only ten more years. Because Ghana is highly in debt, however, and its commodifiable resources, besides gold, are quite limited, making such a capital investment will always be viewed as beneficial as long as it generates hard currency for the country. Within this political-ecological rationality, the alternative of "no gold mine investment"—which is, in theory, always an option for EAs—does not merit serious consideration. (No one in the seminar brought up such a ludicrous idea.)

Environmental assessments also offer Bank staff the opportunity to strengthen the claims of the project's value by downgrading existing conditions. That is, the EA can provide a baseline measure against which the future outcome can always look, comparatively speaking, rosy. If the site can be represented as impoverished and ecologically degraded, as was the case of the gold mine site in Ghana, then the environmental assessment can reproduce the long-standing Bank tradition of describing prospective project sites and beneficiaries in terms of their "lacks." Environmental assessments can confirm, with all the backing of an environmental cost-benefit analysis, that the government and its poor populations need this Bank loan. In the process, EAs also clarify what counts as nature and what counts as development by predicating these concerns on a scientific, economic valuation. The only questions left involve the assignment of responsibility and liability: Who is responsible for a mine-related chemical spill or supplying potable water to the workforce and surrounding community? Even though these elements of the project are defined as costs—specifically *local* costs—they are juxtaposed to the larger *national* benefits of an income-generating investment, such as a gold mine.

Environmentalism, however, is also a discourse that project critics can claim as their own, which presupposes its own possible dangers. Interestingly, in the discussion of the African gold mine, no one in the training seminar seemed at all enthusiastic about the project as it seemed ripe for public controversy. Why put yourself and the Bank at risk by investing in a highly toxic site, even if it will produce gold? By the end of the discussion, the issue was less whether people would support the project than the overriding importance of a well-documented environmental and social assessment. Without it, you not only can get "zapped" by scrutinizing critics, but worse, the project could become an expensive liability down the road. Within this historical moment of contentious development, the significance of doing a thorough EA becomes self-evident.

By the end of the daylong seminar, those attending felt better equipped to confront the critical public, the demanding bosses, and the lawyers and financial advisors who apply pressure on Bank staff to increase their ability to "due diligence" around these large risky investments. It was a painful but rewarding seminar for all. I, for one, certainly will not look at environmental assessments in the same light as I did when I started the day—as just a tool to appease the environmentalists.

## Environmental Monitoring: A Herculean Task

Going from theory to practice is always difficult. Most Bank loan managers are trained in neoclassical economics, and environmental assessment is a trying proposition for them. Despite in-house trainings, most managers feel ill qualified for the task. (Fortunately, they can hire consultants to conduct them.) Nonetheless, loan managers are obliged to ensure that their loans are being monitored for environmental concerns throughout their project work. But many Bank projects are so large and so complex that no one could possibly monitor every aspect for its negative (or positive) environmental effect, even if an infinite amount of time and money were available. Below I describe some of the most obvious constraints for project oversight, however well one may have anticipated problems at the environment assessment stage.

Our first example comes from a loan manager, whom I will call Ted, a recent and young Ph.D. from the University of Chicago's economics department with no previous foreign experience. He is in charge of managing a $900-million rural modernization project, cofinanced by the World Bank, the InterAmerican Development Bank (IDB), which lends to Latin America and the Caribbean, and the borrowing country. This massive loan responsibility was a big step forward in his career; he started out at the Bank as a consultant, helping others on their projects, and this one fell into his lap after consecutive loan managers moved on to other jobs within the Bank. Ted is now overseeing the financing of multiple investments under the rubric of rural infrastructural development: roads, irrigation, drainage, electrical power plants and distribution grid development, land mapping and titling, fishing docks, farmer training, seed distribution, farmer credit, and more.[20] The loan affects every aspect of rural productive life in order to, as the loan's official title suggests, modernize the countryside.

One small component of the project is farmer credit, which Ted estimated would affect more than 90,000 farmers. He could not begin to speculate as to how many people would feel the effects of the main components of the loan, which included a huge power plant and road and irrigation construction projects. When asked about the environmental impacts of this mammoth intervention, he pointed only to the credit program and explained the difficulty of monitoring it. The program's objective ideally is to speedily distribute loans between $10,000 and $1 million to farmers to modernize their farms. Ted's main environmental worry is not soil erosion, land flooding, chemical runoff, elimination of traditional seed varieties, or other common environmentalist concerns associated with agricultural intensification. Local NGOs brought to his attention an unintended consequence of his loan: farmers were using these low-interest loans to invest in clearing adjacent forested area so they can extend their property under agricultural production rather than using the funds to intensify production on existing plots, as lenders intended.

To deter illegal encroachments into the forests, the Bank installed a monitoring system whereby each loan applicant must fill out a two-page environmental compliance form, which is reviewed by local officials, then by the Ministry of Environment, and finally by the Bank task manager. Loans are denied to farmers who acknowledge that they will use the funds to clear trees on public land. Any closer supervision, for example, actually monitoring borrowers' activities, is not feasible, Ted said. As it is, when he travels to the country—once every three months—his agenda is packed with meetings and commitments: "I may look into the files [collected in the capital city] and see one or two applications rejected, and for me, that's a measure that someone [in the ministry] is paying attention. Otherwise, there's no way for me to know what's going on—I have to go on faith. Look, there are so many components to this project. I bring a team with me and we look into each component maybe twice in the year, but we can't possibly look over everything in one week."

Ted says he can barely talk to all the necessary officials during his visits to the capital, let alone do spot checks in the countryside. Most of his time is spent trying to settle technical problems having to do with delays in construction, or incorrectly ordered supplies, or any number of routine problems and minidisasters that would bog down the smooth implementation of a massive development scheme. This is, after all, a $900-million loan shared with the InterAmerican Development Bank and the national government. There is plenty for Ted to oversee in his quarterly visits: "If a farmer is using his loan to cut down trees, well that's not good, but realistically what can I do? I can't stop the whole loan disbursement, that would be a big headache for us all."[21]

Many Bank staff members with whom I spoke made it clear that much rides on the successful completion of loan disbursements; the World Bank cannot afford to be slowed down by surveys or on-site inspections that reveal environmental debacles. Loan managers work under the constant pressure to move loans swiftly, and environmentally degrading project components inevitably slip past these project gatekeepers.

One of the environmental specialists who joins the team with the loan managers on their country visits says these institutional loopholes make his job quite stressful. Recently, this technician, whom we will call Raj, worked on a large loan package that included a credit program similar to the one just described, although this program lent money to individual industrial entrepreneurs rather than farmers. As part of a large in-house team hired to focus solely on environmental assessment, Raj found himself constrained by the institutional norms of project support: "I'm working on a loan in which we're offering credit to small industrial firms. I'm supposed to assess the environmental impact of a line of credit for thousands of small entrepreneurs. Well, believe me, it's not so easy to patrol such projects—it's not possible to pursue every loan. I don't have the resources to do a sample survey. Instead, I have to look around for clues of people complying or not complying with our rules. But, who knows how individuals will use their credit, maybe for good or for bad. . . . An environmental assessment in these cases is fairly meaningless, yet required."[22]

Although employed by the regional technical units to independently evaluate ongoing projects, Raj and his colleagues lack the time, resources, and institutional support to make a studious analysis; instead, they are left with highly fungible, anecdotal evidence, some of which could satisfy or anger their employers, depending on which anecdotes they choose to utilize. Without sufficient information to challenge the validity of projects, environmental specialists inside the Bank have no choice but to affirm project success. In other words, faced with an inability to ask basic questions and gather adequate data during seasonal whirlwind country tours, staff are left with the choice of either demanding more money and time—to the disapproval of their superiors and colleagues—or merely nodding affirmatively. Forced to choose their battles, staff typically choose the latter.

But this freedom to choose is really beside the point. More time, bigger teams of experts, and more money will never tackle the fundamental concern of mitigating the negative effects of a multimillion-dollar investment because project decision making occurs within a temporal milieu dictated by more substantial political-economic concerns. The amount of time allocated for research, assessment, and monitoring of Bank projects is largely determined by the worries, pressures, and threats coming from the private firms that help finance the project (alongside the Bank) or build the dam and run the power plant (with the borrowing government as a minority interest). These multinational firms invariably want the project to start yesterday, and they want to start making money on it now. Bidders on Bank projects will pull out if they do not see an attractive rate of return on their investment due to delays, added costs, and stipulations. The turnover time of capital requires a speed that not even adrenaline-rushing Bank experts can keep up with. The result is not that *no* environmental assessment or monitoring is done, but rather, that a *type* of assessment is done that becomes the protocol for transnational development professionals, NGOs, and governmental agencies complying with World Bank conditions. This protocol is shaped by the rhythms and parameters set by the Bank in conjunction with its corporate investment partners, rather than in conjunction with its expert hydrologists and soil chemists.

## The Knowledge Hierarchy

World Bank staff are also constrained by the Bank's information flow structure in which policy directives typically ignore contradictory findings from the field. In the Bank, information flows through the corridors of Bank hierarchy downward to the rank and file.[23] Few decisions are made by those at the bottom, and Bank staff learn to be careful with what information they choose to send up. One learns quickly what data and analysis please management and what will either be sent back, ignored, or heavily edited. Staff expend a tremendous amount of stressful energy trying to anticipate their superiors' responses to their draft reports.

One Bank economist discussed his experience, first as a young professional (called YPs) producing research reports for different regional departments and then as an analyst working on his own project. He explained that "most decisions are made from above, and projects just follow the framework."[24] As a project analyst, he is asked to produce reports that offer evidence to substantiate policy claims. "I was asked to do an environmental costing of future subsidies. But, what data could I come up with? My boss told me to try anything, so the only environmental data set I could find was on soil leaching. I had to play with it until I could come up with something. What could I know sitting in headquarters about this? But that's what I was told to do. There's great pressure to come up with something, just so you and especially your boss, don't come up empty-handed. When I first came here, I'd protest about how unreasonable these tasks were; but now I realize it's just a crazy part of this place."

An environmental unit economist offered another example, noting: "When the authors of *WDR* '92 [The highly influential 1992 *World Development Report* that featured the environment] were drafting the report, they called me asking for examples of 'win-win' strategies in my work. What could I say? None exists in that pure form; there are tradeoffs, not 'win-wins.' But they want to see a world of win-wins, based on articles of faith, not fact. I wanted to contribute because *WDR*s are important in the Bank, [because] task managers read [them] to find philosophical justifications for their latest round of projects. But they didn't want to hear about how things really are, or what I find in my work."

Some observers note that these influential reports read as if they were sculpted by a Madison Avenue PR firm, full of impressive graphs and sidebars but rarely rooted in what they desire to be known for—serious scholarship.[25] After a few missions with the World Bank, a young economist said that one learns quickly what must go into a report and what must not. "It's hard to deviate from it. This is especially true with this greening thing. I personally think it's absurd to make the link between devaluing currency [part of structural adjustment policy] and environmental issues, as there are so many intervening factors. But that's the policy that's being promoted, that's what I've been told to find data on, and it's hard to think otherwise."

This hierarchical relationship makes it difficult for staff to produce what the Bank's recent chief economist calls "serious scholarly research." Referring to the high-profile *World Development Report* series, Nicholas Stern, Oxford economics professor and former World Bank chief economist and senior vice president (2000–2003), wrote, "many of the numbers come from highly dubious sources or have been constructed in ways which leave one skeptical as to whether they can be helpfully used" (Stern and Ferreira 1997). Stern argues that despite its supreme ability to gather and analyze data, the Bank's work is neither innovative nor scholarly. Stern finds that the Bank's "documentation has fallen far short of that which would be acceptable in a scholarly publication" (Stern and Ferreira 1997). Why is this so? According to Stern: "Researchers are not free to follow intellectual inspiration. They are under constraints of designated priorities. . . . Further, there is the strong hierarchy and an atmosphere much more deferential than would be found in universities. Among researchers there is a considerable concern with what superiors will think of conclusions reached" (Stern and Ferreira 1997, vol. 1, p. 594).

Knowledge is a highly political, cultural, social, historical, and economic phenomenon, deeply reflective of the conditions in which it is produced (Haraway 1989; Hess 1997; Shapin 1985). Whenever we engage in a debate as to what is "bad science," we often neglect to scrutinize that which we assume to be, in the world's scientific hierarchy, the good. We too quickly forget that the supposedly "civilized and sophisticated" European scientists of just a few years ago were proving through science the existence of a "Jewish race" with its smaller inadequate brains, an "African race" with genetic shortcomings, and so on, ideas published in the premier journals and taught at the most enlightened universities in Europe (Beckwith 2002). Indeed, our premier academic disciplines—from economics to anthropology to forestry—were born within the bloody frontiers of Europe's colonial empires, which desperately needed experts and expert science to explicate the perceived inferiority of colonial populations, their natural tendencies to degrade and destroy, and their supposedly intrinsic needs for Europe's civilizing support (Grove 1996; Moore 2003; Stoler and Cooper 1999; Stoler 1995). In other words, science is always produced *within* and not outside of history, so we can never assume that it is objective and impartial, with discoveries emerging from a pure environment untainted by social influence. We should be equally careful to scrutinize the science that comes out of Harvard, the World Bank, or a development research institute in Botswana.

In observing the ways in which knowledge is produced by the World Bank and its counterparts, it does not serve us well to adopt the sentiment of some Bank staff members who feel like the neglected stepchild of serious scholarship, produced at their very own alma maters of Oxford, Cambridge, and the Ivy Leagues. After all, many of the experts who work at the World Bank, uncomfortable with the quality of the science they produce, base their assumptions, models, worldviews, and hypotheses on what they learned from their mentors at elite universities. Moreover, much of the work produced under the Bank's auspices plays a crucial role in Oxford, Yale, and Cambridge, as well as in New Delhi and Ouagadougou, in creating consensus around specific elite ideas and practices. The point here is not to castigate the Bank for its deeply flawed scientific production process, even though, of the hundreds of studies produced by the Bank every year, all roads of inquiry happen to lead back to the Bank's latest policy stance. Instead, we should learn about the knowledge production process itself, in situ, questioning why it is treated as truth and expertise and asking what larger project such faith in global knowledge serves (Jasanoff 2004). When the Bank claims that its global authority and comparative advantage are based on its ability to produce universal knowledge and global expertise, it is important to then try to understand what this knowledge is based on and why it is so important for the Bank's legitimacy and survival. Scholars and economists who demand that the Bank have higher standards for knowledge production only reinforce the assumption that objective and all-encompassing knowledge *can be* and *is* produced. Believing that the Bank needs only to try harder is a stance that lacks a historical and reflexive perspective on knowledge production in general, and on these institutions in particular, ignoring such questions as knowledge for whom, knowledge for what, knowledge backed by whom, and knowledge that silences what alternatives (Fairhead and Leach 2004; Foucault 1994; Haraway 1989; Mitchell 2002).

## Narcissus Redux?

Many Bank publications, in addition to the influential *World Development Reports,* suffer from the problem of dubious scientific claims making. In recent years, the Bank's African environmental unit has produced some important publications, but these works often seem to be in debate with themselves, faithfully avoiding current scholarship and external political debates. *Crisis and Opportunity: Environment and Development in Africa* (Falloux 1993) is a lengthy book written by senior Bank officials that at first glance promises to be an analysis of the complexities of Africa's environmental troubles. In reality it is a self-referential institutional diary of how the Bank persuades government policy elites to adopt its policy of writing National Environmental Action Plans (NEAPs) as a precondition for Bank loans.

The NEAPs, high-profile documents that summarize a nation's plan to tackle national environmental problems, must be drafted by borrowing governments with public participation. Many Bank staff who have worked on NEAPs have dismissed their content, echoing what one Bank NEAP expert exclaimed to me, that "most NEAPs are a joke."[26] They are mostly written by Bank staff members, or by an obliging government official, reflective of the latest Bank policy (down to the word) and absent of inputs from cross sections of society.[27] Since NEAPs are required for International Development Assistance (IDA) countries (which includes most of Africa) applying for loan disbursement, and since most actors within the Bank and in client countries do not take them seriously, NEAPs have been recycled from political speeches and from project wish lists generated by Bank staff.[28] In many African countries, NEAPs were written by "favorite sons" of the environmental minister and were not, as Bank guidelines require, the result of serious consultations with all sectors of society.[29] (Of course, how common is serious consultation to the production of government reports in general?)

For instance, two books written by one of the African divisions, the above-mentioned *Crisis and Opportunity* and Cleaver's and Schreiber's *Reversing the Spiral: The Population, Agriculture, and Environment Nexus in Sub-Saharan Africa* (1994), are full of airy proclamations, offering up an image of Africa as it is reflected in the looking glass of World Bank policies. Distinctions over time and space hardly exist; benchmark scholarship is ignored; historical events are confined to a selective Bank policy timeline. Nonetheless, Bank reports become an important source of authority on Africa's environment and are subsequently cited in other Bank reports, as well as in numerous studies of Africa that depend on Bank references for documentation. Interestingly, if one works backwards and looks into the data used to support the claims made in these documents, one finds that similarly produced Bank materials were *their* sources. Although *Crisis and Opportunity* features approximately ninety citations in its bibliography, almost 70 percent refer to Bank publications and a full 90 percent can be attributed to individuals and organizations affiliated with, or financed by, the World Bank. This is true of many of the Bank's major reports on the African continent, all of which are equally self-referential.[30] One internal document depends on another for its evidence and argumentation, and in this way, an internal body of knowledge is introduced and then reinforced.[31] (Of course, this is not too different from some subfields within academic disciplines.)

I asked a number of Bank staffers why it is that Bank reports, studies, and books never begin with a standard of the academy, an academic literature review of the latest scholarly debates and controversies, nor include many scholarly references in their bibliographies. One suggested that such tasks, routine within the academic community, are too time-consuming, expensive, and beside the point for Bank staff. A second said that such a culture of scholarship at the Bank is strictly prohibited. A third official thought it naive that I would even put Bank research and reports in the same category of scholarship. Instead, he suggested the Bank's publications are more in the realm of spin: "Why does the Bank only cite itself? It's like asking why IBM doesn't refer to the literature on computers. When they say that 'IBM is going to conquer the world' with its latest computers, they don't need to explain or reference. They're selling a product, and so are we."[32]

It is fine to be dismissive of Bank information, except for the fact that Bank expertise and knowledge have a tremendous impact on policy makers and researchers around the world. Bank knowledge is a tactical technology whose power should not be underestimated, whatever one's interpretation of its truth value. Despite their questionable history, NEAPs have become important gateway reports that define where in a national economy the Bank should invest. Under the Bank's prodding, the idea of the environment in the world of development has been stretched to mean something far beyond what a typical ecological conservationist (and certainly an old-fashioned banker) means when she or he defines the term.

Today, the Bank's green neoliberal approach pushes government officials—and therefore environmental NGOs, development consultants, and university scholars—to rethink the way they perceive and manage forestry, mining, agriculture, and aquaculture projects, as well as municipal water supplies and eco-tourism and game parks. As we will see in subsequent chapters, these Bank-driven eco-priorities are also translated into the latest form of structural adjustment policy—"environmental adjustment"—that compels borrowers to restructure their regulatory institutions, reframe land reform and natural resource use policies, and change tax and capital-flow laws as preconditions for new Bank loans. Again, the point is not to debate the relative truth value of Bank environmental science and compare it to a higher order of academic scholarship—after all, World Bank texts and data sets are crucial to university-based knowledge production, as are World Bank high-paying consultancy contracts. Rather, it is more useful to consider how these truths and knowledge become constituted inside the Bank; how they become codified into rules, policy directives, and norms that travel outside of the Bank; and how and why certain aspects become authoritative, however briefly, around the world.

## Maintaining Hierarchical Control

> There's a saying in the Bank, that the job is hard on your rear end: in the office, it gets kicked; on the road, it gets licked.[33]

The World Bank is a hierarchical institution, and the internal controls over this set-up, according to Bank staff, influences the nature of their intellectual work. The Bank's internal authority structure has an impact on more than just the selection of research questions; it also affects who is hired to do research, how consultants are used, who gets promoted and who gets left behind, whose analysis is legitimated, and whose is marginalized. There is an explicit link between knowledge production and career development or, put more directly, what types of research and analysis can get you in trouble.

At the Bank, full-time professionals are hired through two narrow openings. One is the World Bank's Young Professionals (YP) program, which recruits top candidates from the world's most elite universities; and the other is through mid-career appointments. After competing within a massive pool of highly qualified candidates from throughout the world, the handful of successful YPs go through a trial period during which they are taught the tools of the trade in a number of different positions across the Bank. After a year or two, a manager recommends that the trainee receive permanent status; if no manager wants to hire the YP, she or he is released. As graduates of the YP program have explained to me, new hires learn early on how the system works: energetic and happily ensconced in their new environs, YPs learn first and foremost how best to comply with their superiors.[34]

Although many at first find the institutional norms and culture disconcerting, most YPs hang on to become long-term Bank staff. Social scientists who choose to leave the Bank often do so out of concern that they are rapidly becoming ill qualified to compete on the academic or professional job market. The analytical work conducted at the Bank, especially by staff in their first five years, does not count for much in the non-Bank world of scholarship. Bank reports are, as one senior economist put it, "primarily vehicles for selling projects." By contrast, experienced midcareer appointees learn in their first official meeting that whatever respect they may have earned in their previous academic or professional careers is immediately overshadowed within the highly structured Bank hierarchy. One climbs methodically through the Bank system, moving gradually up the patronage ladder through loyalty and compliance, not "through the side door." As a consequence, midcareer hires "can't accomplish much inside, they're hardly ever promoted and tend to leave at the same stratum which they entered."[35]

A third entryway for researchers and analysts is much less restricted. It is the competitive market of consultants, many of whose careers involve shuttling back and forth among international development agencies. This group, with homes (and mortgages) in the Washington, D.C., area, is quite vulnerable to red pen marks in the margins of their reports. Bank consultants survive with "just-in-time" flexible work habits; by the nature of the job, they are enthusiastically available and loyal to Bank task managers. Consequently, task managers view the consultant reserve army and their research reports as a useful vehicle for getting their inner thoughts scripted for them.[36] Through its employment and training practices, the Bank leaves its institutional markings on its workforce, rewarding the "champions" and dismissing the "contrarians." In this way, upper management sees its policy prerogatives confirmed, translated, magnified, legitimated, and disseminated.

## An Anthropologist among the Economists

Sociologists and anthropologists at the Bank have to adapt to the dominant culture, one where neoclassical economics is the sole language of communication and rationality. Everything one sees and understands must be explained in terms of American-style economics. Many sociologists and anthropologists at the Bank have shifted from academic positions at universities; this is a tremendous epistemological leap that requires some serious professional retooling, if not soul-searching.

One senior anthropologist whom I interviewed was working on a politically charged topic: the social and environmental aspects of population resettlement in China. In his attempts to analyze and "put a value on" the unvalued aspects of resettlement in a country that, until recently, has been closed off to most Western researchers, he conceded, "It's quite difficult to measure value in this respect, as it has to be based on local needs." Placing an economic value on the intangibles runs counter to his field of training, which recognizes that notions of land, place, and community are deeply embedded in religious, kinship, and other political and cultural practices—practices that include markets but not exclusively determined by them.[37] His assignment, however, forces him to overlook these complex debates. He is paid to figure out the most efficient way to reduce the potentially devastating social and environmental effects of new Bank investments in China and to calculate an appropriate level of compensation for dispossessed communities. China is the Bank's largest borrower and debtor and the country where the Bank hopes to expand dramatically over the next decade. The Bank lends billions of dollars to China for large infrastructural transport, energy, and water projects, all of which inevitably displace populations and submerge or cut through forests, grasslands, villages, and small cities.

Anthropologists, according to the norms of the discipline, are supposed to develop empathy for the subject's culture and interpret meaning based on the local context. (Of course, since the discipline emerged from the colonial task of studying and codifying the "native" for the purpose of colonial subjugation, empathy is not the accurate sentiment to describe early anthropologists [Cohn 1996; Hymes 1974].) But what if, as is the case the world over, communities do not want to move or choose not to accept the terms of compensation for the destruction of their ancestral land, burial sites, and productive territories? On the rare occasion that they are asked, those about to be ousted by development projects typically choose *not* to move or receive the monetary compensation that is offered (Cernea and Guggenheim 1994; Fox and Thorne 1997; McCully 1996; Thukral 1992). Hence, this anthropologist's job is a difficult one, to understand the conditions and desires of local communities that find themselves living smack in the middle of someone else's development ambition. Under Bank working conditions, however, it is physically impossible, and institutionally inadvisable, for this anthropologist to understand or develop empathy for people in fourteen provinces over weeklong visits. Listening could take years if not decades. Instead, he defers to the prevailing Bank culture that "what's best for the national economy is best for its people," whatever differences of opinion people might have. This, of course, is not the job for an anthropological scholar, but for a claims adjuster. Because Bank resettlement has become a highly contentious issue, Bank anthropologists must come up with alternative tracts of land for the displaced, an alternate livelihood scheme for displaced communities, and, as Bank staff see it, the appropriate carrots and sticks for state bureaucrats. Thanks in part to the incorporation of proficient anthropologists, the Bank is able to demand that borrowers follow its guidelines.

But what about the reliability of such development science? After much external criticism of Bank resettlement activities, and prodded by a retiring Bank sociologist, an in-house review of resettlement projects (within the time frame of 1986–93) was conducted. The study found, as critics had charged, that Bank resettlement work was abysmal and based on shoddy data collection and analysis (Cernea and Guggenheim 1994; Fox and Thorne 1997). Almost 60 percent of the World Bank projects included in the study had failed to include baseline population surveys; less than 15 percent actually included a budget to finance resettlement and rehabilitation; and less than one-quarter included resettlement specialists. Moreover, the internal review task force revealed that the official numbers from internal Bank reports underreported by almost 50 percent the numbers of people displaced by Bank projects. (Since most project reports were prepared without baseline studies, the real numbers of negatively affected people may well have been substantially higher.)[38]

The problem here lies at the crossroads of knowledge production and use. For Bank loan managers, institutional procedures require that loans be conceived, packaged, and sold to the Bank's executive directors and the finance ministers of borrowing countries in a very short time period, sometimes within twenty-four months. Thousands of pages on the environmental, legal, economic, procurement, and technical aspects of the loan must be reduced to a short summary for presentation to the Bank's executive directors, who will make the final approval. Meetings with borrowers in Caracas or Delhi are swift and to the point; one visit may include meetings with high-level finance, legal, and procurement officials, with occasional spot site investigations by project designers and other specialists, whose job is to assess the possible costs and benefits of a proposed loan. In China, our senior anthropologist visits fourteen provinces in thirty months to do his requisite assessments. He readily admits he has shed the pristine cloth of the academy to become a global development specialist, as this approach clearly would not be acceptable as anthropology today. But as development knowledge, it is, wherever the Bank performs its work. The dimension he does not discuss, however, is that as this becomes the big business of development, it draws in hundreds of applied and development anthropologists as its hired practitioners. Thus the type of anthropology being produced for the World Bank becomes a strong influence on the trajectory of anthropology scholarship, writ large.[39]

## Creating Consent

One of the more contentious midcareer hires has been Herman Daly. In the following excerpted interview he explains some of the constraints he experienced working at the Bank. With an international reputation as a founder of the field of environmental economics and a leading expert in cost-benefit analysis, Daly was invited to work at the Bank as a midcareerist during the 1980s.[40]

> I arrived precisely when the Bank was beginning to expand its environmental resources. I was hired to work in the environmental unit within the Latin American division. The team had two missions: first, we were to *sign off* on all Latin American projects. Ideally, we tried to get in on projects as early as possible. Now remember, this is big stuff: environmental auditors with veto power. This was quite new for our Bank colleagues. Second, we were in-house consultants for projects; for this, we were well funded and encouraged. The first task, however, was not funded and was very much discouraged. It was believed to be bad form to do "policing" of other people's projects. As it was, we were only able to audit based on what we found *on paper,* in reports, as there was no money appropriated for us to actually do an on-site inspection.
>
> One of the first projects for me was a nuclear power sector loan to Brazil. I looked over the economic calculations and noted that the benefits of nuclear were not properly dealt with—not so much the costs, as in environmental costs, but simply the

benefits, as in how the military would benefit from this power sector loan. Now, it was clear from the loan statements that the benefits were primarily for the military [as the Brazilian government argued that Argentina had nuclear weapons]; so it seemed obvious to me to disclose what the benefits were in a preparation report. But no one wanted to bring it up; it was only discussed as a positive power project. When I did so, I was severely reprimanded by my superiors. As it was, Brazil had one nuclear plant, which was called "lightning bug" because it would only rarely flash on, yet they wanted two more at the same site. The Bank's cost-benefit analysis was seriously flawed. As the loans would have been heavily subsidized by liability insurance, it seemed that all these issues needed to be considered, but weren't.

Right after I wrote my short note on the flawed analysis, the Bank's central economic unit was drawing up a report on funding nuclear power in general and asked me to submit my note to them, which I did. When the central unit report was drawn up, the regional economic unit from Latin America was furious. My loyalty to the region and to the boss was the main problem. Ultimately, the central report was used against the Latin American region's power loan, and my job was immediately threatened. Now, I was considered an expert in cost-benefit analysis, I wrote and taught on it for twenty years, so I was ready to defend my work, but, of course, that wasn't the issue here. The real issue was the fact that I allowed my notes to get into a central report without the regional boss's permission. Hence, my job was at stake for a bureaucratic act. Since I was too high profile to be fired, and . . . I let it be known that it might not play well in the newspapers, I was allowed to keep my job. But I, and the whole team, was forced to move out of Operations where all the action is, over to the Center, to do policy research and assessment. In other words, we were sandbagged.

Herman Daly's most negative experience at the Bank was with censorship: he had a number of run-ins with his superiors related to his published and unpublished articles, speeches, memos, and research. On one occasion, Daly was asked to debate the distinguished conservative economist, Jagdish Bhagwati, in the pages of *Scientific American* (Bhagwati 1993; Daly 1993). The topic was NAFTA from an ecological economics perspective, and Daly was asked to write on the problems with NAFTA. His article was published on the eve of the U.S. congressional vote on NAFTA, at a time when the World Bank's Mexico desk and senior management were lobbying Congress for votes in support of NAFTA. When the piece was published as the cover story and widely distributed, the Bank's Mexico staff started a campaign to get Daly fired, accusing him of treason for breaking the fundamental rules of the Bank's constitution, which forbid the Bank from intervening in national politics.[41] Daly was amused by this accusation. In his view, it was his colleagues at the Mexico desk, feverishly absorbed in lobbying Congress, who were the ones engaging in politics. But then Daly, unlike his accusers within the Bank, believed that everything the Bank does is politics. "Restructuring the national economy is not politics? Devaluing the Mexican peso is not politics?" he asked. At other times, he had to clear his public speeches with the External Affairs Department, the in-house censors, and once, he was forbidden from participating on a panel on environmental economics in Chile, and after a humiliating protest was allowed to participate only with a Bank staff escort.[42]

As one of the world's most esteemed environmental economists, Daly was hired by the Bank to offer his opinion on projects, on general reports, on in-house processes. But too often, his responses were considered too controversial for the Bank, however respectable his work was considered outside the Bank. Daly explains:

> The Bank considers itself the premier development bank, and they're careful not to publish anything without due consideration. Since the Bank pushes the concept that affluence through development is good for the environment, it's not possible to make a peep about how this might not be true. A few of us tried to get that point across in *World Development Report, 1992* but they would not allow it—not even a couple of pages. We even tried to publish a "minority opinion" as a separate document, with two Nobel prize winners as main contributors, but the Bank's censors in External Affairs wouldn't accept it. The Bank is a tough place to discuss different ideas.
>
> In my day-to-day work, my job was to evaluate projects for their environmental assessment. But, if I ever found a project to be bad for environmental reasons, the response would always be: "No need to put this on the table, there's no reason to upset our

clients. Besides, if we don't support it, then private Japanese investors will fund it without *any* conditions." The belief is that the Bank's way is always more enlightened than private investors', which might be true in some cases. But really, everyone is so eager to push loans, they're not concerned about what private investors might do. It's the same with arguments for structural adjustment loans: Why are we offering loans for policy reforms, which taxpayers have to repay? Shouldn't policy reforms come about through internal financing and political processes? This type of policy discussion could never occur at the Bank. No one would ever be allowed to do a cost-benefit analysis, for example, on Bank macroeconomic policies.[43]

## Between In-House Constraints and External Institutional Power

Despite the many in-house norms that constrain staff from freely expressing their opinions and perspectives, the cumulative effect of working at the World Bank is one of empowerment. Bank staffers have unparalleled access to vital and privileged information and are uniquely able to visit capital cities, call meetings with high- and low-level officials, sift through government materials, and have local or expatriate consultants brief them on details. In their interactions with officials in borrowing countries, they typically set the agenda, request information that can help them expedite the loan process, and frame the discussions in an orthodox neoclassical-economics worldview. Most of all, it is important to remember that these Bank officials would not be visiting the capital city in the first place if they were not selling a loan, discussing a policy imperative as a precondition to a loan, or renegotiating an outstanding debt. These asymmetric political-economic relationships and realities profoundly affect the knowledge production process. Wherever Bank staff go, they have inordinate power in the social relations they establish, even if they often feel frustrated by the limits imposed on them by their superiors or by the stubbornness of borrowers who do not want to conduct the business of development in World Bank style.

An insightful environmental technician working for the Bank in Asia explained to me the dilemma he faces in his work, in wanting to make the Bank a more environmentally and culturally sensitive place yet realizing the difficulty in imagining such a possibility given the institution's structural imperatives. "We run our missions every two months to South Asia, bopping them on the head with our environmental programs. We are quite persistent every time, and yet they don't want any of it. . . . Sri Lanka gives in, but Bangladesh says, 'No, thank you, we want to focus on public health and education; environment isn't a priority for our borrowing.' But ours is a supply-determined agenda, and very prescriptive. There's no culture here for listening; we just go to countries and sell, sell, sell until the borrowers cave in."[44]

On another occasion, he expressed his frustration more philosophically: "You and I may say that our *World Development Reports* are BS. But I go to Sri Lanka and officials there quote from the latest report, word for word. That's music to our ears." He continued: "Once upon a time, 'development' and 'environment' contradicted each other. Now, development [has] co-opted environment and discursively they have grown to complement each other." In the meantime, he and his colleagues have written a series of documents on the region's environmental woes that include a strong plan of action. In each case, the plan introduces World Bank policies and projects, analytic frameworks and concepts of environmentally sustainable development as the vehicle for reversing these trends. The Bank highlights successful local cases where people are managing, for example, their flood plains sustainably. But these cases are rarely interpreted within the complex social reality in which they unfold, and the Bank's role never becomes one of supporting these local endeavors as they exist. Rather, these "best practices" cases are plucked from context and resituated within the Bank's ambitious and multi-tiered action plans. Hence, in Bangladesh, delta flood management Bank-style becomes an expansive plan requiring substantial loans and imported expert technical assistance—the "common sense" alternative to what the Bank describes as endemic flood and famine cycles. Because the World Bank is also Bangladesh's debt manager, delta management becomes one of the many strategies for alleviating debt and stimulating national economic growth through the earning of foreign exchange.[45] The quaint success story of locals protecting their delta becomes a justification for a multimillion-dollar Bank project, distorting this particular meaning of "success."

Over the years, in fact, this Bank official has seen his portfolio of projects in South Asia grow, however much he may be dissatisfied with the priorities and procedures. Bank-style environmentalism is firmly rooted in the Bank's complementary policies of capital-intensive problem solving, state restructuring, market expansionism, and public-sector privatization. In practice, during the 1990s, environmentalism and neoliberalism have coevolved to become inseparable. As Bank staffers learn on the job, Bank-style environmentalism begins to gain credence and spread with legitimacy once they find its "value-adding" opportunity within projects that promote capital accumulation.

## Conclusion

Despite the enormous power and global reach the World Bank has today, relatively little in-depth debate exists on its production of knowledge.[46] A top scholar on East Asian economies, Alice Amsden, has engaged the Bank in a constructive critique of the quality of its research and writes, in utter exhaustion, that it is "like a small firm confronting a multinational enterprise, or a guerrilla army engaging a nuclear power" (Amsden 1994, p. 632). Supported by a small cluster of reputable economists, Amsden reviewed the scholarship of Bank publications on the so-called East Asian miracle development model, the ideological pillar of the Bank's "market friendly" policy on client states. She writes: "A 'veil of money' keeps inquisitive readers from understanding the actually existing world of development. The veil comes in the form of expensive 'background papers' by consultants, hand-picked and hired by the Bank, who collaborate with Bank insiders and personally interpret what they believe happened . . . based, in some cases, on extensive bibliographical references mainly to their own work. Most experts outside immediate Bank circles . . . are rarely cited, if at all. . . . The failure to recognize classic works in the debate and cite the original source—'to get the copyright'—means that all information to the reader is filtered" (Amsden 1994, p. 630).

Amsden finds that since the Bank perpetually fails to scientifically prove its conclusions, its policy justifications are "quintessentially political and ideological" (p. 627). What makes the World Bank so powerful? According to Amsden, it has no real rival. The regional development banks and UN agencies with much smaller budgets fall over themselves to cooperate with the Bank, anxious to get a piece of the action from the large loans that may follow.

Political scientist Robert Wade, a veteran of Bank research, believes that the Bank's legitimacy in the global marketplace of ideas and commerce depends on the authority of its research and policies. "Like the Vatican, and for similar reasons, it cannot afford to admit fallibility." It cannot admit its research weaknesses because financial markets demand the illusion of certainty, an illusion that influences knowledge production. Moreover, World Bank staff members construct their version of environmentalism in terms of a "self-reinforcing congruence" with "the values of the owners and managers of financial capital," the Bank's ultimate provider (Wade 1996b, pp. 34–35).

In spite of the Bank's power and authority in support of its own style of environmentalism, it remains a Sisyphean feat to maintain investors' confidence in the light of real-world project debacles, which are easily documented by outsiders and difficult for the Bank to conceal. To succeed, the World Bank must strictly monitor scientific norms and staff behavior. How else could it be that a nine-thousand-person organization, half of whom are high-level professionals, producing hundreds of public and internal documents and working in 170-plus countries, can produce a singular analysis on the complexity of the human condition?

In sum, the Bank wields tremendous power, especially in the realm of knowledge production. Within the Bank, knowledge production is carefully controlled and represents an important arena of social control. When we look inside Policy Research, the Environment Department, the regional environmental units, and the country departments, we find that data collection and analysis, report writing, editing, and the nail-biting process of getting approval from one's superiors (and one's superiors' superiors) is less a process of discovery, creativity, and refutation than one of *manufacturing consent*. From hiring practices, to hierarchical pressures, to funding decisions for research, to the way information flows are manipulated internally and externally, the assembly line of knowledge production is studded with cultural practices of social control as well as incorporation and hegemony-building.

Ideologically derived findings help Bank staff sell the Bank's version of environmentally sustainable development to the outside world, with low-interest loans and loan guarantees as the carrots. In the process, the Bank's new green science spreads and becomes legitimated and reproduced in many venues, from the (U.S.) National Academy of Science, to the professional guidelines used by ministries of the environment in borrower countries, to the policy reports written by international NGOs. The Bank's scientific research on the environment not only supports the reproduction of its own institutions (of control, knowledge, and finance), but it also exerts its power outside of World Bank headquarters in scientific and professional circles.

Assumptions that environmental improvement comes only through capitalist modernization are so deeply entrenched in these practices that few stop to ask, *Why development projects?* Why the World Bank and its development apparatuses that require expensive and inappropriate inputs from Northern capital good sectors? Can environmental improvement ever be conceived of as a project of "no intervention" or of local practices that do not require Bank capital and economistic advice?

The greening of the Bank has only intensified the colonial gaze with which the North views the South, and which has recently come to rest on the environment and those who depend on it most directly as a source of sustenance, broadly defined. The fate of the project of development depends on it. Development experts continually ask how local environments and populations can accommodate another Bank intervention. The givens in all of these inquiries are the centrality of the World Bank, the development project, and capitalist intervention in the pursuit of solutions to the world's problems, down to the smallest of worries of not enough firewood or potable water. Although the heavy hand of Bank headquarters intimidates Bank staff and consultants into producing a consensus on this approach to the environment, its heavy hand is not the only or even the main determining factor. Rather it is the interplay between "big D," the project of development, and "little d," uneven capitalist development—always changing and always generating the "new," but always overlapping with older regimes of power/knowledge and capital accumulation—that defines what counts as nature and sustainable development (Hart 2003).

# IV

# The Birth of a Discipline: Producing Environmental Knowledge for the World

On Christmas Day in 1990, five thousand villagers threatened by forced resettlement and their supporters set off on a "long march" to a dam site in India's Narmada River Valley, hoping to close down the Sardar Sarovar Dam construction project (Baviskar 1995; McCully 1996; Udall 1995). Eight days into their walk, police blocked their passage, many were beaten, 140 were arrested, and 8 began a hunger fast on the side of the road. Twenty-one days later, with the local police and the national government refusing to budge, the dam's financier in Washington, D.C.— the World Bank—agreed to commission its first-ever independent review panel (later known as the Morse Commission). Although the marchers never arrived at the dam site just a few miles away, they reached a more significant site of contestation, the heart of the World Bank, and helped fuel a growing transnational movement to challenge the legitimacy of this powerful global institution. This movement has focused in part on the Bank's knowledge-production practices.

The deputy chairman of the Bank's independent review panel, Canadian jurist Thomas Berger, described his experience as he began to investigate the Bank's knowledge-production practices: "When we first arrived in New Delhi, we had local hydrologists presenting us papers that showed that drinking water would never get to the two drought-prone regions. We had reports that showed whole fisheries would be lost. Scientists came forward with testimony that the irrigation schemes wouldn't work. Our team hydrologist found fifteen-year-old engineering reports buried in Bank file cabinets that said these schemes weren't feasible. None of this was made available to us by the Bank. In all the information made available to us by the Bank, all of the downstream consequences were omitted."[1]

For Berger, the contrast between the scientific data he received from the Bank to do his evaluation and the evidence given to him by people in India was shocking. "People would stand outside my hotel door in Delhi ready to hand over yet another report. Retired civil servants showed us their studies, community members spoke up—it became an incredible exchange of information and ideas." Yet none of this free exchange occurred between the independent review panel and the Bank staff assigned to it by the Bank's president.

Confronted with the panel's report and the social pressure that brought it about, the Bank's executive directors had little choice but to vote to pull out of the project.[2] This episode was important not only to social activists around the world, who could now see their potential power, but for the World Bank itself. The "Narmada effect," as it has come to be called, is invoked regularly inside the Bank and reminds staff that the

Bank must "reform or die."[3] In 1995, the first significant action of the incoming Bank president James Wolfensohn was to cancel a large dam in Nepal, Arun 3, because of claims that the feasibility studies failed to account for the likelihood of extremely negative ecological and social effects. He did so before a full hearing or, more important, before a social protest movement could fully ignite on the heels of the Narmada embarrassment.[4] Wolfensohn's move sent chilling reverberations through World Bank headquarters, putting staff on alert that any project without rigorous scientific support could evaporate under social movement pressure or presidential fiat. As a result, the World Bank started doing business differently. As Bank staff are instructed in staff training seminars on environmental assessment in Washington, D.C.: "Don't get zapped by the *Narmada effect*, do your EIAs (environmental impact assessments)!"[5]

In this context, and at the suggestion of a senior environmental advisor at the World Bank, I traveled to the Lao People's Democratic Republic (Laos) to observe the newly reformed World Bank in action. Under the combined force of the Narmada and Arun effects, he explained, I would find that Bank projects now followed a new scientific protocol with environmental and social standards. These changes are reflected in one of its biggest Mekong River investments—the Nam Theun 2 Dam project.[6]

Indeed, Nam Theun 2 has become an effective litmus test for the Bank's ability to respond to its critics. The project, from the beginning, was not merely a hydroelectric dam project, as it would have been designed by the pregreen World Bank of the 1980s, but a national project that will consume most of the government's resources to finance a wide range of components, including new regimes of law, regulation, and management of both the country's natural resources (its rivers, minerals, forests, wildlife) and the people whose livelihood directly depends on these natural resources (more than half of the country's population). As preconditions for this dam project, national laws were rewritten, government agencies were restructured, and the use of the government's budget was redefined. Because Laos is one of the most heavily indebted countries in the world, owing most of its external debt to the World Bank and its colleague the Asian Development Bank (ADB), its creditors have taken over the traditional role of the government by financing these institutional changes and hiring Northern consultants to do the work. Laos's creditors are introducing a new scientific protocol into the country, one that has begun to permeate three prominent spheres of Lao society: the capital-intensive, national project of development; new national regimes of law and regulation; and retooled government agencies, especially the Ministry of Agriculture and Forestry (more than half of Laos is forested) and the government's primary environmental agency, STEA. This new scientific protocol and milieu are the focus of this chapter.

Whereas World Bank officials in the 1980s insisted that a strong environmental stance would shrink worldwide demand for its capital and services, today the Bank finds itself in the enviable position of having an expanding loan portfolio *and* a globally adopted environmental agenda, which it calls environmentally sustainable development. Simply put, the Bank has transformed an antidevelopment environmentalist agenda into one that works in its favor in many of its borrowing countries. To best understand the milieu in which the scientists hired for this agenda work, it is important to see the world *not* in simple developmentalist terms detached from the workings of the global political economy, that is, a technical project administered by the "haves" transferring capital, knowledge, and technology to the "have nots." The World Bank, as the primary financier and designer of what we can call "the development world," is a more complex institution (Crush 1995; Escobar 1995; McMichael 2000; Watts 1995; Young 2003). From this perspective, the World Bank functions by borrowing capital from a global bond market (that it helped to create), lending it to governments that are deemed in need, and then requiring these governments to spend a substantial percentage of these loans to procure goods and services from firms of the Big Five creditor countries (George and Sabelli 1994; Kapur et al. 1997; World Bank 2002). Sixty years of this asymmetric triangular relation among the Bank, its borrowers, and Northern firms has left borrowing countries highly in debt from their net capital transfer to the North. This bind gives the Bank a particular authority within borrowing countries, which it has mobilized to restructure a broad array of in-country institutions and social realms according to its latest political rationality: neoliberalism. The question posed here is: to what extent does the World Bank's political economy of capitalist development affect, as well as get shaped by, its production of authoritative knowledge?

In answering this question, in this chapter I will invoke Michel Foucault's arguments on relations of power, right, and truth (Burchell 1991; Cooke and Kothari 2001; Foucault 1994; Rose 1999). Rather than pose the traditional question on power and knowledge or power/knowledge (i.e., what discourse of truth fixes *limits* on power?), which assumes that the exercise of power is always repressive and negating, we can ask the alternative question posed by Foucault: what regimes of truth are endowed with potent effects that help generate the laws, shape subjectivities, and drive people to exercise power? That is, what enables the exercise of power *through* social bodies rather than merely against them, compelling them to act and to act in ways defined in the process of "the production, accumulation, circulation, and functioning of a discourse" (Foucault 1994)? It is useful to think about Foucault's triangle of power, right, and truth in the context of how societal rules are written (or removed), rights bestowed (or denied), and truths constructed (or deemed illegitimate), and how these are generated through the practices of many different types of actors in the world we call "development."

Although it appears that the World Bank is the new global sovereign prince, in fact, many networks of actors have joined in the production of development knowledge and have embraced the concepts of sustainability and sustainability rights. The focus here is on the knowledge-production process that has become so inclusive and integral to large capital projects. In today's climate of vigilant social activism around World Bank interventions, there cannot be an acceptable plan for investment without a strong sense of the ecological and social. Since the World Bank cannot do the enormous task on its own (in Laos as well as in 170-plus other borrowing countries), it requires a growing network of translocal scientists, technocrats, NGOs, and empowered (or "responsibilized" [Rose 1999]) citizens to help generate the data and construct the discursive strategies of sustainability. In this case, the production of truth entails the birth of new experts, new subjects, new natures, and a new disciplinary science of sustainable development, without which power could not be so fruitfully exercised.

## Green Knowledge Production in Laos

Just as its latest self-proclamation as *the* global knowledge bank suggests (World Bank 1999b, 2002), the World Bank is the source for cutting-edge knowledge of global significance. Over the past ten years, the Bank has carved out its own green agenda, producing policies, financing, tools and data for an applied global environmental science, training thousands of professionals in borrowing countries—including Laos—to implement and indigenize versions of it.

Nam Theun 2 (NT2) represents the global flagship of the Bank's green incarnation, a model for other projects in the Bank's portfolio. At the heart of the project is a large dam to produce hydroelectricity for Thailand, which—until its recent economic crisis—had been experiencing a period of sustained (albeit highly uneven) economic growth undergirded by rapid industrialization. Associated with the dam, and reflecting the Bank's new concern with environmentally sustainable development, is a state-of-the-art suite of linked projects that includes investments for a Forest Conservation and Management Project, Wildlife and Protected Areas Management Project, indigenous peoples' extractive reserves, irrigated and modernized agriculture with experimental farms, electricity and new roads, megafauna running corridors and eco-tourism, sustainable logging and tree plantations, and new housing settlements. To help understand the potential impacts of NT2, a series of detailed environmental and social assessment studies were conducted. Because of the controversial nature of the Bank's large-scale projects, two independent evaluation teams were set up to ensure that this project unfolds according to the Bank's new environmental directives: the International Advisory Group, which looks at large dams internationally, and the Panel of Experts, which looks at NT2 specifically. The World Bank's recent annual report expressed the uniqueness of its "Laos model" of sustainable development, explaining that "an unprecedented program of international oversight and local consultation is accompanying environmental and social impact assessment studies" for Nam Theun 2 (World Bank 1999).

Given the scope of the proposed project—costing more

than the country's annual budget and covering substantial territory—and the small domestic professional class capable of meeting the scientific-technical demands ("standards") of multilateral aid conditionalities, the Bank has allocated money to support a wide range of state-oriented activities related to NT2, including state capacity and institution-building, a thorough review of government policies, and environmental law reform. Because neither the World Bank nor the government of Laos has the in-house capabilities to study the feasibility and social and environmental impacts of the proposed investment, the Bank has enlisted an army of Northern consultants to do these studies.[7] In the following sections, I describe how the practices for hiring these consultants and the conditions under which they work reflect shifts in development under the Bank's green agenda.

## THE HIRING OF PROJECT EVALUATORS

The old system of hiring consultants to evaluate a proposed project was efficient, cost-effective, and mutually beneficial for the major players involved. Typically, the World Bank would hire Northern engineering firms that had often worked with the proposed contractors—that is, the firms that were expected to build the infrastructure—to collect and analyze data to assess a project. More often than not, the engineering firms would find that, indeed, the project was feasible (or would be, with certain modifications) and that its negative impacts could be mitigated through some additional investment: for example, a drainage system might be added to resolve a potentially leaky irrigation system. As long as the project was not shown to be infeasible (a highly unusual occurrence), these impact assessments could lead to an increase in the size of a loan and consequently more work for engineering firms and builders. In some parts of the world, the World Bank uses the same firms for all its projects, creating an enduring and comfortable relationship between the loan managers and the projects' reviewers.[8]

This is precisely what happened, at least initially, with the Nam Theun 2 project in Laos. In 1990, the World Bank contracted with an Australian engineering firm, Snowy Mountains Engineering Company, to conduct a feasibility study for Nam Theun 2.[9] Snowy Mountains has worked with the largest stockholder of Nam Theun 2, Transfield Holdings Ltd. of Australia, in the past.[10] The feasibility report produced by Snowy Mountains was quite positive overall; on this basis, the government of Laos, the World Bank, the dam investment consortium (then NTEC, now NTPC), and the Bank-appointed Panel of Experts recommended that the project be funded.

After NT2 got the official green light, NGOs based in Bangkok and Berkeley evaluated the report and made a strong case that it was seriously flawed. In the end, the Bank was forced to admit that the environmental impact assessment (EIA) and social impact assessment (SIA) were inadequate, and that the required "study of alternatives" was missing (e.g., studying alternative scenarios, such as smaller dams or energy conservation). It then contracted with another engineering group, the Thai-based TEAM firm, another old-time Bank consultant, to do the job. Its EIA for Nam Theun 2 met a similar fate and was ultimately dismissed by the World Bank when challenged by international activists.

In 1995, a third round of feasibility studies was commissioned, with some responsibilities contracted out to two long-time Bank consultants, the German firm Lahmeyer International (the study of alternatives) and the New Jersey-based firm Louis Berger International (economic analysis). Repre-

senting a dramatic shift for the Bank, however, the environmental and social assessments were contracted out to two
international NGOs, the World Conservation Union (IUCN)
and CARE International. The decision by the World Bank to
incorporate NGOs into the process reflected a highly conscious sense within the Bank of the need to work with its critics if it hoped to transform them from critical observers into
constructive participants.

## KNOWLEDGE UNDER CONTRACT

As NGOs and private consultants have been incorporated into
the project assessment process, the process has the appearance
of being more open and less subject to conflicts of interest. Yet
even for these independent groups and individuals, important
institutional factors shape the knowledge-production process.
The most general are the "terms of reference" (TOR) under
which hired consultants must work. In exchange for high salaries, unique research opportunities, and access to formerly
inaccessible research sites, the Bank specifies exactly what
kinds of information are needed, a time frame for completing
the research (and by implication, how long the researcher can
be in the field), and a deadline for the written report. Ownership and circulation are also important dimensions of the TOR:
the direct contractor—be it the Bank, the borrowing government, an engineering firm, or an NGO—is given exclusive
right of ownership over the product as well as the raw data.
Legally, one cannot use the data for research or distribute the
findings without permission from the contractor.

By far the most pressure comes from the stringent time
constraints placed on those carrying out the research. Because
social and environmental assessments are not stand-alone
projects but preconditions to a loan process, the amount of

time allocated for data collection and analysis is extremely limited. As a result, the method of development-related social and environmental research that has come to be most widely accepted is "rapid rural appraisal," a form of applied research that well suits the World Bank's constrained timeline for loan processing. Rapid rural appraisal (RRA) is "a systematic means of quickly and cost effectively gathering and analyzing information. The method has an extractive purpose in which outsiders learn about local situations . . . an iterative process of rapid and progressive learning from respondents and secondary data" (Chamberlain 1997). Particularly notable here is the emphasis on speed.

Those who do social and environmental impact studies for Nam Theun 2 are powerfully affected by the fast pace of Bank projects. One consultant for the most recent socioeconomic study of the Nakai Plateau people (the group that will be most directly affected by the dam and its standing reservoir) described his team's working conditions in the following terms:

> At first, we asked if we could get three days for every two villages in the plateau and another four to six days' time for write-up—seven to nine days per two villages—so the data wouldn't get confused in our minds. We figured it would take up to three days just to hike into a village. That's the very least we asked for. But the project was on a very tight schedule, as the World Bank needed the report soon.
>
> It's not easy work, and we were working in completely new terrain. [My partner, an ethnolinguist] discovered at least two previously unknown languages. We were trying to cope with new languages, cultures, lifestyles, and trying to interpret it, all within a very short time period.

Because so much time was being consumed by the arduous task of getting from village to village, covering hundreds of miles of very dense jungle, his team was transported by military helicopter, at the cost of $1,100 per hour.[11] "The helicopters saved us some time. But everything else about working in the jungle takes time. We brought in our own food, which we cooked on our own, and we'd set up camp. We were left with very little time to enter a village, explain who we were, and learn about their lives, only to turn back, return the helicopter, and write it all up in Vientiane."[12]

Similar pressure to do research quickly was noted by several ichthyologists who were hired to assess the effects of a set of proposed projects on the Mekong fisheries. According to these scientists, the task of studying the Mekong fisheries is enormous and requires a large interdisciplinary team to gather data all along the river and its tributaries. At the very least, they believe, data should be collected over several years. One consultant explained: "Everything is geared to the annual flood-dry cycle. Different species appear at different places and different times of the year to carry out critical life-cycle events [spawning, feeding, refuge during the dry season]. Migration enables these habitat shifts to take place and is of course the fundamental reason why any migratory animal needs to make regular seasonal movements."

In addition, researchers need to collect data on fish movements at multiple sites because fish do not migrate in straight lines, and the Mekong is not a single river but a system of rivers, with numerous arteries that house their own diverse fish species. The problem is further complicated by the fact that these rivers are not clear trout streams but are deep, dark, and characterized by dangerous currents.[13] The Bank's approach has been to hire consultants on several different occasions to do the job in three to five months.

The fish biologist who told me the preceding story took care to distinguish these "jet-setters" from "fish-heads" like himself, who prefer to go to a village and work with local fishers who have generations of experience with the river. He was asked to study the downstream effects of the recently completed Theun-Hinboun Dam adjacent to the Nam Theun 2 site (Australian Mekong Resource Centre 2000). (International activists and local villagers had protested that the fisheries were being destroyed, which the government, lenders, and builders strongly denied; consequently, he was hired to conduct a study.) Hired on a "four-day input per month" schedule, he found it impossible to do what his contract required: to study the bypass flows at this postimpoundment stage of the finished dam. He took the view in his report that a whole team of scientists was needed to study the dam's effects on the river over a substantial period of time and space.

Yet, he also emphasized, one did not need to be a biologist to understand that if there should be between 45 and 60 cubic meters per second (cumecs) of water passing through the dam site and if only 5 cumecs were passing through, this will cause problems for downstream biota. "If the 45 to 60 cumecs represents a loaf of bread necessary to maintain the system, then the 10 cumecs represents a slice and the 5 cumecs just crumbs." In other words, the more water the dam held back to produce electricity, the more the downstream fisheries would be destroyed. This was, indeed, the experience of the downstream villagers. His immediate recommendation was to increase the minimum dry season bypass flows from 5 to 10 cumecs, which he noted would result in the loss of electrical sales of $1 million but would save at least some of the fisheries in the short term. In spite of promises to post the report on its Web site, the report's contractor, the Asian Development Bank, chose to suppress it, claiming there were no "clear recommendations" in the report.[14]

This incident of suppression is not unique; in fact, it is common practice.[15] Tyson Roberts, an ichthyologist well known for his work on the Mekong fisheries, was hired to conduct a fishery study for Nam Theun 2. Like a number of his peers, Roberts cautioned the Bank and government against making any rapid assessments without first gathering extensive data on fish migration.[16] But, midway through his consultancy, he was fired and his visa was taken from him: "My [legally contracted] EIA work on Nam Theun 2 was suppressed by the Lao Hydropower Office, probably in collusion with the Nam Theun 2 project sponsors (NTEC). World Bank policy of only employing EIA consultants approved by the World Bank and the host country (thereby assuring the sponsoring company can influence the selection [since they are the ones generating the revenues for the host]) is totally against any honest concept of EIA."[17]

Meanwhile, Roberts and his colleagues have documented more than eighty-five different species on the Theun River, and he suspects that several are endemic to the river and will be threatened with extinction if the dam is built.[18] After he was fired and forced to leave the country, the government, the World Bank, and NTEC hired another Northern scientist to conduct the rapid appraisals they needed to move the project along.[19]

Although the reason for particular acts of suppression varies with context, the most common motivation is that problematic EIAs and SIAs can delay or, even worse, prevent a project's approval. The whole process of having to do these assessments is strongly disliked both by Bank staff, whose job it is to make loans, and by borrower government staff, who often have strong political and economic interests in the kind of large infrastructural projects the Bank funds. As one veteran environmental advisor at the World Bank explained to me, it is never easy to get support for a long-term study unless investors (i.e., multilateral banks, private foreign capital, and governments) are certain there will be a project at the other end.[20] In other words, project investors wag the scientific tail. Since there can be no guarantee by the World Bank for a project investment without the requisite environmental assessments—a direct result of social movement pressure—EIAs are being done, but the process is neither disinterested nor apolitical. For Bank loan officers, the primary concern is to promote their portfolio and avoid getting burned by the activists who are closely monitoring their studies.

In another incident involving the socioeconomic study mentioned above, certain research findings were suppressed although neither the Bank nor the Lao government was directly responsible. As one of the researchers (an anthropologist) explained, what he and his partner found did not please their contractor, IUCN, the world's largest international conservation group, which had its own reasons for wanting the dam project to move forward: it was negotiating a $60-million contract to design and run a series of National Biodiversity Conservation Areas (NBCAs) that would enclose more than 15 percent of the nation's territory. The anthropologist recalled that what they found in the field was deemed too controversial to publish:

> We found that people on the plateau (near the dam site) survived on tubers and foraging, hunting and trapping, rice and corn cultivation, and animal

raising. People in Vientiane (the capital city) had warned that there was famine on the plateau because the rice crops had failed. But we saw that the people survived fine without rice because of their nonfarm activities. This would be impossible if the people were forced out of their villages and resettled [where they could] only cultivate rice. If they were left only with sedentary agriculture and not allowed to forage, hunt, and fish, as current plans call for, they might not survive.

We also knew what happened to other ethnic minorities who have been resettled from the hills to the plains, as the government has tried with others from the hills. . . . Almost half the resettled population had died within the first few years. You know, it takes more than three years to adjust to grow rice or adjust to the new environment and lifestyle. Many just can't adjust fast enough to survive, so they die and are listed officially as famine victims. That's why we made the case that the government and the Bank needed to take this whole resettlement plan slowly.

My partner wrote the section of the report saying that these people should not be classified as "ethnic minorities" but as "indigenous people." But that opened a whole can of worms with IUCN. . . I myself pushed another line that they hated equally. I said instead of moving them out, the best thing for these people are health clinics, schools, and agroecosystem support to keep them going. But IUCN felt it would make the plateau such a livable place that others would migrate in and destroy their project of developing the noninundation parts of the plateau into one large NBCA [National Biodiversity Conservation Area].[21]

The anthropologists found themselves in a struggle with IUCN staff, who disliked their findings and demanded that they rewrite their final report. In particular, IUCN staff did not want the term indigenous people used at all, for fear that the classification would require that the project fall under the Bank's Operational Directive on indigenous people, which could further postpone it. The delay threatened to derail IUCN's negotiations to oversee the NBCA system in Laos.[22] These NBCAs would be financed by a percentage of the government's share of the revenues from the Nam Theun 2 Dam, and the Bank planned to set up an international board of directors that would directly receive these revenues for conservation.[23] In other words, groups like IUCN were on the verge of a remarkable windfall because Laos is one of a number of sites where large conservation projects are being linked to controversial Bank investments.

In the end, IUCN decided against circulating the report. NTEC, the consortium of private dam investors, subsequently hired a consultant from Norway to write up a new social action plan, which did not refer to the silenced study. In record time, he concluded that these ethnic minorities were in fact no different than many other groups living in Laos, and that all the peoples of the Plateau *could* be resettled without harm and to great potential benefit (NTEC 1997). He specifically described the different ethnic tribes as a singular ethnic group, "as a whole, a melting-pot culture," which could survive and benefit from resettlement. This consultant is now the main anthropologist on the Nam Theun 2 project.

Instances of outright suppression and generation of alternate research findings, such as those just described, are well known within the research community hired by the Bank and its contractors.[24] But an equally significant, and invariably more subtle, shaping of knowledge occurs through the omission of information. Scientists whom I interviewed spoke at length about their research, yet much of what they discussed with passion would never be written up in their reports. What happened to these ideas, interpretations, and more nuanced understandings of the complex environmental and social realities they were studying?

The answer is suggested by a biologist who exhaustively described species interdependence and reproduction along the Mekong tributaries, as well as differences in social groups and their relations with different flora, fauna, and marine species.[25] He spoke to me about the people who depend on the seasonal cycle of river floods that revive soils for rice cultivation, replenish river flora for building materials, and increase the harvest of snakes, fish, and frogs. After the river recedes, these people hunt and gather in the forest. It was a startling image of complexity, reciprocity, and knowledge that I had not come across in any official report on the Mekong. When I asked where in his report I could read about this, he replied, "Nowhere." Why? Because the Bank had hired him to explain the ability of the river to accommodate aquaculture aimed at the Tokyo fish market. The terms of reference did not permit an analysis of the intricate relation between the river people and their natural environment. Instead, he responded to the question that he was hired to answer: can this particular Mekong River ecosystem hold up under the weight of a capital-intensive aquaculture investment? In this way, knowledges are selectively isolated and/or adapted into a larger truth regime (Braun 2000;

Burchell 1991; Foucault 1994). It became clear through my conversations with both natural and social scientists that the most sophisticated expertise, analyses, data, wisdom, and practices would never appear in formal scientific reports commissioned by development institutions if they conflicted with those institutions' larger purposes and preconceptions.

Of course with omission there is inclusion; for every concern, data set, interpretation, and recommendation that is omitted or removed from a report, there are as many that fill its pages and circulate as science locally and oftentimes transnationally. In the case of the anthropologists and IUCN, a new framework for understanding ethnic minorities (as a "melting pot" culture) is created. In the case of the fisheries study, what gets created is a scientific framework for rationalizing export-oriented aquaculture.

Catching big fish on the Mekong. Courtesy Elizabeth Price and International Rivers Network.

## THE SUBJUGATION OF SUBALTERN KNOWLEDGES

Coupled with privileging knowledge of "experts" (Northerners, locals, and translocals) is the subjugation of the knowledges of the "nonexperts," the millions of people perceived as the object of study and of development. Surveys typically construct and then characterize populations based on very simple but enduring social categories, classifying people as fisher, hunter, or swidden cultivator when many people can be all or none at different times of the year. Some studies define downstream as being just a few miles away from the dam or project and hence make invisible the ecological and social downstreams of large projects, which can include hundreds of miles and whole groups of people, such as the seminomadic, who remain absent from census data or outside of the project's command area. Although most people affected by Bank projects are accounted for through processes of census, classification, and project incorporation, they become legible and accountable only within the context of a specific capital investment and culture of development; qualities that have little to do with commercial markets are ignored or defined as destructive to the unquestioned goals of (trans)national economic growth and sustainable development. The noncommodified realms of social interaction are considered to have value only within the context of development and become more easily comprehended when they are incorporated within the project sphere. The effects are to normalize asymmetric relations between development experts and so-called development beneficiaries and to make scientific stereotypes of the latter as lacking, irrational, environmentally degrading, and in need of development at almost any cost.[26]

In a short time, the remote environments and societies of Laos—and scientific data, techniques, and perspectives—have been judged in terms of their value to the proposed capital investment, and not the reverse. These formally noncommodified realms have been made legible, but only as new sites of scientific research, new objects for interrogation and betterment. Unknowns have been made knowable not just because the Bank has sponsored research, but also because these objects of knowledge have been translated through the epistemic discourse of development, in its latest green neoliberal (con)version. In the Mekong, this has become the framing device through which authorities speak and through which many become authorities. Some of the effects of power/knowledge production along the Mekong are the rise of new subjectivities of both the sustainable-development expert and the eco-rational citizen (e.g., "destructive" forest dwellers resettled as "ecological" and "productive" rice cultivators).

A small window into the relationship between the World Bank's consultants and its development clients is provided by the story of its public consultations on the Nakai Plateau. The Bank and its contractors have held numerous public consultations on the dam and its affiliated conservation projects with the people who will be most directly affected. The idea behind these interactions was that local people could—and should— help planners understand their needs and concerns, which would lead to project (and therefore stakeholders') "improvement." Indeed, public consultation has been honed to a new development science, especially since the issue of participation has become politically volatile for the Bank (Cooke and Kothari 2001). The Bank takes it so seriously that for Nam Theun 2 it hired an evaluation expert (another new development discipline) to formally assess the effectiveness of the Nam Theun 2 public consultations. According to her final report, the consultant noticed that at these meetings most of the plateau people just stared at the presenters (Franklin 1997). Rightfully so, she wrote, as the presenters had described the dam project in a language "more appropriate to an (U.S.) Army Corps of Engineers meeting." After the day-long sessions of PowerPoint presentations, she interviewed the attendees—forest dwellers who had been brought down to the town for the consultation. She learned that a high percentage of them had absolutely no idea what the meeting was about. Of those who said they did understand the topic, most had no idea that these meetings were about moving them from their land and resettling them as rice farm entrepreneurs. In fact, some thought these men had come to present them with a simple but appreciated gift: not Laos's largest dam, but a village well.[27]

Through these costly attempts, the Bank *fails* at the most direct form of information exchange with its "objects" of development, yet it *succeeds* at formalizing, indigenizing, and replicating the new development rituals of participation, self-evaluation, and communication. Each round brings in more scientific intervention, more actors, and more feedback. Subsequent consultations brought in more local consultants who could better speak the language and explain the project. As the consultation process improves, the clear-felling of the forest for the dam reservoir is almost complete, project stakeholders have been identified and debriefed, rules have been rewritten, the project financing deal has been signed, and the retooled government agencies overseeing everything from electricity generation to people's resettlement are put in place. The subaltern is finally able to speak, but mostly through the overdetermined technologies of the development world and not as decision makers able to influence these powerful capital investments.

NATIONAL POLITICAL INTERESTS

The institutional forces shaping knowledge production converge with the political interests of the borrowing country government, in this case the ruling party, the Pathet Lao. A top priority of the Pathet Lao government is to generate as much hard currency as possible, and developing the country's hydroelectric power industry works toward this end. Thus the government's interest in getting the NT2 project funded and its willingness to go along, however reluctantly, with most of the green neoliberal conditions being placed upon it.

Yet it is not just that the Lao government is cooperating with the World Bank to make NT2 a reality; the World Bank is cooperating with the government. For example, it has figured out ways to rationalize the Lao government's engagement in highly unsustainable logging practices, such as granting unlimited rights to log valuable native forests to the Chinese and Vietnamese militaries in return for past military support (Tropical Rainforest Programme 2000; Walker 1996). The Bank has also ignored the government's ethnocidal "Laoization policy" of deploying the military to forcibly resettle 900,000 people, mostly non-Lao speaking minorities (of the nation's total population of 4.6 million), down from the forested mountains into the plains. Although countless studies have been contracted to analyze the "irrational" behavior of the "backward" peasant, no official ones have been conducted on the environmental and social impact of these massive national projects. Because the client state prefers no public scrutiny, the World Bank systematically sidesteps it, shifting its scientific gaze and logic of inquiry onto more acceptable practices of development.

Of course, corruption in the world's logging industry and bloody nationalist projects are nothing new, and this is not the first time the Bank has colluded with its borrowers. The larger point is that there are institutional effects of this highly politicized knowledge-production process: loans and grants are earmarked for a borrowing country's development problems, as defined by the scientific work conducted to justify the investments. When the World Bank and its partners generate data for particular countries, yet systematically leave out the most socially transforming and ecologically destructive nationalist projects, they are creating a powerful scientific protocol that underwrites a particular ideology of development.

From the money of bilateral and multilateral agencies, an accepted and widely utilized scientific protocol, or concretized set of practices, is emerging in Laos. The hiring practices, terms of reference, complexity of projects, institutional imperatives of the Bank and its partners and the particular agenda of the state have all contributed to shaping this protocol. The rapid rural appraisal method of research, with its tremendous time-space constraints, plus the mechanisms that suppress, omit, and outright dismiss what are considered illegitimate or irrational forms of knowledge, represent the essence of this protocol. But the generative side is as impressive: tomes of reports and new categories, data sets, new actors, responsibilities, and forms of acceptable conduct.

What percolates up from these practices on the ground? What counts as nature, society, and green scientific knowledge within these institutional constraints? How is this knowledge reflected in new institutions and new subjects in the new Laos?

## Subjectivities of Green Neoliberalism

In order to spread their particular approach to green science and environmentally sustainable development, Northern aid agencies and banks have invested in "capacity building" in borrowing countries. These funders have given birth to or helped support research institutes, training centers, and national science and policy agendas. In this way green development knowledge has become entwined with processes of professionalization, authoritative forms of power, and disciplinary mechanisms. Enormous flows of money (relative to GDP) stream into borrowing countries to restructure and "modernize" state agencies and institutions. Consequently, the contentious, uncertain, and tentative process of knowledge production described above has become certain: institutionalized, normalized, and multiplied in local sites through which new forms of knowledge and power (or knowledge/power) now circulate.

In Laos, fifty foreign bilateral aid agencies, multilateral banks, and donors contribute money annually to the state.[28] At a donor meeting (the Roundtable Meeting for the Lao PDR) held not in Vientiane but in Geneva, $1.2 billion was pledged directly to the Lao government for 1997–2000 (Government of Lao PDR 1997; UNDP 1997). In 1994, fully half of Laos's domestic revenue came from foreign grants, and a remarkably high 80 percent of the state's public investment program came from foreign aid (Government of Lao PDR 1997; UNDP 1997). That is, almost every public works project and every state agency related to these large capital investments is financed by foreign money.[29] Much of the funding actually goes to foreign consultants and firms hired to reform state institutions and to train a Lao professional class. Although the net capital outflow from borrowing countries is often greater than the capital inflows from multilateral banks and bilateral aid agencies (World Bank 1999, World Bank 2002), artifacts do remain within the country; these include highways, transmission lines, a cultivated professional class, and discourses and forms of power/knowledge. These artifacts help localize transnational social networks, transnationalize the more effective practices emerging from the Lao experience, and accommodate potential foreign investors.

In the case of Laos, multilateral development banks and Northern agencies have tried to restructure the moribund and highly indebted socialist state into one that can better accommodate the needs of foreign agencies, banks, regulatory regimes, and corporations. In the past few years, many of Laos's property and natural resource use laws have been overhauled to reflect the prevailing ideology of its multilateral creditors—green neoliberalism. Many laws were written by Northern consultants hired by the Bank, bilateral agencies, and even NGOs. For example, Laos's new environmental protection law was written by consultants for UNDP; a U.S. lawyer for IUCN wrote key forestry legislation; and Northern lawyers wrote the rules and regulations that will establish twenty National Biodiversity and Conservation Areas. Although these acts have been mediated and delayed by Lao state officials unhappy with such foreign interventions into the internal workings of the state, these *new regimes of rule* clearly reflect the *new truth regimes* on Lao nature and society generated by Northern experts.

The Forestry Department alone contains more than fifty separate foreign-funded projects that promote sustainable logging, tree plantations, forest conservation, and more. The Ministry of Forestry and Agriculture, the Hydropower Office, and most state agencies overseeing natural resources in Laos are almost wholly financed, and their staff trained, by Northern agencies and their consultants. The National University, the Forest Training School and Training Centre, and the state's central environmental agency are all financed by foreign aid.

In the creation of these new resource use laws, new ecozones, and new rules and regulations for forest access, a whole new lexicon has been introduced to Laos. Conservation, biodiversity, sustainable logging, environmentally sustainable development, and environmental economics are imbued with meanings derived from negotiations among these transnational agencies and experts. What counts as biodiversity in Laos is defined by actors other than the people who live there; the very idea of "biodiversity" is believed to be, according to Northern experts, a completely exogenous concept. In the mid-1990s, when the Wildlife Conservation Society (WCS) and IUCN described the state of the environment in Laos, they unambiguously stated that *no* conservation practices existed. Indeed, one report (IUCN 1993) stated that the word did not exist in the Lao language.[30] Subsequently, Northern agencies funded the training of Lao professionals—often in courses overseas—so that they could properly identify Mekong species. These retrained experts return home to manage multipronged conservation projects within state and nonstate agencies that are dependent on financing from large capital-intensive development projects. Ironically, it was the *untrained* forest dwellers who first guided Northern wildlife experts from IUCN, WCS, WWF, the World Bank, and GEF through the Lao forests to reveal to them the world of exquisite "globally threatened species": the rare tigers, elephants, muntjacs, barking deer, gibbons, langurs, and warty pigs. They guided these curious experts down the inaccessible rivers so they could see the distinctive otters, white-winged ducks, and hundreds of diverse fish species, including the Asian cyprinid, known to locals for its remarkable ability to pluck monkeys off the river banks.

When human populations are scientifically isolated from their environments and categorized as slash-and-burn cultivators, poachers, illegal loggers, and failed rice farmers, and when new rules and regulations prohibit hunting, fishing, seminomadism, swidden cultivation, and forest use in large swathes of inhabited forest, these changes affect not only epistemic politics but also ontological and material realities. The new authoritative logic of eco-zone management that is carving up the Mekong region is designed to ensure that there will be ample high-value hardwood supplies for export, depopulated watersheds for hydroelectric dams, and biodiversity preservation for pharmaceutical firms and eco-tourists.

In this way, the old nationalist Lao project to "Laoize" the ethnic minority forest populations (i.e., forcibly resettle them in the plains) has been transformed by the new transnational project of environmental sustainability, but it has been done in ways that further compel these minorities to get out of the forests and become *positive* actors in their society's development. For the more than sixty different ethnic minority communities incorporated into green-development processes, the effects promise to be enormous and possibly devastating. Not only do these practices lead to the new subjectivity of the transnational eco-expert within the Lao professional class, they also reshape the subjectivity of the subaltern forest dweller. By the time this green project is completed, most forest dwellers may experience "sustainable development" in the form of ethnicity-based oppression and expulsion from the forest.

Certainly, debates are taking place within the Lao ruling party on precisely how much power it should cede to foreign agencies, as government officials are taken aback by the onslaught of project demands, as well as by the imperial nature of Northern actors. In one case, a state planning office wrote a critical conceptual paper on the origins of "the idea of poverty" in Laos (Government of Lao PDR 1997) because Northern experts were asking the government to start using the concept in its policy work. The World Bank liaison officer in Vientiane explained to me that nothing changes in Laos unless a top offi-

cial publicly says it is okay.[31] She said it was not until the recent
Sixth Congress that a Lao official had ever used the term
"poverty" or, for that matter, "the environment" or even "regional integration"—all critical concepts for Bank-style rule
of law. "It was only after that meeting that we could officially
proceed on these issues," she noted. As an afterthought, she
added, "They actually took the phrasing, word for word, from
one of our reports."

## Conclusion

The world of development and its proliferating knowledge-
production practices are strategic sites of power in highly em-
battled North-South relations and in global capitalism. Within
these entangled worlds sits the World Bank, an institution currently under intense scrutiny due to the successes of growing
anti-Bank and alternative-development social movements. In
this chapter I have sought to explain the World Bank's latest
innovation in knowledge production and how it becomes authoritative, locally and transnationally. Such practices are best
understood within the milieu in which they are being constructed, reproduced, and circulated.

   In an attempt to overcome the charges of its critics and
to regain (and sustain) the confidence of its investors, the
World Bank at the turn of the millennium has pushed itself to
become the world's "knowledge bank" (World Bank 1998). In
part, this is a valid claim: the Bank is unique in its ability to access the world's most remote regions and most secretive governments and to emerge with a surfeit of apparently reliable
information. There are no other equivalent institutions. Knowledge is now its greatest asset, and it is generated and used in
highly strategic ways in borrowing as well as lending countries.

As we have seen in Laos, transnational actors (who now include the small professional class in Laos) gather the data, decide their utility, and design the institutions to help indigenize (and hence globalize) particular norms. Moreover, the data collection process reflects the needs and limits of the large-scale capital investments and investors that motivate them in the first place. However contentious and uncertain the localized process of knowledge production may be, the stamp of the World Bank gives it—and the data it yields—tremendous global stability, legitimacy, and circulation (Jasanoff 1997). Professional economists, corporate leaders, policymakers, reporters, and professors in universities in the South and North are among the many who consider the Bank's data and reports authoritative and use them as the basis for action.

Besides being the world's main producer of concepts, data, analytic frameworks, and policies on the environment, the World Bank has also become the world's most powerful environmentalist, teaming up with prominent NGOs, scientific institutions, borrowing states, and Northern aid agencies. This new role of the Bank has led to a cascade of institutional effects. This is particularly ironic because the Bank was pushed into its greening phase by a transnational social movement that demanded that it "reform or die." Up against a wall, the World Bank responded with fervor, ingenuity, and capital. Consequently, the Bank's form of environmental knowledge production has rapidly become hegemonic, disarming and absorbing many of its critics, expanding its terrain of influence, and effectively enlarging the scope and power of its neoliberal agenda.

# V

# Eco-Governmentality and the Making of an Environmental State

*Mountainous and isolated, Laos has decided to try and realize*
*its last hopes for development by building dams to supply its*
*neighbors, especially Thailand, reports* Libération *(France).*
— *"Dams for Development in Laos,"* Libération *2001*

A hand-drawn map of Lao People's Democratic Republic prepared for the World Bank by a prominent environmental organization does not demarcate the nation's capital, its towns, or villages. The only cartographic markings are round, oblong, and kidney-shaped, each labeled with initials, such as WB, SIDA, WCS, and IUCN. That these splotches reflect the rezoning of nearly one-fifth of the territory of Laos for conservation, and that these symbols are abbreviations for the World Bank, Swedish International Development Agency, Wildlife Conservation Society, and IUCN-World Conservation Union, tell an important political story about new efforts to classify, colonize, and transnationalize territory in the name of environmentally sustainable development.

In response to the success of its social-movement critics, the World Bank has been forced to enlist scores of social actors and institutions to help generate its green neoliberal regime. In its latest development programs, the Bank has started to include ministries of the environment, natural resources, and finance, as well as some of the world's largest environmental organizations. While activists and academics build their case against a World Bank that they see as ecologically and socially destructive, the Bank plugs away at greening its works, engaging more ecosystems and populations in its loan portfolio, and involving ever more partners from the private and public sectors.

To explicate this phenomenon, in this chapter I will focus more closely on the Bank's work in the Mekong region. Over the next two decades, the multilateral banks and the Lao government plan to build dozens of hydroelectric dams on the Mekong River, converting Laos into the Tennessee Valley Authority of Southeast Asia.[1] But unlike such projects fifty years ago, the plans for the system of dams on the Mekong are incorporating new ideas and tools of conservation, preservation, and sustainability. In the name of this project, a whole range of actors, from World Bank lawyers to international conservation scientists, have been commissioned to rewrite national property rights laws, redesign state agencies, and redefine localized production practices based on new global norms, and in doing so they have transformed conventional forms of state power, agency, and sovereignty. By generating new state authorities within national boundaries and in the world system, these practices are giving rise to *environmental states* in the global South, but not in the way that ecological modernization theorists suggest, that is, that states are motivated by the inevitable Western rationality of environmental sustainability (Frank 2000; Mol and Sonnenfeld 2000; Schofer et al. 2000; Spaargaren and Mol 1992). Such theories ignore the particular characteristics of the forces pushing for sweeping reforms and the differentiated outcomes. The environmental states emerging around the world today are marked by the specific needs of transnational capital, which are shaping the form of legality and eco-rationality that have prevailed in Southern countries. Green-neoliberal pressures have fragmented, stratified, and unevenly transnationalized Southern states, state actors, and state power in ways that defy simple definitions of modernization.

These changes of power affect what Michel Foucault called the "art of government" (Dean 1994; Foucault 1991), a concept he deployed to question the traditional notion of the state as the main site of modern societal power. He preferred to emphasize the multiplicity and widely dispersed "forms of government and their immanence to the state" (Foucault 1991, p. 91), recognizing that many technologies of power do not originate with or exist only within the state. Our emphasis here is on the porous nature of states and state power and, at its most concrete, state actors, finances, and policies. Part of the current neoliberal agenda is to compel us to reconsider the ways we govern each other, govern ourselves, and have our governments govern us. The point of this political obsession is not to improve the art of government for the sake of making states large and nurturing, but to take on the responsibility of government ourselves and to do so in order to privilege above all the needs of the economy. It is through the nourishment of markets and the economy that we will find sustenance, development, human rights and justice, and environmental sustainability. I call this political rationality of compelling states and citizens to improve their care of nature and their care of each other for the greater good of the economy *eco-governmentality.*

My emphasis, however, differs from the recent literature on governmentality in that here the contested terrain is the arena that Foucault and his interlocutors have overlooked and rendered undifferentiated: nature, qualities of territory, and the political-epistemic rationalities that give meaning, order, and value to them (cf. Braun 2000; Kuehls 1996; Moore 2001; Sivaramakrishnan 1997).[2] It is through the Bank's green neoliberal project—in which *neocolonial* conservationist ideas of enclosure and preservation and *neoliberal* notions of market value and optimal resource allocation find common cause— that this institution has made particular natures and natural resource-dependent communities legible, accountable, and available to foreign investors (Scott 1998). Confronted with what Foucault called the "problem of government," unevenly transnationalized state and nonstate actors have sought to "improve" conditions of nature and populations for international markets by introducing new cultural and scientific logics for interpreting qualities of the state's territory. In doing so, a hegemonic discourse of ecological difference rooted in neoliberal market ideology emerges, defining some "qualities of territory" as degraded and others as appropriate for commodification, and hence for improvement. In this way, new domains of political-economic calculation are forged that facilitate the disciplinary (i.e., normalizing) practices and legitimating devices for *trans*nationalizing access and rights to the Mekong.

## THE NAKAI PLATEAU, LAO PDR

Riding along the mountainous road between Vientiane and the Nakai Plateau, in the central part of the country, one cannot help but feel the presence of colonial and imperial forces. The legacies of the French, Chinese, Vietnamese, and the Americans are clearly visible: their currencies, traders, militaries, banks, political-economic pressures, and ways of seeing clutter the spaces of Lao society. These imperial forces are active in the present as well as in the past. Only from a distance is it possible to maintain the fiction that World Bank-style development is simply a technocratic intervention generated outside of the politics, culture, and history of imperial social relations. The variegated landscape and people tell a much different story. High in the mountains thirty years after the U.S. military ended its secret and illegal bombing of Laos, Lao fishers travel down the quiet Theun River on long metal fishing boats made from the shells dropped on the nearby Ho Chi Minh Trail by B-52 bombers. These bomb-shell boats stir the waters where international capital, multilateral banks, and conservation groups are busy making maps and plans and deciding whom to zone in and whom to zone out of the ecologically diverse Nakai Plateau and the larger Mekong River system. But these groups no longer work in the name of strengthening the glorious empire, civilizing the savage, or stopping the tide of communism, but in the name of environmentally sustainable development.

As a Lao acquaintance and I drive toward the site for the next major new dam, Nam Theun 2, we pass cavernous bomb craters, scorched-earth patches, and small spiky metal balls tucked into crevices of exposed tree roots. These are small

Traversing the Mekong by boats made from B-52 bombshells
dropped during the massive bombing of Laos in the 1970s.
Courtesy International Rivers Network.

"unexploded ordinance" or "bomblets" made to explode when
prodded by something as light as a child's stick or a farmer's
hoe. (Thirty years later, these unexploded ordinance blow up
a Lao villager, on average, every day of the year.) Most scraps
of metal we see along the road or in the villages—in the form
of farming tools, housing materials, road signs, and fencing—
come from U.S. military equipment that was left behind or
shot down. From first blush, it is clear this is not a landscape
shaped purely by local inhabitants and their idiosyncratic habits
of land use or culture, as many development officials would
have it. This is not a landscape or a people isolated from modernity and buried in tradition. They have been in the center
of one of the last century's most violent and world-altering
*modern* events.

On the road to the Nam Theun 2 construction site, we drive past the recently completed Theun Hinboun Dam. At the entrance, workers are laying down rolls of grass turf, which shine an unnaturally bright golf-course green, in preparation for an upcoming dignitaries' celebration. Here, high in the mountains in the forested Nakai Plateau, Souly,[3] who is from one of the few Lao NGOs in Vientiane, reminisces about the last time he visited this area. In the early 1980s, Souly had been a juggler for the ruling Pathet Lao's traveling circus. He and the other members of the circus spent months at a time walking through this difficult jungle terrain, trekking to villages setting up tents, and settling in for a few days of circus entertainment as well as information exchange. "We were the only connection between the people in these mountains and the state. In fact, for the villages here, we were the state," he tells me. He laughs because he was a very young man then, and he and his acrobatic friends, carrying their homes on their backs, could hardly be mistaken for "a state." Ten years ago, there was no road here; in fact, there was no state infrastructure, revenue collection, courts, or schoolhouses. There were no police or tax collectors or health clinics. Instead, the Lao state was in the capital city of Vientiane and in a few other Lao towns that were many hard days' journeys down into the valley.

As we traveled, Souly explained how the circus troupe would hike into the jungle, meet the villagers, talk to them, and tell them about what the party was doing for them and what it could do for them. Mainly, though, they gained the attention and the endearment of the villagers through juggling and acrobatics. The day I visited, the well-paved road was traversed by logging trucks (many from Vietnam across the eastern mountain passes) brimming with logs from the biodiverse plateau, which the Nam Theun 2 Dam reservoir was slated to flood. When the World Bank signed a letter of intent with the Lao government to consider a proposal for a dam here, the Lao state began to balloon in size, thanks in large part to the international development agencies that arrived in the country and lent and spent via the state, fighting over who would build the highway, who would fund the forestry projects, and who would conduct the environmental assessments for this expanding hydroelectricity project.

How can we understand these rapid changes? James Ferguson, in his study of development in the southern African nation of Lesotho, noted that large-scale development projects often fail to accomplish their most basic objectives. Yet these failures still have transformative institutional effects on the ground. In Lesotho, a large World Bank-financed agriculture and livestock project fortified the Lesotho state with bureaucratic power as well as an ideological apparatus that *depoliticized* poverty, the state, and development (Ferguson 1990, p. 256). As Ferguson shows, the state gained a foothold in yet another district, which further enlarged its power even though the World Bank project that brought it there failed to achieve its stated objective, that is, to raise agricultural output and small-scale producer incomes.

Today, almost twenty years after Ferguson's insightful study, the Bank's interventions are not only expanding the role of the state, but are helping to produce a different type of state altogether. In the Lao People's Democratic Republic and many other places around the world, the Bank has instigated the creation of *environmental states,* which consist of much more than just additional administrative units and state agencies. Rather, some arenas of the state are empowered as they become capitalized and transnationalized in an effort to support large capital projects; other arenas, by stark contrast, are completely neglected. In a country deemed by the international development community as having only two commodifiable resources worthy of any foreign support—hydropower and timber—the state is under tremendous pressure to recast itself as a globally competitive player in these two industries. All sails are raised for these Northern winds; it no longer seems to matter whether the political authorities are socialist, communist, vicious militarist (e.g., Myanmar), or liberal-democrat. To access capital, borrowing countries must play by the rules of these higher authorities.

In the making of these new environmental states, key agencies are being restructured. This process is supported by professionals from the United States, Japan, and Britain and financed by multilateral development banks and European aid organizations. The offices that flourish are those most directly linked to large-scale development loans (such as those that fund the dams being built on the Mekong) and those that work to get countries up to speed on international codes, rules, classificatory systems, and new ways of handling the populations who live where the large-scale projects will go.

The World Bank's success in becoming the world's leading expert in environmental state building is reflected in the work occurring in borrowing state agencies whose budgets go primarily to manage and disburse development loans. The values state functionaries and consultants assign to fisheries, forests, farm land, water supplies, and rural producers matter greatly to multilateral financial institutions, state coffers, foreign investors, and the local communities whose future access depends on such decisions. In prodding state agencies to become more environmental and neoliberal, the World Bank prompts them to make a country's natural assets accountable in two senses: first, in being counted and thereby made visible locally and transnationally, and second, in reference to new environmental, economic, and cultural norms and responsibilities, with new institutional policing and extractive capacities. Simply put, for the state to gain power in Laos, it is dam building or nothing, which is not such a terrible proposition for state elites as well as many others who stand to prosper from their involvement in these projects. These dam interventions, however, have unleashed a larger set of power dynamics with potentially long-term and devastating consequences.

## Greening Laos

Transnational development boosters trumpet Laos as the future crown jewel of Southeast Asia, able to offer abundant energy resources and services to the economic fireballs, such as Bangkok, in the more industrialized areas of the Mekong (Traisawasdichai 1997; Usher 1996a; Usher 1996b). The Lao state, the World Bank, the Asian Development Bank, and private consortia of foreign investors have been keen on building hydroelectric dams in the Annamite Mountains and on the major tributaries of the Mekong River. In the 1950s and 1960s, a succession of U.S. presidents pushed dam building as a way to usurp communist power in the region, promising lucrative construction contracts and capitalist development. Some transnational institutions like the Mekong River Commission were set up in the era of the cold war, and scores of engineering blueprints describing technocratic solutions to the region's problems were produced, though none of these plans attracted an audience.

Now, however, the blueprints have been dusted off. In the next two decades the World Bank and others hope to stimulate investment in the newly ascribed "Greater Mekong Subregion"

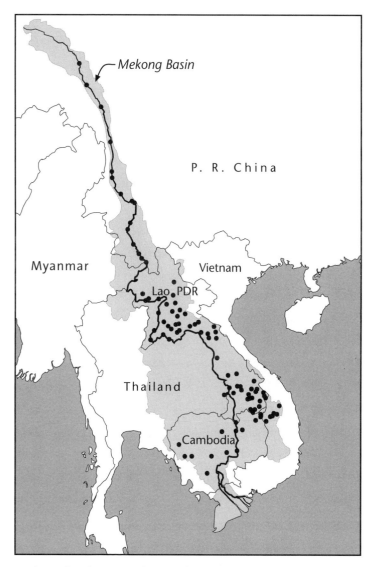

Planned and existing dams in the Mekong River Basin. Map by
Cartography Lab, University of Minnesota–Twin Cities, 2004.

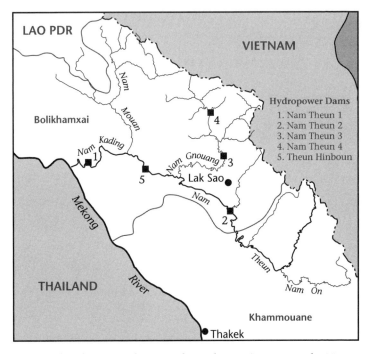

Planned and existing dams on the Mekong River artery, the Nam
Theun, in central Lao PDR. Map by Cartography Lab,
University of Minnesota–Twin Cities, 2004.

by relocating millions of mountain inhabitants in Laos, Cambodia, Vietnam, Myanmar (formerly known as Burma), Thailand, and China in order to construct dozens of hydroelectric
dams (Asian Development Bank 2003; International Rivers
Network 2003).[4] If these plans are carried out, hill dwellers in
these six neighboring countries will become the agro-industrial
workforce in the newly irrigated and electrified plains *and* a
new population of eco-rational natural resource managers.
According to an ADB director, Noritada Morita: "We may need
to reduce the population of people in mountainous areas and

bring them to normal life. They will have to settle in one place ... but don't call it resettlement. It is just migration" ("Relocation in Sight for Hill People" 1996). Morita estimated that 60 million people live in the hill areas of these countries and noted that the ADB has targeted them because "these people are not a part of their national economies." The ADB classifies this project as environmental because its goal is to stop forest destruction through *developing* the hill tribes, whom the development establishment blames for engaging in slash-and-burn cultivation, encroachment, and illegal logging, and too-rapid reproduction. The plan calls for scientists, governments, and NGOs to join the ADB and the World Bank in this $50-billion engineering project ("Relocation in Sight for Hill People" 1996), which would be just the beginning of a trillion-dollar investment scheme for electricity generation and regional industrialization.[5]

Somewhere in the middle of this desire spectrum is Nam Theun 2, the dam, hydroelectric power, and forestry project that is considered to be the test case for these larger transnational plans. Nam Theun 2 is currently the biggest investment project in Laos, with an estimated cost of $1.5 billion, slightly smaller than the country's GDP and almost four times the national budget (GOL 1997; World Bank 1997, 1999a, 2001a). The financial consortium of French, Thai, and U.S. investors (Nam Theun Power Company or NTPC) that will own and operate the project claims that the annual revenues from electricity sales to Thailand will generate up to $233 million annually for the Lao government, equivalent to 43 percent of the country's current income from exports (World Bank 2001b).

Studies in support of the dam claim that given the country's current economic situation (Laos has been designated a "highly indebted poor country," or HIPC, by the World Bank), these precious ecosystems would be better protected *with* large-scale capital projects because the revenues generated for the state could be spent on much needed conservation, preservation, and sustainable development (International Advisory Group 1997; Scudder 1998; World Bank 1999). Without immediate action, this global environmental hot spot will deteriorate under the destructive weight of overpopulation, hunting, slash-and-burn cultivating, fishing, poaching, and tree-felling. As consultants hired to help develop Laos have explained to me, for the future of Laos, *there is no alternative.*[6]

## THE ROLE OF NGOs

The site of the Nam Theun 2 Dam, watershed, and reservoir houses one of the most biologically diverse forests in the world, which includes an amazing array of rare animal and plant species. Some scientists working for international environmental groups argue that local fauna and fish populations will be seriously threatened (to the point of extinction) if the ecological and social landscape is transformed through the damming and rerouting of the Theun River and the inflow of infrastructure-maintenance activities. Anthropologists working on contract for NGOs have raised similar concerns about the human populations, whose communities and cultures could be destroyed by resettlement and the influx of other populations attracted by the opportunities associated with the project (Chamberlain 1997; Chamberlain 1995).

   In all facets of the debate on the potential impact of development projects, international NGOs have played an increasingly crucial role. Indeed, I would argue that they have propelled the process along, in ways that private capital and the multilateral banks could not have done on their own. Moreover, their increased participation has had a powerful impact on the state and the art of government. The NGOs have helped reconfigure the road map for future Bank lending and policy-making, in which NGOs will now play central roles alongside state actors and private firms. In this section I will highlight a few of the key events that led NGOs to shift their stance on dams, describing how that enabled them to become essential characters in environmental state building in Laos and in the Bank's development regime.

One of the key events that defined this development process was the designation of the Nakai Plateau and Nam Theun watershed as a global ecological hot spot for protection and preservation. International conservation groups and the World Bank's Global Environmental Facility (GEF) worked hard to list the area as a global site for protection, a categorization that normally triggers global institutional support at the same time it constrains governments and the private sector from exploiting a fragile environment. But in the early 1990s, when a Bank loan manager expressed an interest in the idea of the Nam Theun 2 Dam, GEF officials were forced to recant their classification so that the loan manager could proceed with her plans.[7]

For a few months, one World Bank loan manager held the world's conservation community hostage. The international NGO community in Laos debated the issue with great fervor and anxiety. After a few months, the Lao government stepped in and forbade a Vientiane-based international NGO forum from holding debates about the dam and threatened to expel the more vociferous NGO staff from the country and to harass the Lao participants. Realizing that their non-dam-related conservation projects in the region would be in jeopardy, the directors of the large environmental NGOs decided, after conferring with their field scientists, that it was better to stay in the country and work with the key actors for conservation, in whatever form that might take.

Many of the development NGOs, such as CARE, Save the Children, Oxfam, and World Education, also decided to stay in the country, continue their development work, and remain silent on the controversy, even though that was interpreted as support for dam building. Consequently, as development in the Mekong region became increasingly defined by dam building, the work of most international NGOs there began to be shaped by dam-related interventions.

Their rationale for withdrawing from the controversy was quite pragmatic: the powerful forces of development insisted that there would be no alternative to dams, and the NGOs felt it was better to be part of the dominant development stream than to be on its banks. Each NGO believed it had a particular comparative advantage (e.g., sustainable forestry, megafauna preservation, village-level support for resettlement and training) that could be used to mitigate a subset of the dam's worst effects. These development NGOs have always worked in conditions not of their own choosing, during civil wars, destructive U.S. foreign policies, and authoritarian regimes. For them, this was just another hostile situation. Their abilities to adapt and compromise are precisely what have enabled them to survive for so many years alongside military regimes and international financial institutions. Moreover, many had become closer to the Bank, as subcontractors for Bank projects, and had decided it is better to try to improve the Bank's work than to stand on the sidelines and criticize. In fact, it is to the credit of NGOs, such as IUCN, Worldwide Fund for Nature (WWF), World Conservation Society (WCS), CARE, and Oxfam, that conservation, biodiversity, farmer training, and carefully mediated resettlement are central components to the project and to the Lao state's agenda.

When senior officials of major environmental groups found themselves in the uncomfortable position of deciding whether or not to throw their organizational weight behind dam building and disavow the global hot-spot designation, they expressed their decision in a publicly circulated letter exchange.[8] In a letter to Patrick McCully, campaigns director of International Rivers Network, David McDowell, director general of IUCN, explained his position:

> I have been very aware of the Bank's sorry past record, its failures, its deceits and its manipulation of people and procedures. I gave a pretty direct anti-dam speech two years ago at the annual Bank jamboree in Washington. I had also had reservations about getting involved at all in the NT exercise. But having made a commitment of time to looking at the Laos proposals I was rather struck by the distance the Bank has moved in the past year or eighteen months. . . .
>
> Having seen the POE report [the Panel of Experts' report, cowritten, coincidentally, by a former senior IUCN official], you will not be surprised to hear that on the environmental side the Groups' view was that the globally important biodiversity hot spot which is the Nam Theun watershed will be more surely protected if the dam is built in association with the Bank than by unregulated, unmonitored private sector consortium. . . . I do concur in the major conclusions. It seems to me that on this occasion the Bank may be getting it more right than wrong, though history will tell. So may I gently suggest that you have another look at Nam Theun and

see if you agree, notably in the light of the limited alternative course of action open to the international community. (August 25, 1997)

In a more convoluted presentation of the position of Wildlife Conservation Society-NY, Dr. John Robinson, vice president and director of international conservation, wrote this letter to IRN:

WCS is neither a proponent nor an opponent of the Nam Theun 2 Dam. WCS is not an advocacy conservation organization. We are a conservation research organization, and we do not comment on issues unless we have considerable relevant technical expertise. . . . WCS is in the position to comment on the impact of projects on biodiversity conservation, and we have very carefully restricted ourselves to this role. As is clear from the context of his 2/7/96 letter to you, Alan Rabinowitz [WCS's conservation scientist in the Mekong] supports the NT2 Project *as it applies to biodiversity conservation.* He is not supporting the dam construction *per se.* The support of the NT2 project is contingent on continued environmental protection and mitigation. Be very clear however in distinguishing that support from the advocacy position that International Rivers Network has taken. We are not a proponent of the dam because of its consequences on biodiversity conservation. We only comment that as the entire project is designed at this moment in time, the impact on biodiversity is most likely to be positive. (April 4, 1996)

At the time, the World Bank insisted that the Lao state and private investors would build the dam; the only question remaining was whether or not the so-called international development community would be willing to come aboard and influence the process. Proponents of "immediate action" believed that a massive intervention was needed to stem the ecological destruction and human poverty in Laos, and that a large-scale project was the best, and perhaps the only, vehicle for changing the way the environment—as well as poverty and development—was managed. These senior environmental officials came to believe that building the dam was inevitable. Because the Lao state was too poor and disinterested in protecting its hot spots, revenue from the dam would be the only source of capital to finance the "saving of the environment," and their NGOs were the best candidates to influence the project as well as the borrowing state. As negotiations began among these different actors, the idea of greening the Nam Theun 2 Dam expanded to the idea of greening the state, state-society relations, and transboundary relations with its adjacent neighbors. With dozens of dams being planned, NGOs felt that the moment was ripe for a major transformation in the whole Mekong region.

Once the intense dam debates died down, megafauna and biodiversity conservationists such as the IUCN, WWF, and WCS teamed up with the Lao state, the World Bank, and corporate investors to help create and implement the Nam Theun 2 project.[9] Although this unified coalition included individual dissenters, the net effect was to move ahead with the World Bank's green neoliberal agenda.

Even as it sought to appease those concerned with improving the conditions of populations and ecosystems, the World Bank was more concerned about its ability to interest private capital in its new ventures. Large fixed-capital investments are not like speculative capital; they require secure and unambiguous property rights and minimal political risks over a substantial period of time to ensure sustained profit rates. Yet to achieve this required a number of fundamental changes in Laos and other borrowing countries, starting with the state and its regulatory, legal, and political institutions. Bringing the NGO community around was only one task of many for the Bank. As important, before the World Bank could persuade Northern investors to invest in "hardware," it had to persuade the borrowing country to invest in the "software" of state restructuring.

The effect of this effort to become more environmentally and socially proactive has been that the World Bank's interventions have become much more inclusive, authoritative, and disciplinary. In general, the World Bank has successfully engaged the nascent professional class in the neoliberal discourse of entrepreneurial, individual responsibility. It has also begun the process of converting the previously inconsequential forest, hill, and river communities into visible, communicative, and accountable populations. In short, the Bank has instigated a proliferating domain of human activity—*the activity of government and subject creation*—that works to make sites and populations more compatible with these large-scale capital investments, even as these investments change to include new ways to "improve" biodiversity, mountain populations, and the professional class.

## New Laws, Agencies, and Projects

Under the rubric of state restructuring, there are three types of interventions in which the World Bank is engaging: rewriting laws (particularly related to the regulation of natural resources, the environment, and property rights); restructuring state agencies that regulate environments (broadly defined to include many state ministries); and funding large-scale "green" infrastructural projects. All three interventions are inextricably linked. The development of fixed capital infrastructure (in this case, a joint-ventured hydroelectric facility) requires laws that establish certain property rights, which can occur only through the restructuring of state institutions. The environmental projects are the legitimizing vehicle for the dam: without a strong public commitment to environmentally sustainable development, the World Bank and its counterparts would encounter robust resistance from highly effective campaigns to stop "business-as-usual," Bank-style development. In effect, the Bank's proactive response to transnational environmental organizations, networks, and movements are new strategies of global environmentalism that have become institutionalized (with greater and lesser effectiveness) throughout the world.

Before 1975, the French created the Lao legal, juridical, and administrative systems to maximize social control, resource taxation, and forced labor for the French empire. Upon taking power, the socialist Pathet Lao abolished the French system and replaced it with a general declaration that all land and resources would belong to the people and be held in a public trust (Evans 1995). By the late 1980s, as foreign aid from the USSR dried up and its foreign debt ballooned, the Pathet Lao introduced a market-oriented set of economic reforms that were in part a response to pressure from its main creditors, the World Bank and the Asian Development Bank, as well as to dramatic shifts already occurring in Vietnam and China. Foreign fiscal advisors, natural resource planners, and lawyers soon moved to Vientiane to facilitate these changes in policy and economic orientation. Subsequently, the prime minister's office passed a number of important decrees relating to property rights and natural resource use, especially forests, water, and land. Each was motivated and largely written by foreign consultants to international finance institutions (IFIs), donor trust funds, or international NGOs. Each was followed up with Northern loans, aid, and direct foreign investments, leading to larger and more permanent offices and staff in Vientiane for Northern aid and development agencies. With each legal change came institutional restructuring in Laos.

In 1989, the country's first national forestry conference produced the Tropical Forest Action Plan (TFAP), which was drafted and funded by UN agencies. It was a boilerplate plan and was criticized by the international environmental groups that were leading successful campaigns against TFAPs in other borrowing countries as being too sympathetic toward timber industry interests (Hirsch and Warren 1998; Lohmann 1990; Parnwell and Bryant 1996). Undeterred, the Lao government and the World Bank pushed ahead with an extensive campaign to document the social and ecological processes occurring in the populated forests of Laos. The prime minister ordered a formal ban on all logging operations until a national audit could be properly conducted with international support (Decree No. 67). The government acknowledged that it lacked sufficient or reliable data to fulfill the demands of both the international development institutions and their detractors to monitor forest clearing. In fact, it lacked the capacity to enforce the ban: Because Lao generals finance their military units through logging, logging of the Nakai Plateau has expanded (Southavilay 2000; Tropical Rainforest Programme 2000; Walker 1996; Watershed 2000). Meanwhile, the World Bank commissioned studies documenting ecological resource supplies, ecosystem dynamics, and utilization patterns of forest users. Since the early 1990s, the government's growing professional staff and transnational consultants have been busy inventing and implementing techniques and tools for rapid appraisals and diagnostics of the Mekong.[10]

As these scientific studies were being completed, the government passed more decrees that incorporated the findings, imposing classificatory systems from the development banks' environmental consultants. The prime minister's Decree No. 169, established in 1993, created a classification system for the nation's forests: *protection forests* for watershed catchment areas as well as for the supply of timber and nonwood products; *conservation forests* for biological diversity and the promotion of scientific and cultural values; *village forests* for subsistence production only; and *degraded forests* for sedentary agriculture. Three years later, the National Assembly approved this decree as forestry law, thereby legalizing state control over forests, a law that nullifies hundreds of local customary-use practices. Decree No. 164, passed in the same year, further classified nearly three million hectares (or one-seventh of Laos's total land mass and one-fourth of Laos's forested land) as conservation and protection forests. This decree also established eighteen (now expanded to twenty) National Biodiversity Conservation Areas (NBCAs), a concept promoted by the World Bank's Global Environmental Facility and the largest international conservation NGOs. Emerging from these Northern-financed initiatives is a new classificatory system and knowledge regime for land relations: socially diverse, semi-nomadic, shifting, kinship-based, interdependent relations of production are "out" in the new framework, while biodiversity conservation, sustainable timber production, and watershed management are "in."[11]

These forestry decrees and laws systematically reconstitute administrative and cultural boundaries into rationalized *eco-zones* delineated by new attributions of the value of the forest and of different groups of forestry users. Every user group—from the timber industry to semi-nomadic forest users, pastoralists, nature preservers, pharmaceutical producers, the global energy and eco-tourism industries—receives rights over a part of the nation's forests. These plans seek to clarify property rights and resource use rules through the transnational environmental science of tropical forestry management, matching newly collected data on ecological resources and capacities (i.e., degradation and recovery rates) with the demands of diverse new markets for these natural goods and services, from hardwoods to biodiversity aesthetics to electricity.

New forestry laws have also authorized the shift of the fiscal and taxation dimensions of forestry from the provincial government to the central government and centralized all these new undertakings under the Ministry of Agriculture and Forestry. The ministry is growing rapidly as a result of the influx of millions of dollars and is creating additional branches and divisions every year, most of which are skeletal units in which transnationally funded projects and programs are housed. Even UN and bilateral agencies spearheading forestry projects to *decentralize* authority over local resources and land are contributing to the strengthening of the central authority of the state through the rents that the central bureaucracy demands from the dollar-based aid money that flows into the provincial and district government agencies and into the villages. The money to support the neoliberal agenda of decentralization also serves to fortify central state power, as well as institutionalize aid-based corruption and rent-seeking.

The 1992 Land Decree and 1997 Land Law have had the joint effect of establishing a land market and new standards for land use. New land titling projects in pilot villages are taking

cadastres and drawing up state-sanctioned land titles to re-
place a decentralized system of customary property rights.
These new titles guarantee rights of usufruct, transfer, and in-
heritance to their owners and allow for land to be bought and
sold. According to the new laws, any land left fallow for more
than three years can be claimed by the state, and any land can
be expropriated for development projects as long as the users
receive compensation. The 1997 law, when enforced, is devastating to upland cultivators who rotate cultivation in eight- to
twenty-year cycles to maintain the land's long-term fertility.
Land use that results in "degradation" or "neglect" based on
new criteria and priorities (e.g., land left fallow for three
years), can be confiscated—even if such lands will regenerate
fruitfully in these long fallow cycles.

A unique characteristic of these new green laws is the role
of a new World Bank-facilitated network of transnational actors in their creation. Evidence of the World Bank's authority
and influence is apparent in its confidential Staff Appraisal Report for the Forest Management and Conservation Project
(FOMACOP), which actually named a deadline by which the
Lao National Assembly was required to pass into law certain
policy changes as a precondition for the project (World Bank
1994; World Bank 1993).[12] Regulatory reforms and state restructuring have always been preconditions for Bank loans
and private investments (George and Sabelli 1994; Kapur et al.
1997), but these green preconditions are unique for being so
encompassing, disciplinary, and neoliberal.

The threat of being denied a large loan makes it difficult
for states to say "no." Such financial withdrawals would be devastating to a state's ability to function. Like other highly indebted countries, the Lao state depends on external development grants, loans, and resources for its operating budget.

Indeed, by 1993–94, fully half of Laos's domestic revenue came from foreign grants, 80 percent of the state's public investment program came from foreign aid (Government of Lao PDR [GOL] 1998; UNDP 1997), and its per capita debt load outstripped its per capita GDP by $140 per person ($500 vs. $360). These are typical features of many states in the South.

By 1999, the National Assembly had passed more laws that effectively created new state authorities and regulatory mechanisms over natural resources. One of the most significant is the environmental protection law. The United Nations Development Program (UNDP) helped write and push this law through the assembly and, along with the Swedish aid agency SIDA, is providing substantial support for the fledgling environmental ministry it helped create, called STEA. Northern aid and finance institutions have helped establish the government agency that oversees all protected areas and wildlife activities (CPAWM) and strengthened the Ministry of Agriculture and Forestry, which receives most of its budget as grants and loans from these aid agencies. The budget of the Hydropower Division of the Ministry of Industry has grown exponentially due to foreign contributions directly related to big dam investments.

The amount and breadth of environmental programming within the state is impressive. The Forestry Department alone is buckling under the ballast of more than fifty separate projects, named with such English acronyms as FOMACOP and NAWACOP and official titles that reveal their origins and nationality. In 1999, the Lao Department of Forestry found itself responsible for the Lao Swedish Forestry Programme, the Lao ADB Commercial Tree Plantation Project, the Lao-WB-Finnida [Finnish] Forest and Management and Conservation project, the UN-FAO Benzoin Improvement Project, and the Lower Nam Ngum Catchment JICA-FORCAP [Japanese] Project. Some of the larger projects, such as the World Bank's FOMACOP, or Forestry Management and Conservation Programme, represent a major wing of the organizational structure of the Forestry Department. Together, foreign donors and creditors finance almost all of the department's annual budget, which goes to implementing these transnational projects (and paying the high cost of their foreign staff), managing the forests in a huge expanse of Lao territory, supporting the Forest Training School and Training Centre, collecting and analyzing the data required by these new projects, and implementing the laws and decrees described above (Department of Forestry 1997).

As such agencies as the Ministry of Agriculture and Forestry and the Ministry of Industry and Handicrafts become more involved in the receipt and management of foreign capital inflows, their staffs have the opportunity to integrate themselves into the transnational professional class, which increases their relative power and influence at the domestic level. At the same time, this flow of foreign money reshapes these agencies' domestic priorities to focus on the large-scale investment projects they are now financed to implement and regulate. As the Lao government readily admits, because of the region's currency crash in the late 1990s and the fiscal austerity programs demanded of it by the World Bank, there is a growing disparity between public expenditures on health, education, and public services and expenditures on the increasingly transnational energy, forestry, construction (to house these new development actors), and transport sectors (Government of Lao PDR 1997). Indeed, 84 percent of total state investment was in the latter group of sectors (UNDP 1997; World Bank 1997). In short, the new Lao state, like so many other states today, must starve the social sectors to nourish the newly capitalized ones.

## Generating Hybrid State Actors

In these upgraded state agencies, the traditional work of state actors is now being dispersed across a new array of hybridized state actors. The most common is the Lao civil servant—the privileged of whom have been retrained in new skills and norms and, if lucky, sent abroad for special training programs. The second type is epitomized by the Northern (semi-nomadic) transplant who works inside the Lao state as a consultant and invariably wields enormous power relative to his or her Lao counterpart. The third is the Northern expert who sets up or staffs a shadow organization that conducts the work of an existing state agency, but without the obvious representational or bureaucratic constraints. Both the work and the actor of the old regime are paradoxically underfunded and yet judged ill equipped for the highly valued and transnational state work of the new regime.

A striking feature of government offices in Vientiane is the sharp degree of contrast among them. Some are dusty, hot, and slow paced, whereas others are air-conditioned, computerized, and run on international clocks—typically European. At one forestry department office, for example, Finnish consultants work with Lao assistants in the redesigned top floor of a dilapidated government building behind sliding glass doors in air-conditioned offices; they are busy reorganizing the "subsistence" forestry sector.[13] The Lao counterparts to the Finns work on the ground floor in pre–gold rush style and calm.

In an effort to provide them with highly specialized technical training, the World Bank and Lao government send civil servants to workshops and conferences abroad, and to short courses in environmental assessment and management designed by the World Bank Institute. These international excursions are quite a departure for a country that is still unable to afford the membership costs of joining, and the travel costs of sending, high-level delegates to international meetings of the United Nations, ASEAN, and other groups to which the country is regularly invited. Indeed, this process of building up Lao human capital takes more than just time; many civil servants are paid a tiny fraction of what their Northern counterparts earn ($20 per month salary versus $3,000–$5,000 per month). Scientists with the country's lead environmental agency, STEA, have told me that they are often treated as second-class citizens by foreign consultants and staff, regarded more as translators than scientists, assisting consultants as they quickly traverse the countryside and computer data bases gathering evidence, yet left with little but the authoritative, English-written report.

Officials from STEA explained that although their budget has grown substantially, almost all of the funds coming from Northern agencies funnel directly to Northern scientists, consultants, and employees from engineering firms shuttling back and forth between Laos and their home countries. As one senior official described the situation: "The problem is that our whole agenda and budget is project driven. We can grow and do the job of an environmental agency *only* if Nam Theun 2 gets funded. Meanwhile the donors demand so much from us. Even though a lot of foreign money flows through our agency, most of it goes to pay for foreign consultants."[14]

Besides writing the new environmental laws and regulations, these traveling hybrid actors are critical conduits for the transnationalization of ideas (i.e., green neoliberal programs). They are also the ones who are paid to construct environmental data, without which STEA (and the World Bank's loan and guarantees packages) cannot move forward. In short, these foreign "state" actors are designing and carrying out the mandates of Laos's new laws and regulations.

With World Bank funding and initiative, and an eye toward readying Laos for large-scale capital investments, Finnish, Swedish, and German government aid agencies have de facto taken over major wings of, for example, the Forestry Department and thoroughly restructured them. The budget of each Northern agency includes a portion for training Lao civil servants in environmental technocracy and management, as well as in English. The fact that most of Laos's public investment funds are voted on and allocated at a meeting in Geneva, Switzerland, suggests the power of these transnational actors (Government of Lao PDR 1997; UNDP 1997). That the skills, worldviews, and conduct of the Northerners in Laos are being indigenized by savvy Lao staff is progressively more apparent.

Listening to some Northern consultants portray the Lao people and their "lacks," it is clear that within the discourses of development, progress, and sustainability lie some very neocolonial attitudes and practices on the part of those "doing the development" toward those "being developed." For example, most Northern conservationists work under the premise that the Lao people know nothing about conservation. Their funding proposals and projects reflect the view that it is best to start from scratch with Lao nationals: first teach these protoprofessionals English; then send them abroad to learn how to identify endogenous flora, fauna, and fish species; and then return them to Laos to staff the newly designed wetlands, watershed, and conservation agencies (Chape 1996; IUCN 1997; IUCN 1993; McNeely 1987). Yet such a perspective ignores, among other things, the fact that the actors being produced are the ones who made it possible to generate this knowledge in the first place. As one Thai forestry specialist suggested, "It's not as if only people with [the Northern experts'] kind of knowledge are equipped to conserve forests . . . if it were not for those villagers with their knowledge of the terrain and animals, Northern wildlife scientists . . . would not be able to make those amazing 'discoveries' of rare or newly found animal species" (Watershed 1996, p. 40). Some Lao government scientists expressed frustration: they had already undergone scientific and linguistic training abroad during the 1980s, under different world-systems imperatives, in Bulgaria, Hungary, and Czechoslovakia. Why retrain again?

Reflecting this powerful neocolonial attitude, the Australian public relations specialist with the Nam Theun Power Company (NTPC, formerly NTEC), on being asked about the possible negative effects of the dam, listed the issues raised by the antidam critics, and then remarked, "Remember, these people on the Plateau are primitive and anything is better than what they have." This representation does not seem to be lost on the people who are "being professionalized" through the development process. For example, a Lao environmental specialist explained the asymmetric nature of his relationship with Northern scientists hired to conduct work for STEA: "We want to learn the consultants' trade, but we are pretty much left carrying their bags."[15] While the "modernization" process associated with the Bank's investments is supposed to reduce uncertainty and risk, the nascent class of Lao state actors has expressed a sense of *increased* uncertainty and risk in engaging in a process over which it has little control. These Lao actors describe the time-space compression of having to get on or off this fast-moving vehicle called environmentally sustainable development.

The discursive field in which these development actors work is so powerful that it is hardly possible to speak with expertise of Laos today except by using these eco-rationalities. Indeed, the proliferating body of scientific research on the Mekong is produced either as a condition of multilateral bank loans and development interventions, or as a reaction to them. Fish biologists, cultural anthropologists, environmental economists, development professionals, and Lao citizens participating in World Bank public consultations speak mostly within this discursive field. As a consequence, international conservation groups have framed their megafauna discoveries and their mechanisms to protect biodiversity exclusively in terms of a commensurable trade-off between dams and conservation. "The old," as David Scott argues of colonial governmentality, "[is now] imaginable along paths that belong to new, always already transformed sets of coordinates, concepts, and assumptions" (Scott 1995). In this way, localized forms of scientific production proceed along highly prefigured political fields of development.

## Uneven Development

Laos's new green neoliberal forestry laws rezone the country's forests into distinct administrative categories. *Protected forests* are so designated because they protect ecological services, such as watersheds and soil, from erosion and ensure national security, which is threatened by porous international borders. *Conservation forests* protect high-value biological diversity while permitting limited competing uses, such as nontimber forest production, tourism, and hydroelectric dams (Department of Forestry 1997). These new environmental zoning classifications carve up territory and sovereignty through scientific distinctions of forest use (e.g., sustainable timber production, transboundary protection parks, subsistence production). They have also served as a catalyst for resettlement plans, requiring numerous public consultations and scientific studies that seek to demonstrate the rationality of transplanting people who do not fit the required social characteristics for eco-zone habitation (Franklin 1997; Government of Lao PDR 1999; Sparkes 1998).

In addition to this forest classification system, Lao's new policies identify corridor zones, controlled-use zones, total protection zones, and National Biodiversity and Conservation Areas. There are clear regulations as to what people are and are not allowed to do within these various eco-zones. In NBCAs, for example, no firearms are allowed, entry by motor vehicle is limited, and commercial logging is banned. In total protected zones, no hunting, fishing, or collection of nontimber forest products is allowed, nor entry without permission, agriculture, or overnight stays. In controlled-use zones, there is no inmigration and only limited village rights to grazing, fishing, and fire wood collection. The only requests allowed "by special permission" relate to eco-tourism and hydro-dam reservoirs (Department of Forestry 1997). In other words, dams and tourism receive greater weight than the forest dwellers' right to hunt, gather, and sleep in their forests. Indeed, the implementation of these newly ascribed eco-zones is shifting the rights and access to the forests' vast natural resources from forest-dwelling communities to the energy, conservation, and tourism industries. The NBCAs, which comprise an estimated 15 percent of national territory, will be managed by a transnational board of directors and financed by a percentage of the revenues generated by the dam's sale of electricity. The money will bypass the national government and go directly into an off-shore fund to ensure that the Lao government "takes conservation seriously" and that conservation in Laos unfolds as this transnational board of directors sees fit. On the ground, dam revenues will support "responsibilized" natives trained as guides, rangers, and park police (i.e., productive citizens). With this shifting of rights and access comes the ontological transformation of the forest dwellers, hunters, gatherers, fishers, and swidden cultivators of the Vietic, Brou, Tai, and Hmong ethnic groups, among many others. And in the process, Lao officials become beholden to foreign conservationists with their own sense of rights and truths about Laos.

In Vientiane, real estate prices have skyrocketed and urban resources have become expensive and relatively scarce.[16] The eco-development business boom has had the immediate and inadvertent consequence of depriving some locals of basic resources while increasing the city's consumption of goods like petrol, water, and public funds, needed to service the transnational class in their new settlement enclaves. In this chapter, however, I have emphasized some of the less obvious political effects of this highly uneven process—for example, the focusing of the investigative lens on rural peoples and environments where development elites inevitably find degradation, mismanagement, poverty, and backwardness. Ironically, these human populations are being thrust onto center stage as their conduct becomes the scrutinized subject of the new global technologies of government, which has become routinely known as environmentally sustainable development.

The new legal, institutional, and investment modalities are all buttressed by corresponding forms of knowledge, such that state-building is not just about gaining new forms of control over territorial space, but also about control of epistemological space. Moreover, the newly emerging art of government is being framed by a global environmental scientific discourse that includes a politics of ethics that requires accountability to the global community (Goldman 1998; Rose 1999). Percolating up from the investigative modalities in Laos is a classification system and a new set of disciplinary technologies. EIAs and SIAs, NBCAs and the "best practices" of Nam Theun 2, FOMACOP, and STEA, are all critical effects of power circulating through Laos, constituting the double movements of state-building and global institution-building, on the one hand, and the science and art of government, on the other.

In addition to constructing an environmental state, the World Bank is instigating the rise of an inclusive global environmentalism that is based not on mere rhetoric but on powerful regimes of science, regulation, and capital investment. It is no coincidence that these power/knowledge interventions come at a time when the World Bank has had to wrestle with a demand crisis for its services, largely due to a combination of trenchant social activism and increased access to private sources of capital with fewer disciplinary strings attached on the part of prosperous borrowers. The Bank's response has been to create new demands for its services and to broaden the scope of the services. In the process, it has gained access to new populations and environments to the benefit of its main clients, the Northern-based capital goods and financial sectors.

## Conclusion

As an employee of a Lao NGO, Souly, the ex-juggler, is regularly invited to participate in various projects connected to environmentally sustainable development. All sorts of organizations would like to employ him. Lao government agencies would like him to help resettle people and train them to live in their new environment. The World Bank would like to hire him to design development projects that will integrate ecological territories and natural-resource-dependent communities into Bank projects. International conservation groups—among the Bank's subcontractors for the multimillion-dollar conservation and resettlement projects related to the hydroelectric dam—want him to conduct conservation-training sessions in the villages. Activist groups based in Thailand, Cambodia, and the United States would like to hire him to organize alternative development campaigns in the region. All seek out Souly and his colleagues to join the new development campaign to enliven the space of civil society.

In deciding which job to take, or whether to take any at all, this social worker must navigate through a sea of activity shaped by the environmental and structural adjustment policies that are preconditions for the Nam Theun 2 Dam project. In all his forays into the realms of governance reform, biodiversity conservation, or civil-society participation—that is, the new activities of development—he must engage with the prevailing political rationality of supporting large capital investments for dams and for biodiversity-conservation projects, even if the rationality evolves as new actors come on board. Under such conditions, people's actions are highly circumscribed by the practices of green neoliberal development. Souly's dilemma—in what form should he participate in Bank-style development—illustrates one of this book's main conceptual themes: the commingled roles of civil society, the state, international capital, and transnational policy networks of development. In sum, everyday cultural practices of employment and civil-society engagement are shaped in Laos today by the overwhelming force of green neoliberal development.

Souly must work in an environment where the role and character of the state is changing fast. As the example of Laos demonstrates, even with the expansionary powers of financial and speculative capital, multilateral development banks, and transnational regulatory regimes, state power is not vanishing. Instead, states are rapidly changing. Some state functions are being created or strengthened whereas others are being defunded and devalued. States are being reconfigured with new regulatory regimes and hybridized transnational state actors. The World Bank has been in the vanguard of state restructuring, helping states to better respond to the forces of capitalist development.

Souly must also grapple with a highly volatile NGO environment. Many of the smaller local NGOs have become dependent on larger organizations, and the largest ones are changing fast. In the mid-1990s, the largest environmental organizations were on the fence about whether or not they could work with the development community to build dams. Just a few years later, a sea change occurred. In June 2000, the Worldwide Fund for Nature founded the Center for Conservation Finance (CCF) in a bold move to marry the world of conservation with the world of international finance. The center's mandate is to cultivate "the next generation of conservation-finance models—models that can be replicated in every corner of the world" (WWF 2002). The WWF hired financial consultants from Wall Street firms to develop financial instruments to "generate conservation capital" on their own, as well as to "leverage money for the environment" through environmental taxes, conservation easements, trading systems, environmental investment funds, and more. Its work is presented in the form of "business plans" and through the discourse of *financial investments,* with biodiversity mapped as investment portfolios and ecosystems measured, evaluated, and valorized for their natural capital and ecological services. Also in 2002, a transnational partnership was created by IUCN, Conservation International, the Nature Conservancy, WCS, and the World

Bank, called the Conservation Finance Alliance (CFA) (Alliance 2002). The CFA's mandate is "to catalyze increased and sustainable public and private financing for biodiversity conservation" as well as to develop a "communication strategy" that explains to key audiences the significance of "sustainable conservation financing."

Ten years ago, one could argue that these environmental organizations had their backs to the wall and were forced to either work with the World Bank or get out of the business of development. Today, however, it is clear that they have developed their own business plans to raise conservation capital, which reflects a synchronicity that is proving beneficial to them, to the multilateral banks, and to their overlapping corporate sponsors.

In this chapter, I have sought to demonstrate not only how the world of sustainable development is constituted in situ in a borrowing country of the World Bank, but also the regimes of power, truths, and rights on which these new institutional practices are based. These knowledge/power relations run through the scientific and legal practices of the World Bank's new work and become concretized through loan conditionalities, classification systems, new laws and regulations, and large-scale foreign capital investments. Newly transnationalized state agencies, staffed with hybrid actors, emerge with the strengthened mandate to oversee the reterritorialization (Brenner 1999) and re-evaluation of borrowing country landscapes, resulting in a radical alteration in the ways people interact with each other and with nonhuman nature. In analyzing this process, we find the making of hegemonic forms of rationality that translate into effects of government: constructing the environmental science and art of targeting populations, production practices, and behaviors vis-à-vis nature that are judged as guilty or innocent of ecological degradation. In this way, the modern eco-rational subject and the environmental state are mutually constituted.

Interestingly, this strategy was not anticipated by the leading actors. The fiercely nationalistic Lao state and rigidly economistic World Bank did not originally intend to hinge new capital investments on transnationalized eco-zones of biodiversity and conservation. At the start, international conservation NGOs did not want to sign on to large-scale projects that dam rivers, submerge forests, and threaten the health of natural species and even human populations. These conservation NGOs were part of the larger NGO community questioning the motives and impacts of the World Bank. Yet within a decade, in the process of establishing the epistemic and ethical differences of territory and nature (e.g., the ways in which some species have become more important than others, some knowledge privileged over others), the cognitive mappings of this strange collection of bedfellows have, remarkably, converged. These epistemic and legal interventions have triggered new cultural and political rationalities in this transnational scramble for the Mekong.

New environmental regimes do not roll quietly into town on the train of progress but rather storm in on the wild bull of uneven development. Any resources that might be harnessed for environmental protection and maintenance are concentrated on the natures (social and ecological) that will support large capital investments. Other natures are differentially defined based on the needs of development-related rationalities. Some are valorized for rice cultivation through privatization, others are judged to be best for export logging.

Although Laos may seem like an extreme case, one finds similar trends in larger borrowing countries, even those with more robust state institutions and more active and autonomous civil societies. From Mexico to Nigeria, the World Bank's green neoliberal framework finds resonance in diverse ways in different institutional settings. Laos is an example of how transnational efforts are transforming one country in the name of green neoliberalism, but the Bank also influences policies, politics, and cultures across national boundaries and in the realm of so-called global civil society where some of today's most volatile development policies are being forged.

# VI

## Privatizing Water, Neoliberalizing Civil Society: The Power of Transnational Policy Networks

*Public-sector reform and privatization constitute a large part of the World Bank's lending and technical assistance programs. Such reforms go to the core of the social norms around which society is organized. Such reforms affect the relationship between institutions and citizens, requiring of all parties a radical change in beliefs and perceptions about the nature of public goods and the balance between government responsibility and private-sector opportunity. They require a shift in the rights and responsibilities of all players*

*and call for a national mobilization of civil servants, ministries,*
*businesses, academics, media, managers, unions, consumers,*
*associations, nongovernmental organizations and the*
*public-at-large to pull together to move reform forward.*
—*World Bank 2003, p. 8*


*Civil society is made up of international organizations . . .*
*[for which] citizenship is therefore not a necessary qualification.*
—*Guyer 1994, pp. 21–22*




"Africa—do you want to make a difference?" reads the headline of an advertisement in the *Economist* in the January 25, 2003, issue. Under this heading, Oxfam UK is looking for a governance and civil society adviser, and on the next page the African Development Bank is searching for a Sustainable Development and Poverty Reduction unit head. Historically, most professionals in the field of development were trained in agricultural or development economics, with experience in irrigation, forestry, or the like. Today, however, the market is demanding professionals equipped with expertise in neoliberal forms of public-sector privatization, good governance, and civil-society advocacy. Where does one learn such new trades? A primary source for training in these new fields is the World Bank itself, at its headquarters, where it trains thousands of professionals each year, or at one of its

thirty-seven Distance Learning Centers or four hundred partner institutions around the world. For Oxfam, the Asian Development Bank, or the Ugandan government to be players at
the table, they need to work within the changing parameters of
the latest development regime. Interestingly, the ad's headline
can be read two ways: it is as much an alert to development
professionals around the world as it is to "Africa" about what
the new development trends are. These shifts in the professional development worlds are not simply rhetorical; they
are real and substantial and worth many millions of dollars.
How are these power/knowledge regimes established and supported, how do they become common sense, and to what extent do they bring about change?

In this chapter I will explore these questions by looking
at one of the fastest-growing areas for the World Bank and
the development industry at large—capacity building, civil-
society promotion, and transnational policy networking. Graduates from the global training and hiring programs of the
World Bank play an important role in translating and indigenizing the Bank's neoliberal lending and policy interventions,
and with their help, the Bank has been able to spawn new
transnational policy networks (TPNs). According to the World
Bank, it is through this dynamic that active civil societies are
constituted as a viable mediating force between ineffectual and
often corrupt states, on the one hand, and emerging (albeit
distorted) free markets, on the other. In this way, development
and state bureaucratic professionals have become the hand-
maidens to a globalizing neoliberal politics.

To illustrate the powerful synergies among the Bank's
global training and outreach program, these new transnational
policy networks, and the Bank's latest interventions, in the sec-

ond part of this chapter I will look at the global policy of water privatization, a potentially lucrative initiative for international firms bidding on third world public-sector goods. Since the mid-1990s, a new transnational policy network has arisen with the ambition of generating a global policy agenda on water. Its arguments are constructed in situ, in the process of building alliances, writing policy statements, negotiating plans, and soliciting expert advice and opinions. It has grown as it moves from one venue to another; each year, new ideas, initiatives, coalitions, and networks are born—while others disappear— in the process of constituting a green-neoliberal water-policy action plan. These transnational sites overflow with policy-making activities directed at trying to "find the right price" for water and overcome barriers to supplying clean water to the poor. It is a discourse that has developed an enormous reach, ranging from the *Financial Times* of London to the World Water Forums in The Hague and Kyoto, from local NGOs in Ghana (Berry 2003) to city mayors in Bolivia (Laurie and Marvin 1999). During the ten years between the 1992 Earth Summit in Rio and the 2002 World Summit on Sustainable Development in Johannesburg, global water privatization policy has gone from a nonstarter to the main event. How the policy rose from obscurity is the topic of this chapter. The World Bank successfully transformed a "potentially explosive political question about rights, entitlements, how one should live, and who should decide *into technical questions* of efficiency and sustainability" (Li 2002, p. 1, my emphasis). Critical to the politics of this policy shift is the fact that it has thus far been an extremely fragile accomplishment and one that has begun to arouse the political ire, and transnational activist networking, of tens of millions of angry people.

## The Rise of Transnational Policy Networks

Transnational policy networks have always played an important role for the World Bank; indeed, the Bank has been one of the great motors behind these networks and has benefited enormously from them over the past sixty years. During Robert McNamara's tenure the idea of cultivating networks of experts became a well-funded priority for the Bank. For most of its history, these networks were peopled by a narrow, elite strand of professionals, mostly high-level state and United Nations officials, Northern economists, and a smattering of agricultural scientists. The recent crop of Bank-inspired TPNs, however, are distinctive for their growing ubiquity, authority, and centrality to transnational issue formation; the greater diversity of their participants and geographical loci; and the shortened time frame from when policy is debated to its global dispersion. They are also marked for their close tie-ins to important international meetings and conferences and their access to generous funding, which enables them to dominate multilevel policy debates as well as to convert talk into action. The efficacy of TPNs derives from the fact that they are able to include within them a wide range of actors and institutions, giving them broad credibility and influence as well as a self-acclaimed comparative advantage in the field of transnational policy expertise with apparently few viable competitors. Such networks typically include officials and/or representatives from large corporations, state ministries, NGOs, engineering firms, media conglomerates, UN and World Bank agencies, national and international scientific councils, and even eminent personalities, such as former IMF director Michel Camdessus and billionaire George Soros.[1]

A critical element of TPN building is the World Bank's ambitious worldwide training program that generates many qualified actors (including heads of state) as well as the material, epistemic, and cultural basis for developing effective knowledge networks. Starting in the McNamara era, the Bank began training its own staff, members of borrowing state agencies, staff of NGOs, academics, and employees of engineering firms that the Bank would later hire for its projects. By the late 1980s, the Bank's training center was preparing more than 3,000 professionals annually in the field of economic development alone (Kapur et al. 1997). In those days, the center was called the Economic Development Institute because development economics was its core curriculum and the primary knowledge good the Bank marketed. By the late 1990s, and with a change in name to the World Bank Institute (WBI), those numbers dramatically increased, as did the sites and topics for trainings.[2] In 2002 alone, the Bank delivered 560 "learning activities" to "more than 48,000 participants in 150 countries through collaboration with more than 400 partner institutions." According to this same report, it broadened "its reach to include parliamentarians, policymakers, technical specialists, journalists, teachers, students, and civil society leaders, as well as World Bank staff" (World Bank Institute 2002).[3] Under a broad rubric of technical titles, these training programs teach the types of expertise required to generate, tailor, and manage the lending efforts of the Bank and to contribute to the production of green neoliberalism around the world.

For example, in China, which is the Bank's largest borrower, the WBI has run environmental management courses for the directors of China's State Environmental Protection Administration, trained senior and deputy officials from district and central governments in sustainable urban development and management, and plans to offer these courses to more than 600 mayors through the Chinese National School of Administration (WB Institute 2002). The WBI ran a decentralization program in Pakistan after that country was subjected to a Bank-enforced reform aimed at devolving its central fiscal and regulatory powers to local governments.[4] Pakistan now has 6,455 new local "self-governments," and the WBI plans to train the newly empowered local government officials in governance, regulation, and management to integrate Pakistan into the global economy (WB Institute 2002).

The WBI recently shifted its curriculum from a focus on development economics to a much broader set of courses on the environment, public-sector reform, and public-private partnerships and now utilizes tools of cost-benefit analysis and the mandate of "full cost recovery" to help trainees assess the efficiency of their public sectors (e.g., health, education, welfare) and define ecosystems (e.g., river basins, forested water sheds) as arenas that require economic valuation and rationalization. Senior government technocrats are encouraged to evaluate diverse state-managed realms ranging from rural primary school systems to public aquifers for their cost recovery ability. The idea of contracting out public goods and service provision to the private sector, and in particular, to globally competitive bidders, becomes more than an ideological fantasy but a "best practices" case that gets explored in the classroom, with experts flown in to demonstrate its utility and viability, and then gets realized in the field through development projects.

The World Bank trains state and nonstate professionals in such topics as "educational reform," "community empowerment and social inclusion," "social risk management," and "poverty reduction and economic management" specifically to help it and its client countries overcome the twin obstacles to implementing its desired policy shifts: the lack of local champions capable of turning neoliberal ideas into practice, and the difficulty for state actors to counter the challenges offered by animated and wide-ranging campaigns against neoliberalism, privatization, and structural adjustment (World Bank Institute 2002).

Courses, such as "Improving Trade Competitiveness," "Making the WTO Work in Developing Countries," "Conflict Resolution for Natural Resource Management," "Corporate Governance and Social Responsibility," "Macroeconomic Policy," "Banking and Finance," and "Infrastructure Finance Training and Financial Sector Learning" help inform professionals in the art of macro-policy management—an expertise that is now a prerequisite of the development industry. These training programs help the Bank implement its latest round of structural adjustment programs and are offered wherever poverty reduction support credits (PRSCs) are being implemented. For example, the Bank sponsored the Dakar Poverty Forum in 2001, which brought in more than 270 participants from 32 African countries to promote continent-wide harmonization of the Bank's neoliberal policies in Africa (World Bank Institute 2002). For most of Africa, PRSCs have become not only the main source of capital from the World Bank, but also the primary topic in the Bank's professional training programs, reinforcing the Bank's political significance as well as its economic role as a source of employment for those within the marginalized African professional class willing to embrace its policies.

The WBI offers certain courses to state administrators, others to private investors, a third set to journalists, and still others to staffs of NGOs. Such courses feed people directly into consultancy positions with the World Bank; steer them into fledgling regional professional networks, such as the Environmental Economics Network for Eastern and Southern Africa, the International Network for Environmental Compliance and Enforcement, or the China Health Economic Network; and provide them with opportunities at major global policy conferences, such as the World Summit on Sustainable Development and the World Water Forum. In a context where many people live with drastically reduced salaries and/or the quotidian threat of losing their jobs because of World Bank/IMF imposed cuts in the public sector, there is no shortage of people who are willing (indeed, anxious) to become part of the Bank's ever-expanding network.

One set of courses specifically caters to borrowing-country journalists as a way to encourage the major presses, television, radio, and wire services of the South to run stories on the issues the Bank promotes. The World Bank Institute runs courses called "Journalistic Reporting on Water and Health Reform," "Investigative Journalism in Africa," and "Human Rights and Economic Development" to help educate journalists about these potentially explosive political issues. These courses come with a major career opportunity for Southern journalists: a free trip to cover a major world conference. With such training, they are presumably better equipped to interpret the claims made at these global forums by the Bank's vociferous critics, who often steal the limelight and embarrass the Bank in the media.

Just as the World Bank helps teach journalists about how to cover its global conferences, it also hires some of its own trainees to help with its media and public relations campaigns. The Bank now trains staff and consultants in public communications to better argue its case for public-sector reform, privatization, and other desired policy shifts before skeptical public audiences.[5] Improving its public image has become such a priority that the World Bank's public relations expenditures have surpassed its research budget in recent years (Kapur 2002; Standing 2000).

More than simply offering courses on an as-needed schedule, the Bank is institutionalizing its training process in borrowing countries, legitimizing one path, while marginalizing others, to professionalization.[6] The WBI has opened up thirty-seven distance learning centers on six continents for its Global Development Learning Network, with the short-term goal of having one hundred centers worldwide, including thirteen in China alone. Five years after launching the Fiscal Decentralization Initiative for Central and Eastern Europe (FDI) to train trainers and offer research grants on decentralization and privatization (a funding arena worth hundreds of millions of dollars to the region over the last few years), the FDI has become a financially stable Budapest-based NGO, which now delivers the WBI's fiscal decentralization core courses and manages a nine-language Web site.[7] In Brazil, the Ministry of Finance took over a WBI training program and offers courses with WBI training materials on a regular basis.

In the early 1990s, the World Bank, along with UNDP and the African Development Bank, set up the African Capacity Building Foundation (ACBF) to help build up local institutions able to run programs and implement policies originating in the international finance and development institutions. In less than a decade, the ACBF has created fifty policy centers and training institutes throughout Africa, from which has emerged the African Policy Institutes Forum, whose agenda mirrors the World Bank's newest agenda for Africa.[8] Many of these African policy centers serve as national secretariats for Bank-sponsored professional skills training programs. They also serve as the site for the preparation of Bank-required

Poverty Reduction Strategy Papers (PRSPs), poverty reduction action plans, economic reform programs with the IMF, development projects funded by international aid agencies, and trainings for participation in upcoming WTO conferences. Closely reflecting the Bank's ideological bent, the African Capacity Building Foundation recently expressed its unambiguous support for the highly controversial New Partnership for Africa's Development (Nepad), which critics have described as a World Bank blueprint for fast-tracking economic neoliberalism across the continent (Bond 2002)—derisively referring to Nepad as "knee-pad." According to its own promotional materials, ACBF is committed to realizing and mainstreaming Nepad's objectives through its institutional networking and training capabilities.[9]

In sum, within a decade, the World Bank's training programs have found new homes outside of Washington, D.C., and inside borrowing-country state ministries, private universities and privatized wings of public universities, international institutes, and the Bank's own growing network of global learning centers. This knowledge circulation process becomes cemented once its World Bank label is replaced with an indigenous one and when the knowledge-production process gets "scaled up" across the African continent, for example, with trainers and policy advocates being Africans and working on such Africanist agendas as neoliberal trade, environment, and growth policies.[10] Media professionals, government officials, and professionals at large become cultivated through these activities; they are also giving back much in the process—ideas and their professional time that circulate back through the networks to Washington, where their contribution can become quite pivotal to the Bank's ability to effect change. But local trainers still adopt Bank training materials, and the professional networks in which trainers and trainees actively participate are still Bank sponsored. So well instituted have these practices become that the training materials I received as a participant observer in a 1995 two-week World Bank seminar for African economists are now available through training programs run by an all-African network of economists, which the Bank helped start. Whereas in 1995 the trainers were Washington-based Bank officials and consultants, today the trainers are mostly African graduates of Bank-related training programs. This is but one example of the networks that become generated over time and through which World Bank exercises its power.

## Networking For a New Global Agenda on Water

As recently as 1990, fewer than 51 million people received their water from private water companies, and most water customers were in Europe and the United States. Just ten years later, more than 460 million people were dependent on global water firms for their water supplies, and the high growth areas were Africa, Asia, and Latin America. Industry analysts predict that by 2015, 1.16 billion people will be buying their water from European-based water firms (Shrybman 2002).[11] These days, an indebted country cannot borrow capital from the World Bank or IMF without a domestic water privatization policy as a precondition. The world's largest firms, French-based Suez and Vivendi (now Veolia Water), control about 70 percent of private water markets, and in the mid-2003 economic downturn, competitors were bought out and the market became even more concentrated. Industry analysts predict that private water will soon be a capitalized market as precious, and as war-provoking, as oil (Barlow and Clarke 2002; Global Water

Report 1996; Grusky 2002; International Consortium of Investigative Journalists 2002; Shrybman 2002). Dealing in water has become one of the most lucrative markets for transnational capital investors. According to one water analyst, "the global market for municipal and industrial water and sewerage goods and services is currently estimated to be in the region of US$200bn–$400bn per annum" (Owen 2001).

Perhaps as no surprise to many of us who study the world of development, these industry trends mirror larger tendencies in the global development industry. From the 1950s through the 1970s, in response to colonial expropriation, national leaders emphasized repatriation and nationalization of extractive and industrial sectors. But since the debt crisis and the precipitous rise of structural adjustment impositions worldwide, states have been forced to sell off their public enterprises even if these had successfully produced national wealth, widespread employment, accessible public goods, and social stability. By the late 1990s, under the neoliberal logic of privatization, even the most essential public-sector services, such as education, public health facilities, water and sanitation, were being put on the auction block. The issue of public-sector privatization rose to the top of the agenda of governments, NGOs and aid organizations, business forums, UN agencies, and major global conferences. In 2002, for instance, at the world's most attended international conference in history—the World Summit on Sustainable Development held in Johannesburg—the question of water privatization dominated official and unofficial agendas.

The way this agenda became dominant in such a short time illustrates the escalating power of transnational policy networks and their institution effects. It shows how the World Bank has been able to mobilize champions and generate social

networks capable of innovating on and implementing World
Bank-supported policies through their own diverse contributions, and to accomplish it far from Washington, D.C., and
without the Bank's sole authorship. These activities have generated the space of what development advocates call "global civil
society," a realm in which transnational professional class activities—training programs, networking conferences, and professional labor markets for policymakers and implementers—
powerfully converge. The case of global water policy reform
demonstrates another way the World Bank has managed to
proliferate and exercise its power.

## Spaces and Flows of the Water
## Privatization Discourse

An article on a report on water scarcity, released at a major
global water conference by an eminent panel of experts,[12] carried the headline: "Poor countries 'must raise water prices':
World Commission Warning on Shortages of Vital Resources."
The journalist reports:

> Prices paid by water consumers in developing coun-
> tries must rise substantially to avoid life threatening
> shortages and environmental damage, according to
> an international report published yesterday.
>
> The report by the World Commission on Water,
> supported by the World Bank and the United Na-
> tions, calls for radical changes in the way in which
> water services are subsidized in some of the world's
> poorest and most disadvantaged regions.
>
> It says annual investment in water facilities need
> to more than double from $70bn-$80bn to $180bn

to meet rising demand and reduce the numbers without clean water—1bn—and without sanitation—3bn—to just 330m by 2025.

Governments unable to finance this huge investment must encourage the private sector—which provides less than 5 per cent of urban water to consumers in developing countries—to fill the gap. The single most effective stimulus for private-sector investment would be to adopt "full cost pricing of water use and services" says the commission. . . . Without full cost pricing the present vicious cycle of waste, inefficiency and lack of service for the poor will continue. Private parties also "will not invest unless they can be assured of a reasonable return on their investments." (*Financial Times* March 12, 2000)

The authors of the much-cited report referred to in this article, "A Water Secure World: Vision for Water, Life and the Environment,"[13] are among the world's policy elites, collected together as an eminent panel of experts called the World Commission on Water for the 21st Century. Their message and relational biographies reveal an important story about the lofty goals of finding global solutions to a global water crisis.[14]

Formed in 1998, the World Commission on Water for the 21st Century includes former heads of state, such as Mikhail Gorbachev of the USSR, Fidel Ramos of the Philippines, Ketumile Masire of Botswana, and Ingvar Carlsson of Sweden. It also includes former and current senior World Bank officials, such as Robert McNamara (also cochair of the Global Coalition for Africa); Mohamed El-Ashry, who is the CEO of the Bank's Global Environmental Facility; Enrique Iglesias, president of the Inter-American Development Bank; former World Bank vice president Wilfried Thalwitz; and Ismail Serageldin, who is both a senior World Bank environmental official and the commission's chair. Corporate leaders play an equally prominent role: included on the panel are Jerome Monod, chairman of the board of Suez, and Maurice Strong, former CEO of Petro-Canada, Ontario Hydro, chair of the Earth Council, and a frequent commissioner and special envoy for the United Nations. From the foundation, NGO, and state sectors come such dignitaries as the president of IUCN, Yolanda Kakabadse; president of the Rockefeller Foundation, Gordon Conway; chair of the World Commission on Dams and former South African minister of water affairs, Kader Asmal; and the former president of Canada's foreign aid agency (CIDA) and current member of the Population Council, Margaret Catley-Carlson. Well-connected heads of major transnational research and policy institutes, most of which receive funding from the World Bank and the bilateral aid agencies of the North, fill out the ranks.[15]

These people, well recognized in both the business and development worlds, have come together to form a transnational policy network on water. This particular commission was started and is funded by another important actor in the network, namely, the World Water Council.[16] The World Water Council, established in 1996, is a self-described international water policy think tank which aims to provide policymakers with up-to-date research and advice on global water issues. It is sponsored by UN and World Bank agencies and is governed by board members hailing from the World Bank, CIDA, the United Nations Development Program, IUCN, Suez and other European water firms, and water-related professional associations. A 300-member group, the World Water Council played a pivotal role in organizing the Second World Water Forum in The Hague and the Third World Water Forum in Kyoto. It also produced the well-circulated "World Water Vision" report quoted above with its unambiguous water privatization agenda for the future—one that mimics as well as extends the World Bank's policy position and economic analysis on water reform.[17]

Another important player in the transnational policy network on water is the World Business Council for Sustainable Development, or WBCSD.[18] Representing a coalition of 160 transnational corporations, the WBCSD is made up of some of the world's largest corporations involved in the business of water, energy, and waste management.[19] In August 2002, the WBCSD released an influential report entitled, "Water for the Poor," with a battle cry of "No Water, No Sustainable Development!" The report strongly endorses (as well as puts its own spin on) the Bonn Action Plan, a plan developed during the multistakeholder International Conference on Freshwater held in Bonn, Germany, in December 2001. In its "Water for the Poor" report, the World Business Council's main policy prescriptions reflect a political rationality that weaves together the needs of corporations and public institutions with those of the poor. From its perspective: "Providing water services to the poor presents a business opportunity. New pipes, pumps, measurement and monitoring devices, and billing and record keeping systems will be required to modernize and expand water infrastructure. Industry not directly related to the provision of water services will be able to enter new markets because water for production, and to sustain a productive workforce, will be available. Thus this program has the possibility of creating huge employment and sales opportunities for large and small businesses alike" (World Business Council for Sustainable Development 2002, p. 9). In short, everyone wins—the firms that form partnerships with the global development community and governments to bring water to the poor, and those who are at the receiving end of the water pipeline. This is the same perspective the World Bank promotes in its professional training seminars and its policy work.

Another key actor, the Global Water Partnership (GWP), also established in 1996, supports countries in the "sustainable management of their water resources." This support is channeled through the ideological lens of interpreting water strictly as an economic good, and its main programs seek to reform public water utilities around the world. The chair of its steering committee is, again, Ismail Serageldin, longtime World Bank senior official, and its funding comes from bilateral aid agencies of the North (especially those with large water corporations), the World Bank, UNDP, and Ford Foundation. As of January 2003, GWP's executive secretary is Emilio Gabbrielli, who is also the managing director of Thames Water Do Brazil, a subsidiary of the German conglomerate RWE-Thames. The chair of GWP's Panel on Financing Water Infrastructure is Michel Camdessus, former IMF executive director, structural adjustment guru, and member of corporate boards of directors.

Representatives of states, international financial institutions, development agencies, think tanks, and firms are not the only actors in the new and expanding transnational water policy network. The oldest and most prominent water NGO to get involved is WaterAid of Great Britain. WaterAid joined the World Bank and UN agencies in calling for "new millennium development goals" of halving the proportion of people without access to water and sanitation in the world by 2015,[20] and in the process, connecting 230,000 people to a safe water source, providing 500,000 people access to adequate sanitation each day for the next thirteen years, and raising and disbursing $25 billion each year to provide for these connections.[21] Water-Aid also endorses the increased participation of NGOs, civil-society groups, and transnational water companies in water reform: "One solution to this crisis is to call in the private sector. The idea is that more actors (not just governments) would enter the sector and deliver the services. In an environment of relatively free markets, the private sector can deliver not only investments, but also the reforms and efficiencies that are urgently needed in water and sanitation service delivery."[22]

In other words, the world's most influential water NGO has embraced the World Bank's and IMF's clarion call for water privatization as the most sensible way to avoid catastrophe.[23] Moreover, WaterAid also endorses the Bank's and IMF's controversial policy of making water privatization a precondition for access to desperately needed capital and debt relief. That is, Poverty Reduction Support Credits (PRSC, with PRSP as one component), the latest structural adjustment policy for highly indebted countries, has water privatization commitments as one prevalent feature of their conditionalities for access to loans for poverty reduction and debt relief, and WaterAid supports this approach: "WaterAid has joined with other civil society groups in engaging with the PRSP program in some of the countries we work in to ensure that access to water and sanitation remains a priority in the PRSP. . . . The PRSPs present the clearest and most important opportunity for translating these policies into plans that will be prioritised, resourced, implemented and monitored."[24]

The British public has an intimate connection with WaterAid in the form of monthly pleas for charitable contributions for "pro-poor" water projects in the South that come with the monthly water bill. WaterAid also has high-profile promotional fundraisers that are written up in major British newspapers. Formed in 1981, it is one of the earliest and largest advocates for "water for all." WaterAid raises money from corporate and individual donations and works in fifteen countries in Africa and Asia delivering water to the poor; in 2001–2, it had an income of 11 million British pounds. In contrast to many other high-profile development NGOs, WaterAid was started by large water corporations and still receives support from them, along with individual donations and government contributions (from the UK and the European Union).[25] Almost every one of its trustees works or has worked for a major water firm: Vic Cocker retired as CEO of Severn Trent, Hugh Speed is the vice president of Suez, David Luffrum and John Sexton have been directors at Thames Water, Stuart Derwent is from Southern Water, and Colin Skellet is the chair of Wessex Water. WaterAid, among the best networked of the water-related NGOs, ran a number of panels at the Kyoto Water Forum, including one that tellingly asked "How will the poor become customers?" which is precisely the question the World Bank and the largest water firms have been pushing the past few years—with its embedded answer, that is, turn the poor *into* good customers. WaterAid responds with its own "successful" case studies on private-sector participation and "the role of civil society in promoting a pro-poor agenda."[26]

Tracing the discursive genealogies and relational biographies of dominant global policy forums on water reveals the enormous role the World Bank has played in constituting and supporting these networks and their agendas.[27] Three of the highest profile transnational water policy network actors came into being with World Bank support: the Global Water Partnership, the World Water Council, and the World Commission on Water for the 21st Century. All are key production nodes for transnational water conferences, training seminars, and policy papers and are ultimately a highly mobile set of global experts on water that comprise the leadership and establish the guiding principles of the new water reform movement. The Bank has also helped start and sustain the triennial World Water Forums[28] and funded the International Symposium on Water,[29] the Global Panel on Financing Water Infrastructure,[30] the Water Media Network,[31] Water Utility Partnership–Africa,[32] and a variety of other high-level networks that bring together state, private sector, NGO, and corporate officials by region, theme, and agenda.

The World Bank and these key nodes in the global water policy network are educating journalists, development consultants, state officials, and the world at large on the necessity for water policy reform. In 1998–99, WaterAid, Vivendi, the World Bank, and the International Chamber of Commerce's Business Partners for Development organized a series of influential meetings on water and sanitation where they invoked the reports and arguments produced by these networks to make the case that these TPNs reflect widespread agreement on how to solve the crisis of water scarcity.[33] At high-level meetings, forums, and policy-generating conferences throughout Europe, Asia, Latin America, and Africa, the topic of water reform moves forward, creating the appearance of worldwide consensus. Consequently, these uniquely situated and well-funded transnational water policy networks have effectively filled the spaces and saturated the marketplace of ideas on water policy in global civil society. Who can afford to attend global forums, speak up with reliable global data, and sit at these roundtables on water but their own members? Indeed, a well-known insider, the journalist John Roberts of one of the top industry newsletters, *Platts Global Water Report*, publicly scolded these network actors for considering themselves as leaders of a "global water community" (Roberts 2002). At the Fourth International Symposium on Water, Roberts criticized symposium attendees for being too narrowly doctrinaire and for acting as ideological advocates of water privatization, rather than as neutral sponsors of open dialogues on global water policy reform. Even to an insider, the self-referential work seemed a bit too gratuitous.

## Creating a Global Consensus on Water Reform

Although seemingly diverse interests are represented in this debate, the positions of these organizations, the strength of their voice, and their roles in transnational policy networks have converged to create what they describe as a "global consensus" on water. The TPN argument begins with the compelling "facts" that the global water commons is being threatened and the world's poor are suffering the most both because of their lack of access to water and their inability to become productive contributors to society (Goldman 1998). The second step has been to construct a narrow historical time frame and simple political landscape that governments inhabit. According to the TPN analysis, the main actors causing the degradation of water service systems and depletion of the global water commons are inefficient and politicized (i.e., monopolistic and corrupt) governments that treat water *as if* it were a free natural resource. Governments' failure to price water in a way that reflects its *true* cost has inculcated a culture of wastefulness among the world's populations, and as a result, water has become scarce. (As Peter Spillet, senior executive for Thames Water recently put it, without a hint of irony, "clearly people do not understand the value of water and they expect it to fall from the sky and not cost anything" [Carty 2002].) Yet because it is scarce, it has now become an arena that has begun to interest "value-seeking" corporations. According to Spillet, "There is a huge growth potential.... We think there will be wars fought over water in the future. It is a limited precious resource.... So it's a very viable place to put your money" (Carty 2002).

In sum, the majority of the world's water consumers lack access because of a history of government indifference and a failure to charge people adequately for its use.[34] Indeed, the poor are in part impoverished *because of* this irresponsible government behavior. According to the political rationality of the transnational water policy network, this causal argument is applicable throughout the ailing South.

To solve these problems, governments need to adopt international accounting methods for water services, submit to grading by international credit agencies, and, most important, put a market price on water. These standards should steer governments to invite the help of experienced Northern private water companies, since the private sector is assumed to be more efficient, more capable of increasing water supplies, and more likely to improve conservation. This argument is one that has evolved since 1996 and has been contrived through the hard work of the vast transnational policy network of actors that present themselves, in this self-referential and intertextual narrative, as neutral global-problem solvers trying to reverse water scarcity trends.

Perhaps what is most striking about the many different transnational policy actors I have described in this chapter is that they invoke the same origins story, declarations, and principles—all coming from the 1992 Rio Summit and Dublin Conference. They all refer to a meeting in Marrakech as a defining moment when a diverse community came together to devise a global plan of action. This is true even though those original participants were from a small circle of World Bank and UN institutions, major transnational corporations, development and bilateral aid agencies, and a few state agencies with large stakes in water projects.[35] By the Second World Water Forum, held in 2000 in The Hague, a handful of NGOs were invited to participate. In the third forum, held in Kyoto in mid-March 2003, organizers promised that the meetings would be more diverse and participatory, even hosting an open Internet discussion. (Tellingly, the Kyoto World Water Forum Web site was available in only three languages: English, French, and Spanish.) Yet for all the innovative ways that these global water forums try to incorporate different people and worldviews—with the list growing to include concerns related to gender, disability, indigenous peoples, orphans of HIV/AIDS victims, and noneconomic uses of water—the fundamental "Dublin principle" on economic valuation remains a pillar of truth around which all competing ideas revolve. That is, water has an economic value and, in the name of sustainable development, must be considered as an economic good in all of its uses.

The major global water policy event of 2002, the World Summit on Sustainable Development (WSSD) in Johannesburg, reflected the realization of this global consensus, the product of six years of transnational networking. Although a number of sustainable development issues were on the agenda at the WSSD, including the famine in southern Africa, the HIV/AIDS crisis, and sustainable forestry and mining issues, the main theme was water privatization. Indeed, the summit's main media event was the christening of the glamorous corporate—and UN-sponsored—WaterDome. This gala spectacle was hosted by Nelson Mandela and the prince of Orange surrounded by the paparazzi and the global "water lords" and celebrated in ostentatious splendor the public-private partnership (PPP) agenda of the water lobby.[36] The water agenda aired at the WaterDome and the WSSD was identical to the one developed by the transnational water policy network, from the global diagnosis of a "world water crisis for the poor" to the solutions offered of greater efficiency in water service provision, better cost recovery, and a shift from public-sector to private-sector providers through partnerships. The strength of this consensus can also be seen in the seemingly unrelated launching of the African Union as well as its bold report on the New Economic Program for African Development (Nepad), both of which embrace and echo the TPNs' analysis and plan of action. This new global policy consensus reflects the collective policy mandates of the World Bank, IMF, and World Trade Organization, which are now being instituted by governments throughout Africa, such that Africans are feeling the repercussions of these global mandates, even as they debate, indigenize, and resist them.

In the mountains of policy papers, technical agendas, investment portfolios, and legislation on water and sanitation reform that have been produced since the mid-1990s, one discovers a remarkable global consensus on the options available to countries that have large populations living without clean water or decent sanitation. In less than a decade, there has been an unequivocal and narrowing set of the terms of reference, of economic models, of ethical concerns, and of the roles of actors offered as a synthetic global regime of truth, rule, and right. This phenomenon is not unlike the many other discursive strategies and artifacts that comprise the age of green neoliberalism. Paralleling these other discursive offenses, debates on the global water crisis have been driven by the immediacy that surrounds any self-stated crisis: we have no time to bicker or defer, because there must be "water for all, quickly!" (Mestrallet 2001). The argument becomes that much more persuasive and effective when backed by the full force and authority of the international institutions of finance, trade, and development. Consequently, in a world where state leaders and vulnerable professional classes from the South seem to have few alternatives, the global water policy boosters offer the best choice in the classic Friedmanesque "freedom to choose" paradox in which choice is in fact quite limited and overdetermined (Rayack 1987). That paradox becomes clearer when we look at the latest round of conditions placed on heavily indebted borrowers by the Bank and the IMF and the way that water privatization has come into Africa roaring like a lion, even as elements of it just as quickly limp out like a lamb.

## Imposing Water Privatization

The most direct way the network's idioms, technologies, and water action plans get translated into action is, of course, through the imposition of conditionalities on World Bank and IMF loans. In fact, almost all recent public utility privatization deals (outside Western Europe and the United States) have occurred through active Bank/IMF participation.[37] That participation comes in the form of a threat, since every government official knows that the Bank/IMF capital spigots can be shut off if governments refuse to conform to their loan conditions.[38] As overwhelming debt burdens have put tremendous pressure on borrowing-country governments and created dire social conditions (most recently reflected in the 2002–3 famine in southern Africa), and as populist movements have demanded that governments stop servicing these odious and un-just debts, the Bank and IMF are using the carrot of debt relief to foist water policy reform on borrowing-country govern-ments.[39] In 2001, for example, all eleven of the World Bank's water and sanitation loans carried conditionalities that re-quired borrowing governments to either privatize these ser-vices or dramatically increase cost recovery from them (see table 6.1). Because the Bank and IMF often give indebted coun-tries a very short time to construct a "viable" water action plan, the transnational water policy network's expertise and action plans are likely to be invoked to satisfy the Bank and IMF's water reform demands.

In addition to targeting water and sanitation services, the Bank also imposes stringent conditions on its large structural adjustment loans, the Poverty Reduction Support Credits (PRSCs) referred to earlier. The selling-off of state owned en-terprises, utilities, and public services has become a prerequisite for continued access to Bank and IMF loans (Grusky 2002).[40] In 2000 alone, Benin, Honduras, Nicaragua, Niger, Panama, Rwanda, Sao Tome and Principe, Senegal, Tanzania, and Yemen agreed to conditions placed on IMF Poverty Reduction and Growth Facility loans before receiving much-needed capital and/or debt reorganization. These loans and debt renegotia-tions had water privatization and cost recovery as key con-ditions. The IMF's Emergency Post-Conflict Policy loan to Guinea-Bissau and Tanzania's acceptance of its Poverty Re-duction loan were predicated on privatization of public water services. Indeed, in order for most "highly indebted poor countries" (or HIPCs) to receive debt relief, it has been neces-sary to lease their water services to private—and invariably Northern—firms.[41]

**Table 6.1  World Bank Water Supply and Sanitation Loans for Fiscal Year 2001**

| Country | Total Amount of Loans in Millions of U.S. Dollars | % of Total Loans | Cost Recovery Conditions | Privatization Conditions | Both Conditions |
|---|---|---|---|---|---|
| Burkina Faso | 70 | 12.6 | yes | yes | yes |
| Comoros | 11.4 | 2.1 | yes | yes | yes |
| Ecuador | 32 | 5.8 | | yes | |
| India | 65.6 | 11.8 | yes | yes | yes |
| FYR Macedonia | 29.3 | 5.3 | yes | yes | yes |
| Niger | 48 | 8.7 | | yes | |
| Russian Federation | 122.5 | 22.1 | yes | | |
| Senegal | 125 | 22.6 | yes | | |
| Ukraine | 24.3 | 4.4 | yes | | |
| Uruguay | 6 | 1.1 | | yes | |
| Yemen, Republic of | 20 | 3.6 | | yes | |
| Total | 554 | 100 | | | |
| *Percent of total value of loans* | | | 80.9 | 51 | 31.8 |

*Source:* World Bank reports compiled in Grusky 2002.

At the end of 2001, the Bank had outstanding loan commitments in water-related sectors of nearly $20 billion (World Bank 2001). Most of the Bank's water service loans have started out with cost-recovery mandates, only to be ratcheted up to partial or full privatization when governments prove themselves unable to comply with the Bank's requirements for cost recovery, and when few communities are willing or able to afford the associated price increases (Grusky 2002; World Bank 2002). Without compliance, the public-sector choice is judged as inadequate, and private alternatives are introduced. By 2002, most of the Bank's cost-recovery agreements led to some form of privatization and were presented as a bail out of sorts by foreign firms "willing to help" indebted and floundering public agencies meet World Bank and IMF targets. In effect, corporations are placed in the role of charitable trusts, offering a helping hand, technology transfer, and expertise where it is needed the most. Under this political rationality, it is not International Chamber of Commerce members who are being attracted to a new business opportunity, but rather private-sector development actors who are on an ethical mission of poverty alleviation, ecological sustainability, and social justice.

One finds this worldview expressed by Gérard Mestrallet, CEO of Suez, in the French newspaper *Le Monde*:

> Two years ago, I set up a committee of twenty independent world-class experts from 17 different countries, all of them internationally recognised specialists in water and sustainable development. For a private group it was a new initiative, but one that was needed. Someone had to think to the future, to rethink policies for sustainable management of water resources and services in megacities around

the world. ... For the past ten years, international institutions and the World Bank in particular have extolled public-private partnerships as a focus for renewing water policies, to lever new sources of finance and apply more efficient management methods.

For a Group such as ours, possessing more than a century of experience in managing water services for local authorities, we have seen extraordinary change. The numbers of our customers have multiplied by five, such that our subsidiary Ondeo today serves 115 million people around the world, from Buenos Aires, to Santiago in Chile, La Paz, Casablanca, Atlanta, Budapest, Mexico City, Djakarta, Manila, Amman, Barcelona, Indianapolis, New Delhi, Gaza. ... The partnership model has produced tangible results. Many governments are undertaking reforms to promote it and are collaborating closely with local authorities and international institutions.

The universal right of access to water must be recognised. Our work consists in turning that right into a reality every day. Nine million of our customers in the world live under the poverty line. Serving those people is one of the main objectives to which we are committed by contract. ...

We involve local communities in decision-making and sometimes even in carrying out the construction work, backed by efficient, local NGOs. Where these solutions have been adopted, the price of water has been divided by ten in comparison with that of water dealers, and its quality is incomparable. Elsewhere, the poorer you are, the higher the cost of water, and the lower its quality. Connecting underprivileged districts to the public water system is a basic tenet of social justice. For us, it is not a question of corporate philanthropy: we are merely doing our job, and our duty, and we are proud of it. . . .

These people expect solutions now. The world needs the efforts of each and everyone. Opposing political and economic standpoints where water is concerned is detrimental to the interests of the underprivileged everywhere around the world. The war for water needs all our resources.

If nothing is done, however, by the year 2025, four billion men and women will not have satisfactory access to drinking water. That is the reality behind the commitment expressed in our appeal for "water for all, quickly." It will only be attainable if the political authorities in every country take immediate action to lay the groundwork for a more ambitious, efficient water agenda. (Mestrallet 2001)

If, however, we shift the analytical frame and see the problem in terms of the two-decade-long process of structural adjustment in which World Bank clients have been exporting more capital in interest repayments than they have been spending for public health, education, and welfare at home, then the way we judge the cause of ineffectual public service sectors changes. If the global community of actors articulating the rationality of privatization comprises the same actors who pressured states to dramatically reduce spending on public infrastructure and services, including in the water sector, then the network's "at-a-distance" objective standpoint becomes subject to question.

Indeed, there is good reason to critically question the "global water scarcity" and the "crisis" discourses of the transnational water policy network and to examine the very real political-economic interests that lie behind it. First, as noted above, these practices are a product of a particular agenda of the international finance institutions and the global water industry and have not arisen because of demands made by water-deprived poor communities. This is not to say, of course, that urban squatters and slum dwellers, the rural poor and subsistence producers do not lack access to clean water and sanitation. But this particular policy initiative has come from above and is part of the neoliberal capitalist transformation being promulgated by the IFIs and their development partners. Since 1990, the World Bank has not only helped finance the birth of these transnational policy networks but it has also underwritten the widespread privatization of public utilities, industries, and goods. In the realm of water alone, the World Bank awarded 276 water supply loans between 1990 and November 2002, one-third of which require the borrowing country to privatize some aspect of its water operations as a condition of receiving funds.[42] Indeed, the number of loans requiring privatization as a precondition has tripled since 1996 (International Consortium of Investigative Journalists 2002, p. 16). Of the 193 structural adjustment loans approved between 1996 and 1999, 112, or 58 percent, required privatization as a condition (see table 6.2).

In Africa, there has been a particularly marked trend toward privatization. Until 1997, privatization of water services had occurred only in a few West African countries, but in 1999, the number of contracts rose sharply. As of May 2002, more

**Table 6.2  Countries with IMF Water Privatization and Cost-Recovery Conditions, 2000**

| Country | IMF Program | Loan Condition |
|---|---|---|
| Angola | staff-monitored program | –adjust electricity and water services tariffs |
| Benin | Poverty Reduction and Growth Facility | –revise regulatory framework<br>–privatize before the end of the third quarter of 2001 |
| Guinea-Bissau | emergency post-conflict policy | –privatize management of electricity and water management services |
| Honduras | Poverty Reduction and Growth Facility | –approve framework law for the water and sewage sector by December 2000 |
| Nicaragua | Poverty Reduction and Growth Facility | –continue adjusting water and sewage tariffs by 1.5% a month<br>–offer concession for private management of regional water and sewage subsystems in key regions |
| Niger | Poverty Reduction and Growth Facility | –divest from key public enterprises, including the water company, SNE |
| Panama | Stand-by arrangement | –privatize management of public water company service<br>–allow contract with private-sector operators<br>–adjust tariffs |

(*continued*)

**Table 6.2** **(Continued)**

| Country | IMF Program | Loan Condition |
|---|---|---|
| Rwanda | Poverty Reduction and Growth Facility | –privatize management of the water and electricity company (Electrogaz) |
| Sao Tome and Principe | Poverty Reduction and Growth Facility | –adjust water and electricity services tariffs to provide for full cost recovery |
| Senegal | Poverty Reduction and Growth Facility | –reform regulation through creating regulatory agency for the urban water sector<br>–adjust tariffs through transferring the recurrent costs of water pumping and distribution equipment to the communities<br>–increase the involvement of private-sector operators |
| Tanzania | Poverty Reduction and Growth Facility | –assign the assests of Dar es Salaam Water and Sewage Authority to private management companies |
| Yemen | Poverty Reduction and Growth Facility | –adjust tariffs in water, wastewater, and electricity services to provide for full cost recovery |

*Source:* Letters of intent and memoranda of economic and financial policies prepared by government authorities with the staffs of the International Monetary Fund and World Bank. The documents are available at the IMF Web site, www.imf.org.

than eighteen water privatization contracts had been signed between European firms and African governments, five in South Africa alone, with eight more countries in the process of negotiation. Vivendi (now Veolia Water), Saur (France), Biwater (England), Aguas de Portugal, and Northumbrian Water (England) are most frequent lead companies; the contracts, with durations ranging from five to fifty years, sometimes combine control over both electricity and water (see table 6.3). By 2002, more than 460 million people worldwide were purchasing their drinking water from European-based companies. The six largest companies work in more than fifty-six countries, and their revenues have grown dramatically over the past six years (Barlow and Clarke 2002; Global Water Report 1996; Grusky 2002; International Consortium of Investigative Journalists 2002; Shrybman 2002). In sum, this remarkable shift from public to private serves a particular set of economic interests, with the world's largest firms and dispersed comprador classes eager to be part of this new wave of third world investment.

## Cracks in the Pipe

One measure of how these privatization efforts have fared is the durability of the contractual agreement. For this measure, the process has not been smooth. Many of the new contracts with transnational corporations have been, and are being, widely contested. Many communities threatened with rate increases have begun to network within and across national borders, sharing information and organizing strategies in their campaigns against water privatization. In Cochabamba, Bolivia, where a mass uprising closed down the city for weeks and forced the government to nullify its water contract with Bech-

## Table 6.3 Water Privatization in sub-Saharan Africa, November 2002

| Country | Lead Company | Local Company | Contract Duration and Type | Year |
|---|---|---|---|---|
| Republic of Congo (Brazzaville) | Biwater | Biwater (Congo) | contract awarded but details not known | 2002 |
| Uganda | Suez-Ondeo | Ondeo (Uganda) | 2-year management contract | 2002 |
| Burkina Faso | Vivendi | Vivendi (Burkina Faso) | 5-year management contract | 2001 |
| Niger | Vivendi | Vivendi Water (Niger) | 10-year renewable contract for water and electricity supply | 2001 |
| South Africa | Suez-Ondeo | Johannesburg Water | 5-year management contract | 2001 |
| Chad | Vivendi | STEE | 30-year concession (management contract initially) | 2000 |
| Mali | Saur | EDM | 20-year lease | 2000 |
| Cape Verde | Aguas de Portugal/ EdP | Electra | 50-year lease | 1999 |
| Mozambique | Aguas de Portugal | Aguas de Mocambique | Maputo and Motola, 15 years; other 3 cities, 5 years | 1999 |

| | | | |
|---|---|---|---|---|
| South Africa (Nelspruit) | Biwater/NUON | Metsi a Sechaba | 30-year lease | 1999 |
| South Africa (Dolphin Coast) | Saur | Siza Water | 30-year lease | 1999 |
| Gabon | Vivendi | SEEG (Gabon) | 20-year concession | 1997 |
| Senegal | Saur | Senegalaise des (Eaux) | 10-year lease | 1996 |
| South Africa (Stutterheim) | Suez | none | 10-year lease | 1993 |
| South Africa (Queenstown) | Suez | none | 25-year lease | 1992 |
| Central African Republic | Saur | Sodeca | 15-year lease contract | 1991 |
| Guinea | Saur | SEEG | 10-year lease | 1989 |
| Côte d'Ivoire | Saur | Sodeci | contract started in 1960; renegotiated in 1987 for 20 years | 1960 |

*Source:* Information gathered from two tables from Public Services International Research Unit (PSIRU) database. See http://www.psiru.org/reports/2002-12-W-DSAAfricawater.doc and http://www.psiru.org/reports/2002-06-W-Africa.doc.

tel, a citywide protest united for the first time disparate groups from urban and rural areas, women's groups, professionals, trade unionists, irrigators, and the poor (Finnegan 2002; Laurie and Marvin 1999).[43] A number of attempts at privatizing municipal water services have been prevented (e.g., in Poland, Honduras, Hungary, Sweden), some contracts have been terminated and reversed (e.g., in Argentina, Trinidad, Bolivia, and the United States), and other antiprivatization campaigns are building (e.g., in Brazil, Ghana, Indonesia, and South Africa) (see table 6.4).

Amidst the recent wave of privatization, two main actors are balking: firms and consumers. In February 2002, John Talbot, the chief executive of Saur International, the world's fourth largest water company, spoke before a World Bank audience, arguing that the needs of the Bank's clients were so great that although extending water to all made good sense in terms of sustainable development, he had to ask whether this "is [a] good and attractive business."[44] Cost recovery from the poor is not feasible, Talbot suggested, and the private sector may not be the place to tap for investments in these sectors. In his words, it was "simply unrealistic" to believe "that any business must be good business and that the private sector has unlimited funds. . . . The scale of the need far out-reaches the financial and risk taking capacities of the private sector." As a result, subsidies and soft loans would be necessary to make the endeavor worthwhile. "Even Europe and U.S. subsidize services," Talbot coyly noted. "If [subsidization] does not happen, the international water companies will end up being forced to stay at home."[45] Talbot's proposed solution is particularly ironic because it turns existing logic on its head; rather than provide subsidies to consumers (which many actors in the network believe is wastefully wrong), the World Bank and

## Table 6.4 Campaigns against Water Privatization

| Country | City | Year | Type |
|---|---|---|---|
| Poland | Lodz | 1994 | privatization prevented |
| Honduras | Honduras | 1995 | privatization prevented |
| Hungary | Debrecen | 1995 | privatization prevented |
| Sweden | Malmo | 1995 | privatization prevented |
| Argentina | Tucuman | 1996 | termination and reversion to public |
| Germany | Munich | 1998 | privatization prevented |
| Brazil | Rio | 1999 | privatization prevented |
| Canada | Montreal | 1999 | privatization prevented |
| Panama | | 1999 | privatization prevented |
| Trinidad | | 1999 | termination and reversion to public |
| Bolivia | Cochabamba | 2000 | termination and reversion to public |
| Brazil | Limeira | 2000 | incomplete termination |
| Germany | Potsdam | 2000 | termination and reversion to public |
| Hungary | Szeged | 2000 | incomplete termination |
| Mauritius | | 2000 | privatization prevented |
| Thailand | | 2000 | termination and reversion to public |
| United States | Birmingham | 2000 | termination and reversion to public |
| Argentina | BA Province | 2001 | termination and reversion to public |
| France | Grenoble | 2001 | termination and reversion to public |
| Brazil | | current | continuing campaign |
| Ghana | | current | continuing campaign |
| Indonesia | Jakarta | current | continuing campaign |
| South Africa | | current | continuing campaign |
| Uruguay | | current | continuing campaign |

*Source:* Gathered from http://www.psiru.org/reports/2002-06-W-Africa.doc.

other development funders should provide government subsidies, soft loans, and guarantees directly to private firms that know how to use them best.

To wriggle out of their existing contractual (and ethical) commitments to provide water for all, water service companies are redefining the language of their legal contracts. For instance, in its contract with the city of La Paz, Bolivia, to connect the shantytown of El Alto to the water system, Suez recently argued that "connection" would no longer mean a "piped connection" but "access to a standpipe or tanker"—precisely the condition that CEOs and elite transnational policy networks once called deplorable under public regimes.[46] Water companies are also demanding that poor communities donate labor to help build the supply system. In essence, these firms are creating a nonmonetary barter system (which rests on self-exploitation by the poor, who have few options) so they can live up to their agreements and shore up their profit rates. Is this déjà vu globalization of the old imperial order? Or is it the next frontier of uneven and combined capitalist development where twenty-first-century technologies (such as prepaid water meters) will become available only if combined with indentured labor conditions reminiscent of the nineteenth century?

In Ghana, privatization ended abruptly when the World Bank withdrew funding because of public outcries about corruption on the part of the parent company, Enron. In Gambia, Guinea, Kenya, Mozambique, South Africa (Fort Beaufort), and Zimbabwe, either the government or the water company pulled out amidst controversies raised by angry communities. In some places, firms have withdrawn because they were unable to make their expected profits without substantially changing the rules or interpretation of the contract. The response by poor "customers" has been a vociferous refusal to accept dramatic increases in price and no improvement in service, pressing elected officials to demand equitable service and lower prices from foreign firms. One-third of the contracts in Africa have been nullified because of mass-based political actions, and this is also happening throughout Latin America, Eastern Europe, and Asia. Tellingly, in Grenoble, France, home of Suez, the firm that promises to bring Africa its "European services," Lyonnaise des Eaux, a Suez subsidiary, was expelled for gross violations of overcharging, theft, and corruption in its water and sewage services (Barlow and Clarke 2002; Lobina 2000). The irony of this event, of course, is not lost on either French or Ghanaian water consumers. It is the flip side to the neo-colonial discourse that deems corruption, theft, and collusion as attributes of third world public sectors and not of France or French firms. It flies in the face of the old European tune of good Western conduct that the World Bank and its transnational policy networks sing to non-Western borrowers.

In 2002, a controversial suit was filed with the World Bank-run International Centre for Settlement of Investment Disputes (ICSID) by the California-based Bechtel Corporation. Throughout April 2000, tens of thousands of Bolivians gathered in the streets of Cochabamba to reject the water privatization policy of the government negotiated by the Bank and its sell-out to Bechtel. After eight days of continuous protest, the local government relented, repealed the contract, and expelled the Dutch subsidiary of Bechtel. In February 2002, Bechtel filed a $25-million lawsuit with ICSID against Bolivia for the loss of future profits. "We could use that money," reported a Bolivian community leader Oscar Olivera speaking in Johannesburg at an alternative World Summit forum, "to pay 25,000 teachers or to build 120,000 water-gathering structures in Cochabamba. Instead, we must hire lawyers and fight a company whose annual revenues are $14 billion, or double Bolivia's gross national product." Olivera continued: "The problem is that the World Bank, who supported the privatization deal in Bolivia, is now also the judge of this case. And to whom is the Bank accountable?"[47] Although the World Bank is not literally the official judge in the case, the ICSID is under the auspices of the World Bank and is the legal arbiter of disputes for the Bank's aid and loan agreements. It has also become the preferred site for arbitration by large multinational firms filing suits against Bank borrowers who want to avoid government courts and their public juries.[48]

The motive for these protests and contract nullifications is the steep rise in water prices for the poor. For poor households, water fees now consume a substantial percentage of household income, sometimes as much as one-third. In Cochabamba, the cost of water equaled one-fourth of a typical family's income after the Bechtel subsidiary increased its prices to reflect water's "true cost."[49] For some social groups, the price of water spiked more than 200 percent (Laurie et al. 2003). Bechtel also insisted on charging communities for water gathered from handmade rain-catchment systems, the water conservation technology that predates unreliable government taps. This action best exemplified the attack on enduring local ecological practices and fundamental community rights and produced the rally cry that Bechtel was charging for the use of the rain (Finnegan 2002).

In the black townships of Johannesburg, South Africa, where most water consumers are underemployed or unemployed, the price of water rose more than 50 percent after the public water system was privatized. Moreover, these township communities have experienced a proportionally greater price hike than that experienced by middle-class consumers in neighboring white suburbs and by large industrial and mining firms (Bond 2003). Critics have called this the neoliberalization of apartheid. In Guinea, water prices rose more than five-fold after privatization, resulting in a steep drop in bill collections and a steep rise in inactive connections (Grusky 2002). Given these realities, it is hard for anyone to argue that the shift from public to private providers has increased water access for the poor.

## Awash in Contradictions: The Rise of Decidedly "Uncivil Society"?

On the drive from the Johannesburg airport to the wealthy white suburb of Sandton—host to the 2002 World Summit on Sustainable Development—colorful billboards cajoled summit delegates to taste and enjoy the city's tap water, boasting that it was as pure and clean as bottled water. Billboards suspended above the airport freeway display pictures of black township boys splashing joyfully in an endless bath of fresh blue tap water. The messages imply that, unlike bottled water, Johannesburg's water is free, clean, and for all to enjoy. But after two weeks at the summit, it became crystal clear that these ads were not selling the idea of safe potable water to European delegates anxious about drinking the water in the third world; on the contrary, they were selling South Africa's water systems to interested European bidders in town for the World Summit.

In painfully stark contrast, ten kilometers down the road, the rigidly segregated and decrepit black township of Alexandra ("Alex") houses Sandton's underpaid labor force. Without good public transportation, health clinics, schools, or basic public services, Alex stands as a grim reminder of all that has not changed since the end of apartheid. Three hundred thousand people in Alex are jammed into just over two square miles of land without access to affordable clean water, electricity, safe housing, or basic sanitation services. The key word is "affordable," as many of these services *have* been provided but have now been shut off because people cannot afford to pay for them. In a dramatic political U-turn, the new politics of the postliberation African National Congress (ANC) conforms to the view of the Washington Consensus of the market as "willing buyer, willing seller," which has been imposed on poor black South Africans in the most draconian fashion.

At the time of the 2002 summit, South Africa was still reeling from a deadly cholera outbreak that erupted after government-enforced water and electricity cutoffs. At the outset of the epidemic, which ultimately infected more than 140,000 people, the government cut off the (previously free) water supply to one thousand people in rural KwaZulu-Natal for lack of a $7 household reconnection fee. South Africa has an ongoing water supply problem as is evidenced by the 43,000 children who die annually from diarrhea, a disease endemic in areas with limited water and sanitation services. The Wits University Municipal Services Project[50] conducted a national study in 2001 that identified more than ten million out of South Africa's forty-four million residents who had experienced water and electricity cutoffs (McDonald 2002). (These figures are disputed by South Africa's Water Ministry.)

In the black township of Orange Farm, just days before the start of the 2002 World Summit, the French firm Suez rushed to install water meters as a test run for other parts of the country.[51] The French insist its "pay as you go" system avoids nonpayment or theft. But in Orange Farm, meters were installed at homes with no income earners. Some of the new taps already leaked, and residents, with no way to recover the lost water, feared that their first month's free water would be their last.[52] As it is, many households can afford only four to five days per month of electricity from their recently privatized electricity meters. Township homes replete with fancy new French meters are otherwise ill equipped: toilets are outhouses, there are few sewage connections, and homes are constructed from either thatched materials, concrete slabs, or collected pieces of scrap metal. Along with the ten million people suffering from water cutoffs, and ten million from electricity cutoffs, two million people have been evicted from their homes and many more live in substandard conditions. With more than one million formal sector jobs lost since 1994, the full-throttle move by the ANC to privatize the heavily unionized public sector will cause many more jobs to disappear soon. However much the ANC wishes it could constitute a willing consumer culture amenable to foreign investors, the only thing thus far being consumed are the township residents themselves. The government and its police can do only so much to contain this political pressure cooker.[53] The tensions running through Johannesburg exemplify the troubling reality found around the world as neoliberalizing governments face mounting public protest.[54]

The changes that have occurred in the townships were in many ways the mirror image of the World Summit agenda. As a follow-up to the momentous Rio Earth Summit in 1992, the mission of the Johannesburg Summit was to assess the accomplishments and failures of the past ten years and to agree on a program for the future. The agenda emphasized five basic issues: water, energy, health, agriculture, and biodiversity. After a series of preparatory committee meetings held throughout the world, attended by government officials, staff from major intergovernmental agencies, NGOs, and international environmental organizations, the final WSSD document nonetheless read like both the latest World Bank policy paper and a wish list for the world's largest service sector firms. That such a seemingly diverse set of actors should carve out a document that is so familiar, so full of "common sense" to many sectors and professional classes, including environmentalists and development activists, should give us pause.

## Conclusion

The economic and ethical arguments for Bank-style development are always changing based on pressures from diverse political forces, ranging from the Bank's Northern country and corporate clients to antiprivatization activists cropping up across the postcolonial map. But whichever way the wind blows, there is an ever-widening cadre of professionals ready to learn and a new set of Bank training courses available. What is so remarkable is the rapidity with which the Bank's new political rationalities shift and often contradict one another, yet circulate and become legitimate. In this chapter, I have sought to highlight the rise of a particular eco-rational logic that has sprouted up from the activities of Bank-facilitated professional networks. This logic has circulated within training centers, gained authority and voice in high-echelon circles of policymakers, and has congealed as a policy framework implemented through existing political-economic imperatives managed by the Bank, such as structural and environmental adjustment regimes. Even though disparate actors represent vastly different perspectives on the role that private capital should have in the control of public water supplies and services, in practice a consensus has temporarily emerged on the way that public water should be managed—a fragile consensus orchestrated through World Bank technologies of power and knowledge.

In the case of water privatization, the shocking tragedy that much of the world lacks access to affordable and clean water is an image that may create new opportunities in development though it may have little to do with ultimately quenching those basic needs (Barlow and Clarke 2002; Bayliss and Hall 2002; Grusky 2002; Hall 2003; Hall et al. 2002). The "problem" of water scarcity for the world's poor has been analyzed by the World Bank as one in which the public sector has failed to deliver and has therefore prevented development from "taking off" and the economy from modernizing. If the state cannot deliver something as basic as water and sanitation, the argument goes, it is a strong indication of a general failure of public-sector capacity. Water scarcity becomes simultaneously indicative of a problem of poverty, of modernization, and of governance. The third world state is typically portrayed by the Bank and its partners as stuck in "arrested development," often depicted as corrupt, inept, and politicized. In this colonial framing, the state is the main hindrance to a country's successful integration into the global economy and hence to the economic fruits that such integration supposedly bears.

Within the interpretative framework of "pro-poor" development, the best decision the Bank can make is to insist that as a precondition of future access to capital, the state must clean house and package degraded public assets for sale on the international market. Such services and goods as housing, water, electricity, and sanitation can no longer be left to decay, for their inefficiency affects not only the health of the poor majority, but the whole country's ability to participate in the global economy. For many reasons, not least a neoliberal ethics of poverty reduction and ecological sustainability, this new political rationality of development views public-sector industries, utilities, and goods as best serving the public only after they are partially or fully privatized. In this scenario, the state should regulate but not run the public service.

Yet with the sale or lease of a public good comes more than simply a privatized service; alongside it comes a whole set of postcolonial institutional forces that intervenes in state-citizen relations and North-South dynamics. The World Bank's policy campaign for water privatization has been much more than a leasing program for dilapidated public plumbing and sewer infrastructure. Rather, it has marked the entrance of new transnational codes of conduct and procedures of arbitration, accounting, banking, and billing; a new ethics of compensation; new expectations of the role of the public sphere; and the normalization of transnational corporations as the local provider of public services and goods. It also marks the apocryphal last stake into the heart of nationalist revolutionary politics in the ex-colonies.

Within the world of development, a consensus has emerged claiming that private firms can do no worse than the inept state, and will more likely do much better. Those who constitute the world's transnational water policy networks believe that the poor are already paying above-market rates for water from private water tankers and taps when public systems are inadequate. To European-based water firms and World Bank economists, this evidence indicates that the poor (as well as the middle classes) represent a large population of "willing customers" eager to be provided with an efficient and reliable service, something the private tankers and public taps apparently cannot offer, especially on the scale required.

In today's dominant discourse, the distinction between public and private is assumed to be sharp and clear, such that one can make the sweeping generalization that the world's past and present water problems are due to the public sector. Yet even the most conventional historical readings of the world's largest water projects—e.g., the Hoover Dam, Suez Canal, Indus River waters projects—reveal that this distinction is a specious one and that, in fact, the public-private distinction has always been blurred. The world's largest water projects have been joint public-private ventures with states typically the lead investors and with private firms doing the infrastructural and contract work and receiving most of the benefits they provide. Whether they are feeding industrial farming, mining, or energy production, most grand water schemes have had highly subsidized state support in order that a minority elite could profit (Cronon 1991; McCully 1996; Scott 1998; Worster 1985). Indeed, often it is the very same actors who are generating and awarding the contracts (in their roles as state officials) as receiving them (in their roles as goods and services providers, investors, or landowners).

Many of the world's largest water projects have also been inextricably tied to state-building and imperial military projects, a two-for-one territorial and capital accumulation process, such as the Indus Water Treaty of 1960 and the subsequent Indira Gandhi Canal that created a massive irrigation moat in an otherwise porous desert border between Pakistan and India, or the damming of the Colorado River to ensure that Mexico would not get any water overflow from U.S. rivers (Goldman 1998; McCully 1996; Worster 1985). In these cases, public utilities have been set up as quasi-public ventures, with private firms managing or leasing them, often with guaranteed profit rates that are voted on by "public" oversight boards.

Finally, it is important to note that in the colonies vast amounts of valuable "public" natural resources (including water, watersheds, and river systems) were controlled by "private" trading companies awarded contracts by "public" European royalty and imperial states. Zambia, for example, was colonized by the British South Africa Company, a private multinational corporation led by Cecil Rhodes (Ferguson and Gupta 2002, p. 992). Today, Zambia along with many other African nations are ruled "in significant part, by transnational organizations that are not in themselves governments, but work together with powerful First World states within a global system of nation-states that Frederick Cooper has characterized as 'internationalized imperialism'" (Ferguson and Gupta 2002). So, how can we say without batting an eye that the public has failed such that, now, it is time for the private sector to take over the experiment? It requires the violence of abstraction and the denial of colonial-imperial history to derive such a simplified narrative (Scott 1995).

In sum, the relation and identities of development NGOs, state professionals, firms and business councils, and international aid agencies should not be taken for granted, as their genealogies and biographies *do* matter. Who is billed as local and who is transnational, public or private, charitable or profitable, above, below, or in the civil middle? The categories are highly problematic and politically strategic. Not only is the realm of *newly emerging* civil society romanticized as the space of progress and ingenuity, but the process of constituting civil society—or *transnational networking*—is a "globalization project" that has received tremendous philanthropic support from elite sectors within the North and become uncritically assumed as *the* inevitable social process of agile and flexible globalization (Florini 2000). Important questions to pursue are: why has the process of networking become the privileged site of transnational social relations for political civil-society actors (Riles 2000), and what other types of political processes are erased, undermined, and subordinated by this privileging? Networkers, it seems, are best able to generate and work in spaces of just-in-time, flexible, deterritorialized, and depoliticized expert realms. The instant expertise certification one earns as a member of the jet-setting transnational class of networkers suggests we need to give greater attention to this power/ knowledge nexus. The largest international conference ever, the 2002 World Summit, reflected the ultimate accomplishment of World Bank-financed transnational policy networking. Making this claim is, however, not to suggest that its outcome is singular or overdetermined. By focusing on the remarkable rise and legitimacy of the powerful transnational policy network promoting global water reform, I have tried to shed light on the increasingly significant phenomenon of this type of elite policy networking and its basis in the Bank's expanding regime of green neoliberalism. Although Western media repeatedly question the "representation" and "accountability" of the green-haired anarchists who demonstrate outside of major international finance meetings, our attention needs to turn to the question of who comprises the "official" transnational expert networks, interrogate from where their authority derives, what the institutional effects of their extraordinary rise and influence in the global political economy are, and, finally, the process by which this enormous global influence of the World Bank gets (re)produced. The political stakes in such inquiries have never been higher, and the immanent possibilities never as grand.

# VII

## Conclusion:
## Can It Be Shut Down?

F
ew moments in history rival this moment, a time when so many diverse people have come together to challenge the existence of a single institution. Such worldwide unity is a direct consequence of the Bank's enormous reach and highly invasive work practices. This oppositional political momentum could only have been produced within the milieu of the Bank's latest development regime of green neoliberalism—a regime that is embedded in and emboldened by the rapacious accumulation strategies of global capital. Although the Bank's earlier regime of structural adjustment and debt management was draconian and poverty-inducing, it was an insufficient "hothouse" for such mass-based oppositional politics. The World Bank has offered a gift to the people of the world that it might wish it had not.

The beauty of the Bank and the IMF's structural adjustment interventions was that they occurred behind closed doors among a handful of men, restructuring the inner workings of government financial and budgetary structures. To most people, structural adjustment was an abstraction and a mystery. In spite of widespread food riots and marches by the unemployed in major third world cities throughout the 1980s, the opportunity to build cross-sectional movements was lacking largely because it was difficult to understand precisely the source of these oppressive changes. A huge wave of job loss coupled with the elimination of major social programs often lead to the overthrow of one government and its replacement with another. But the successor inherited the same mess: the burden of generating revenues to repay old debts by firing public workers and selling off public-sector enterprises and goods. In the 1980s, mass-based despair did not translate into mass-based movements working across social groups and national boundaries. It was only when this painful and repressive regime of "fiscal austerity" was succeeded by a much more generative regime that mass mobilizations began to erupt in concert. Dubbed "a movement of movements," oppositional politics arose in a highly innovative and unpredictable fashion (Mertes 2004). Whereas the "battle in Seattle" at the 1999 WTO meetings surprised everyone and gained unparalleled worldwide media coverage, it was only one of a series of protests that closed down major cities around the world, with millions of people hunkering down with determination to protest a multitude of interrelated neoliberal policies.

In its surveys of borrowing countries—a job typically performed by management firms like Arthur Andersen and PricewaterhouseCoopers—the World Bank found health services, water aquifers and water services, fisheries, garbage and parking fee collection, cable TV and telephone services, national airports and breweries, and richly diverse forests seriously undervalued and potentially attractive to foreign capital investors in search of higher profit margins. In effect, the World Bank argued that every place has its own special and hidden treasures that are poorly managed by local populations, states, and markets. Together with local professionals, the Bank dressed up these public goods and services for sale on international markets. While this strategy became palatable to the professional classes enlisted in this neoliberal project, many other social groups found it to be grand larceny. When government resources stop flowing to localities, people often challenge the party in power. But when the water gets turned off, and the controller of the water tap comes from France or the United States, people see the translocal nature of both the problem and the solution. Success stories like the Cochabamba "water wars," pitting the people against the Goliath Bechtel, have mobilized similar communities worldwide.

These social movements are anything but ephemeral; their durability parallels the neoliberal structures they oppose. Activists whom I have interviewed describe their personal and organizational histories as deeply rooted in major political transformations, with their antecedents in the struggles against apartheid, military authoritarianism, and Western imperialism. Experienced activists stumbled upon the World Bank as a focal point for their politics because of the growing role of the Bank, and the IMF, in their lives. Some, for instance, followed the path similar to the Thai environmentalist who started out organizing his neighbors against a dam being built in his home province then "scaled up" to challenge international finance institutions once he traced the relations of power infused in the provincial dam to the World Bank and the Asian Development Bank. The husband of a Filipina activist was murdered while the couple participated in the anti-Marcos student movement. After the Philippines dictator Marcos fell from power, she turned her attention to the issue of indebtedness that plagued small farmers and farming communities, a campaign that expanded nationally with the spread of the oppressive effects of structural adjustment. In the process, she has helped organize a transnational antidebt campaign that strives to reform the global financial system. These are not fair-weather protestors on spring break from their real careers. They are not planning to retreat with the introduction of new World Bank reforms.

What does this political landscape tell us about the future trajectory of the Bank and its detractors? Since 9/11, the Bank has been compelled to redirect its finances to a handful of countries supporting the U.S. war. In 2002, the World Bank put together loans for an unprecedented $800 million to Pakistan, $2.2 billion to India, and $3.5 billion to Turkey, much of which appears unconnected to plans the Bank had before September 2001. Countries in southern Africa suffering from horrible famine received little financial support. In 2004 and 2005, the Bank's flagship investments have been Afghanistan and Iraq. The future of the Bank seems to be in the mopping up of the destruction caused by the U.S. military, the rebuilding of societies in the name of antiterrorism, development, and democracy. It is certainly an important historical rupture that for the Bank will require innovation and change, but routed through its pre-existing regime of green neoliberalism. The new is always produced from the enduring old. Some facets, such as environmental and social assessments, have been jettisoned in the rush to "rebuild" before people's movements organize themselves and propose alternative plans for public goods, such as oil reserves and river basins. Such an imperial project led by the World Bank to win the hearts and minds of the people of Iraq and Afghanistan—and Iran, Syria, North Korea too?—will likely provoke a bloody future.

What about the oppositional forces to the World Bank? As the Bank moves into Iraq, it will be guided by a cadre of high-rolling corporate interests (e.g., Halliburton, Bechtel, the U.S. oil industry) that will reveal more clearly than ever the myths of development and the twentieth century's "wars against poverty." It can only engender a broader base of opposition to the hypocrisies that built up World Bank power over the past sixty years. It will embolden and focus activist organizations that work on transnational political issues, building on both the successes of antineoliberal movements as well as the proliferation of antiwar campaigns that mobilized millions of people in 2003 and 2004 in opposition to U.S. military aggression. But it will also empower people working on issues of local or regional significance, as they make connections between the Bank's work in Iraq and at home. If the next set of priorities for the Bank is to clean up after the U.S. government, it may mark the death knell of the perception of the World Bank's project of development as humanitarian and apolitical. To survive such an agenda shift, the Bank will need widespread support from its employees, and professional allies in universities, on Wall Street and from its borrowers. A global "coalition of the willing" for such imperialist interventions by the Bank is, in my opinion, highly unlikely. Like the U.S. military, the Bank might have to go it alone. But can it? The Bank stands on the precipice of a crisis of legitimation due to the type of global institutional stature that it has been working so hard to create, one built upon allegiances cultivated across sectors, interests, and national borders. Simply put, the Bank's hegemony as a global institution is thoroughly dependent on the support of others. But to be the top global institution in a world of U.S. empire requires that it be, perhaps more than ever before, an intimate collaborator. Does it have any choice but to work on the behalf of the United States? In expanding its imperial nature, the World Bank would be planting the seeds of its own demise.

Irrespective of how the Bank acts in these particular circumstances, the opposition to the World Bank is becoming increasingly robust, geographically dispersed, and durable. Oppositional activists have learned where the Bank's vulnerabilities lie. Using tactics from the international antiapartheid movement, for example, the World Bank Bond Boycott has persuaded institutional investors to disinvest from Bank bonds. Since its start in April 2000, nearly ninety institutional investors have committed either to disinvest or not further invest in Bank bonds. Boycotters include U.S. cities, such as Milwaukee, San Francisco, Boulder, and Cambridge; investment firms, such as ASN Bank (the Netherlands), Citizen Funds, Calvert group, and Parnassus Fund; and church-based and union-based pensions funds, such as the 1.5 million member Teamsters and the 1.4 million member Service Employees International Union.

The Bank is also vulnerable to the default of its largest borrowers. In late 2002, Argentina stopped payments of more than $800 million to the World Bank, leading Moody's Investor Services and others to express grave reservations about the value of Bank bonds. Moody's and Bear Stearns in Latin America commented in different publications that Brazil was likely to default, and Russia and Indonesia could also default on Bank repayments as well. These four countries owe almost 30 percent of the Bank's gross outstanding loans. These defaults would have powerful ripple effects through both borrower and investor communities. Social movements throughout Latin America, Asia, and Africa are pushing their national governments to refuse payments to the World Bank and IMF and to kick them out of their countries; they see current inequitable development debt relations as an affront to national sovereignty and an obstacle to national development. A few well-timed political victories could send tidal waves through the international financial system and create many new opportunities for social movements to create alternative structures.

## Reflections from Political Activists

The gamut of people challenging the World Bank's latest regime is wide, ranging from some World Bank professional staff and consultants working on retainer, to critically minded government officials, to disenfranchised development subjects. This odd assembly is brought together by a desire to change the parameters of development. The spectrum of their political interests is equally broad, ranging from the desire to transform the contours of development—that is, to make it more green, democratic, just, equitable—to a commitment to dispose of development by refusing to allow the dominant institutions and the ruling elite to determine, in Gramsci's terms, "the questions around which the struggle rages." As development is so deeply embedded and articulated within larger structures of power, the latter goal is no easy task.

In this final section, I offer two short excerpts from a series of interviews with Southern activist leaders who are deeply engaged in the politics of the World Bank and neoliberalism to illustrate the depth and breadth of anti-Bank activism. Work-

Young South African protestor at the World Summit on Sustainable
Development, Johannesburg, 2002. Photo by author.

ing together, the transnational networks of activists have helped empower Southern legislators to pull out of the pivotal 2004 Cancún WTO meetings, for instance, and to force a substantial retreat of the World Bank and the water conglomerates from the cities of Manila, Atlanta, Cochabamba, Montreal, Rio, Lodz, Panama City, Grenoble, and possibly also Jakarta, Johannesburg, and Akra. Here, by quoting directly from interviews I conducted with activists, I will highlight a few themes that emerged. The first excerpt comes from a Haitian activist, who explains how he and others became focused on the World Bank and yet how difficult it is to live and organize in crisis-ridden Haiti. I quote him at length not to reveal the tragic consequences of neoliberalism in Haiti or its historical roots, but rather because his particular mode of interpretation and analysis can help us understand the way activists are carving out their own "war of position." "Michel" (a pseudonym, as are all names used in this chapter) is fully aware that the World Bank does not stand on its own, nor do he and his colleagues. The story line cannot be reduced to the neoliberal World Bank on the one side and socially conscious activists on the other; history does not unfold so simply. Michel situates the present struggle within a past of complex forces and events. His narrative makes us aware of the historical conjuncture where neoliberalism takes root and how the same institutions that imposed or helped to support previous oppressive regimes have lined up behind this one—in the case of Haiti, the U.S. military and corporate and political interests from the United States and France. The people of Haiti have experienced worse—slavery, dictatorship, and military invasion. With support from around the world, they have the potential to overcome the worst of the neoliberal forces under which they currently suffer.[1]

## Michel, an Organizer from the Central Union of Electricity Workers of Haiti

I was raised in a modest home and from early on I saw a lot of injustice in the most direct way. Many of us from the South were born under dictatorship, so I'm quite aware of how dictatorships work and who finances them. I developed a critical consciousness at a young age as a result. To understand how a movement against the World Bank emerged in Haiti, it is important to remember that Haiti was the first country of blacks to fight for independence and win; Haiti is a country with a history of militancy. When the United States invaded in 1915, the people resisted until 1934, when the United States pulled out. But Haiti continued to be pillaged by the Western powers as it supplied most of the world's sugar, and coffee and cacao as well. One effect of this history of enslavement and resistance is that the people of Haiti have always been radical. We had soldiers fighting in Savannah, Georgia, against slavery in the United States!

In 1971, our dictator Duvalier died, and his son Baby Doc took over. The Bank and IMF had the power to force him to liberalize the economy; by 1982, he backed a neoliberal plan for the economy. As a consequence, U.S. goods flooded our markets and destroyed our local industries, from pig production to rice cultivation. The Bank had two objectives: first, to dismantle the agriculture sector, which it did by forcing our government to import cheaper U.S. goods subsidized by the U.S. government. And now, the Bank is privatizing our public enterprises: power, health, education, and water, all are critical to our survival. My union organizes against the World Bank because we are public-sector workers, working for the electricity sector, and our jobs are at greatest risk under this privatization program. So our objective is to inform the public that these changes are not coming from the heavens but from the World Bank and its people. Because electricity is so important to the future of Haiti, we feel we're in the mouth of the lion with this struggle. Right after the coup d'état in 1991, the first union attacked by the state was the electricity union. The return of the Aristide government was contingent upon conditions agreed upon in Paris. Aristide could not come back to power until he agreed to the Paris Plan, and the heart of the plan was privatization, currency devaluation, the elimination of tariffs on imports, and to fire people from the public sector. The nine most important enterprises in the country were to be sold. This is all expressed formally in World Bank documents: reduce all social services! The IMF, the World Bank, the minister of finance, the WTO, and U.S. representatives, including some from U.S. firms, were all in Paris and in agreement. After he signed the agreement, Aristide was escorted back into power in Haiti by thousands of U.S. marines. But his power could fit into a small box; he had no more power; Americans and the World Bank held all the power.

What happened next? Phantom firms were created with Haitian elites and U.S. corporate money and Canadian people. The electricity sector was sabotaged as the state stopped funding it so that it could barely perform. Without electricity, the country was in real crisis. While we have been trying to fight the corruption in the sector and bring in decent managers, the World Bank has been trying to convince the government that because of such bad performance, the sector should be privatized. Since 1996, half the public employees of the nation have been laid off.

Besides our unions, we have NGO networks, such as PAPDA [The Haitian Platform of Advocacy for an Alternative Development], working against neoliberalism and privatization, and for development alternatives. But things are so bad in Haiti that the movement itself struggles to survive. One of its leaders recently committed suicide. The movement is evaporating as the situation for organizers has become grave. The last big activity we had was a hunger strike at the National Cathedral, which ended when we were all arrested. I would say there are three main reasons why the movement is failing. First, people have lost trust in everything. Second, the economic situation is so dismal, so desperate, that people can no longer work for political change. They put all the energy into just trying to survive. They have no jobs, no money, no food. They spend their time just meeting their most basic needs, like trying to grow vegetable gardens. Third, the military repression is getting worse for protestors. I've spent a lot of my life in prison; I've suffered from torture. Many of my colleagues are very weak, despondent, and feel helpless. The country is in deep trouble.

But those of us who have come to Washington for these protests are getting new energy from other people who also suffer from Bank programs. I have been promoting the idea of an international tribunal for the people who have committed these crimes against humanity. Just as we are trying Pinochet, and would have [tried] Hitler, we should do the same for the people at the World Bank.

Michel's perspective is clearly rooted in what Howard Zinn calls "people's history" (Zinn 1980), which is quite distinct from the history conjured by the World Bank and development experts, of a country that *alone* "lacks" the ability to develop. In Michel's analysis, the inequities and deprivations of Haitian life are seen as the result of power struggles, rather than through technical questions of economics and markets. It recognizes the transnational character of Haiti's past and present, rather than deploying the "national model" of inquiry that is dominant in development. Michel's explanation of suffering is not based on Haiti's "lacks," deficiencies, mistakes, bad planning, or corruption but on its structural relations with French and American geopolitical interests. Finally, Michel makes connections between Haiti's national elites and the promoters of these inequitable divisions—the World Bank and IMF. He recognizes historical ruptures and continuities, and he understands that the recent neoliberal deluge has a particular history with particular consequences. Hence, he has an acute sense of why he, a public-sector worker and union organizer, is engaged in transnational struggles against the World Bank and its latest development regime of green neoliberalism.

Haiti's dismal situation can be generalized only so far; after all, the World Bank is most able to practice strong-arm tactics in countries where its actions are matched by U.S. strong-arm tactics. The situation in Zimbabwe, a country on the verge of complete disorder, with regular street riots and military repression, offers a different picture.

## James, an Organizer with the Zimbabwe Coalition on Debt and Development

In the 1980s I worked in ecumenical support services and with the antiapartheid movement. The churches were active in the front-line states supporting liberation movements in Namibia and South Africa. After independence, all of a sudden, we found ourselves without work or focus. By 1990, Zimbabwe had a new economic structural adjustment policy. The government went all out to sell the program to the public, without much local criticism. But since thirty African countries had already experienced it, with disastrous effects, there was a lot we could learn from others. Economies had suffered, currencies were devalued, there was disinvestment in education and health services, and many people lost jobs. We found ourselves with a new political agenda.

As we became aware of the situation, we started a policy analysis training program for midlevel managers in the NGO sector, to train ourselves and also engage decision makers in our government, as well as people inside the Bank and IMF, and to relate our experiences and come up with alternatives.

From this, the Debt and Development Coalition emerged, which is a network of twenty-three organizations associated with the Jubilee 2000 campaign for debt relief.

In contrast to a growing NGO sector that questioned these new policies, we also had our national collaborators. The World Bank, for instance, did not go to parliament to talk to [elected officials], but straight to the Finance Ministry, and the technocrats. The Bank and IMF worked to create a token nation-state here, unable to protect its people. If you look at who are the top officials in the ministries, they are not homegrown, but brewed in D.C. and parachuted down into Zimbabwe. Low-level civil servants were implementing policies without understanding them at all. The World Bank works very aggressively here and engages in very little dialogue. Our NGO network has taken the lead in creating public dialogues on these policies and offering alternatives.

Our earliest struggles in Zimbabwe were political: national independence and apartheid. Now, we see this struggle as economic. We have been compartmentalizing our struggles in the past and we should not. The World Bank says we can have our country and our political power but we can't have economic power. The values these policies promote are individualism and competition instead of sharing and solidarity. So, in fact, it's a much broader struggle than an economic one.

This struggle today is unique because people around the world are not just offering solidarity, as in the antiapartheid movement. This struggle is my struggle and it is your struggle. It is global, and so is the movement. In Zimbabwe we used to say that we are a depoliticized society. But the World Bank has politicized us. People are now taking to the streets as never before. So thank you World Bank, you have brought us back to the streets, and I think we are better prepared than before. And thanks to the global movement, our resolve is growing.

James interprets politics in Zimbabwe in two historically distinct periods—the unified struggle against apartheid and for national independence, and today's struggle against neoliberal capitalism. Although people were caught off guard by the rise of neoliberalism, the leadership in Zimbabwe is now quite vulnerable to mass rejection and revolt. Finally, James notes that the struggle cannot be reduced to a single phenomenon or analytical frame, such as the political or the economic. Society is being transformed in such profound ways—cultural, ecological, religious, social—that to reduce it to an economic question misses out on the multiple and diverse ways that people experience neoliberal capitalist development.

In neighboring South Africa, an organizer from the Soweto Electricity Crisis Committee reflects upon an important point that resonates with what others have told me: that the movement against green neoliberalism has exploded in size because of the challenge to people's basic rights to livelihood.

We have had workshops on the World Bank, the IMF, the WTO and we've got strong people working on these issues. We've set up structures for the Campaign against Neoliberalism in South Africa.

But in the end we had to get down to the most basic questions: *What are the problems facing people on the ground that unite us most?* In Soweto, it's electricity. In another area, it is water. We've learned that you have to actually organize—to talk to people, door-to-door; to connect with the masses. But you have to build with a vision. From Day One we argued that electricity cuts are the result of privatization. Privatization is the result of GEAR [national neoliberal policy]. GEAR reflects the demands of global capital, which the ANC is bent on pushing through. We cannot finally win this immediate struggle unless we win that greater one. (Ngwane 2003)

Examples from Latin America suggest the rise of a new form of national politics. In Bolivia, Ecuador, Chile, Peru, and Mexico, indigenous peoples' movements have rejected conventional notions of national politics, and are rearticulating the meaning of nation, borders, and territory. Indigenous Mapuche activists, for example, are remapping their relations and territorial rights across the Argentina-Chile border, stirring up politics in the Southern Cone. Breaking out into armed insurrection on the eve of one critical neoliberal turn, the signing of the North American Free Trade Agreement, the Zapatistas have forced the Mexican government and people to seriously rethink the nation-state and the role of indigenous peoples in society (Collier and Quaratiello 1999; Nash 2001). As a way to counter this subversive discourse on indigeneity, which eschews national borders, neoliberal land policies, and international agreements and bodies, the Inter-American Development Bank and World Bank are pumping money into "indigenous education" institutes and courses that try to take back from social movements their radical framing of "indigenous" knowledge, history, and politics.[2] In other words, as social movements articulate a new politics in terms of economic and cultural injustice and alternatives embedded in struggles over meaning, history, culture, nature, territory, spirit, and kinship, the World Bank has jumped in to offer its own programs on indigenous rights, albeit linked to projects of development capital. In a complementary fashion, cross-class coalitions are forming around antineoliberal politics in Argentina, where the middle class has suffered much under recent neoliberal shifts. In Bolivia, the "water wars" have succeeded in more than the expulsion of Bechtel and its control over municipal water supplies; they have spurred new municipal political formations based on direct democracy and powered by a coalition of urban professionals and rural irrigators, men and women, trade unionists and farm laborers, politicians and activists. As one of the organizers declared in a public speech, "The mayor can never make such a backroom deal with a multinational corporation again!" No decision is now made, he insisted, without the active participation of La Coordinadora, the antiprivatization coalition. In sum, aggressive World Bank policies have triggered unanticipated democratizing responses.

And yet, we should not romanticize the battle social movement activists face. Murder—indeed massacre—is a common prospect for people who challenge such power. Moreover, as Michel's comments show, mobilizing people is difficult when most of their energy must be used for basic survival. Solidarity across class and national boundaries therefore becomes essential. But one must not idealize transnational networking either. Well-funded and well-staffed transnational environmental groups, for instance, can be found co-opting and even closing down local environmental groups, converting them from small populist organizations rooted in radical and anticapitalist politics into their own large technocratic NGOs. When the discourse of environmentally sustainable development becomes the rallying cry for NGOs and multilateral banks, together promoting a global enclosures movement or what geographer David Harvey calls "accumulation by dispossession," then we know that this green neoliberal turn is generating dangerous consequences (Harvey 2003).

Have these protests sparked a world-historic shift in oppositional politics? Are they laying the foundation for new political institutions? Do they have the power to shut down the Bank? The World Bank is not working merely through deception: the Bank is deeply embedded in multi-tentacled structures of power, culture, and capital. Even if every activist across the globe came to Washington, D.C., to protest, the Bank would likely remain standing. Yet it is also possible to speculate that just as the World Bank arose from the ashes of World War II and remained a fairly minor actor until the 1970s, it could return to those ashes as a result of persistent revolt and cross-class coalitions boycotting and confronting their political leadership's agreements with the Bank. Perhaps the Bank's main source of capital—large institutional investors—would prefer to switch to more secure, less volatile investments. Without legitimacy, there would be no capital to lend; without capital to lend, the Bank could conceivably become irrelevant.

The global political economy has changed substantially since the 1970s, and the role of Wall Street and Washington power brokers has expanded and intensified immeasurably (Gowan 1999). Today, the policies the Bank thrusts upon sovereign states in the South and in Eastern Europe work in part to sustain this highly inequitable set of power relations. Although Northern firms and interests *could* produce an alternative vehicle to do their work, it would require a level of legitimation that could not be generated overnight. Indeed, the main argument of this book is that the World Bank has cultivated institutional and class-based support for its global agenda of development over many years, with hard cultural work and powerful capital forces and incentives spread across the globe. We know that this type of complex power regime does not reside *just* within the New York-Washington corridor. Nonetheless, North-South power dynamics would look profoundly different—indeed, become much more vulnerable—without the World Bank and its development regimes. It would be a very different world.

We need a much deeper understanding of the development myths we choose to believe and of the ways we participate in and consent to the forces that constitute North-South power relations today. Recognizing the roles we play in reproducing the structures that are the bedrock of our highly exploitative and commodified world is the first step to a more emancipatory one; democratizing and socializing these powerful capitalist structures becomes the obvious second step. Another world is indeed possible.

# Notes

## Chapter 1.
## Introduction

1. As Timothy Mitchell notes of the effects of Bank/IMF policies in Egypt: "It is not uncommon, among the proponents as well as critics of the [IMF/World Bank] reforms, to admit that structural adjustment and the opening of markets may be accompanied by political repression . . . an unforeseen, unfortunate, intermittent, and probably temporary side effect of the shocks that accompany the expansion of the global market" (Mitchell 2002). Mitchell documents the repression, violence, censorship, and humiliation that are everyday effects resulting from the alchemy of military rule, U.S. foreign policy, and Bank/IMF policies.

2. John Williamson, who coined the phrase "Washington Consensus," notes that the consensus consisted of ten basic axioms that formed "the common core of wisdom embraced by all *serious* economists" (Pincus and Winters 2002; Williamson 1993).

3. While at the World Bank, Stiglitz (2002) was shocked and dismayed by his peers at the IMF who told him that countries needed to "feel the pain" in order to recover.

4. I challenge this interpretation in chapter 2, with a different reading of Bank and IMF history.

5. I focus on postdevelopment scholarship because I share much of the same intellectual foundation, with the exceptions highlighted in the next section.

6. This information is based on an interview with a senior environmental officer, World Bank, 2001.

7. See the Web sites of Center for Economic Justice (www.economic justice.net) and World Bank Bond Boycott (www.worldbankboycott.org) for updates and background on the global campaign to boycott Bank bond investment, with international unions, city and state legislative bodies, investment firms, and umbrella church organizations participating.

## Chapter 2.
## The Rise of the Bank

1. The authority of Treasury, State, and Wall Street concerning the policies and the trajectory of the Bank are unmistakenly clear in the collection of oral histories of early senior Bank officials, archived as the World Bank Oral History Project in the Columbia University library and at the World Bank.

2. The World Bank Group consists of five associated institutions: the International Bank for Reconstruction and Development (IBRD), established 1945, 184 members; the International Finance Corporation (IFC), established 1956, 176 members; the International Development Association (IDA), established 1960, 162 members; the International Centre for Settlement of Investment Disputes (ICSID), established 1966, 134 members; the Multilateral Investment Guarantee Agency (MIGA), established 1988, 157 members. http://web.worldbank.org/WBSITE/EXTERNAL/EXTABOUTUS/ 0,,contentMDK:20040580~menuPK:34588~pagePK:34542~piPK:36600 ~theSitePK:29708,00.html. The World Bank is actually composed of a group of five agencies. The International Bank for Reconstruction and Development (IBRD), established in 1945, is the main branch of the Bank, lending money to "creditworthy" borrowing countries carrying lower-than-market interest rates. But because Wall Street from the beginning had deemed most third world countries as "uncreditworthy," IBRD lending started off slow.

In 1960, the Bank established the International Development Association (IDA) for those borrowers that could not qualify for IBRD loans, with the intention of helping them become creditworthy. Borrowers were offered no-interest loans with a small (0.75 percent) administrative charge. Some middle-income countries have "graduated" out of the IDA and have become full-fledged IBRD borrowers; many lower-income countries continue to receive a mix of IBRD and IDA loans. The International Finance Corporation (IFC) was established in 1956 as the largest multilateral source of loan and equity financing for private-sector projects; it has blossomed into a major global player only over the past decade, as the world of development shifted into this neoliberal privatization phase. The International Centre for Settlement of Investment Disputes (ICSID) was established in 1966 to settle disputes outside national court systems. Over the past few years, a steady flow of transnational corporations have been using the ICSID arbitration process to resolve disputes they have with Bank borrowing countries. Finally, the Multilateral Investment Guarantee Agency (MIGA) came into existence in 1988 and has also recently become quite active in providing investment insurance and political risk guarantees for high-stakes investments in third world countries. For the sake of clarity, I chose to focus on the World Bank as a single entity and specifically emphasize the work of the IBRD, the main lending and policymaking arm of the World Bank Group.

3. World Bank presidents: Eugene Meyer (six months, June 1946 to November 1947), John McCloy (two years, March 1947 to April 1949); Eugene Black (fourteen years, July 1949 to 1963); George Woods (five years, January 1963 to March 1968); Robert McNamara (thirteen years, April 1968 to June 1981); A. W. Clausen (five years, July 1981 to 1986); Barber B. Conable (five years, July 1986 to August 1991); Lewis T. Preston (four years, September 1991 to May 1995); James Wolfensohn (ten years, June 1995 to May 2005) (World Bank 1995).

4. See, e.g., Keynes's quotation in this chapter's opening epigraph.

5. From the start, questions arose about the Bank's purpose and intentions, compounded by reasonable concerns about its ability and legitimacy to lend money for a concept as unstable as "development" in the newly invented role of a "world" bank. All of this resulted in heavy constraints in its growth by the founders themselves—the United States and England.

6. See also Hurni 1980; Mason and Asher 1973.

7. Mason and Asher, in their respected 1973 history of the World Bank, reviewed the first twenty-five years of the Bank in these terms: "[Bank leadership] recognized that investments of many kinds were needed for development but frequently implied that one kind was more essential than any other. The relative ease with which [the Bank] could finance electric power, transportation, and economic infrastructure projects . . . made it an exponent of the thesis that public utility projects, accompanied by financial stability and the encouragement of private investment, could do more than almost anything to trigger development. . . . At the same time the Bank was led to eschew certain fields traditionally open to public investment, even in the highly developed free-enterprise economies: namely, sanitation, education, and health facilities. . . . The contribution of [these] *social overhead* projects to increased production, however, is less measurable and direct than that of power plants. . . . Financing them, moreover, might open the door to vastly increased demands for loans and raise hackles anew in Wall Street about the 'soundness' of the Bank's management" (Mason and Asher 1973).

8. I borrow the phrase "Big Five" from George and Sabelli (1994).

9. See interviews with Cavanaugh and others in the Columbia University Oral History Project collection (Cavanaugh 1961).

10. See Mitchell (2002) on the genealogy of the idea of economic worthiness.

11. It is worth noting that most of the first professionals at the Bank were ex-colonial officers (Mason and Asher 1973).

12. McNamara, who graduated from UC–Berkeley and taught at Harvard Business School, often used his social networks for promoting the Bank.

13. The World Bank under Rotberg began a whole new set of currency and financial transactions that marked the world with "rate setting, 'tap' facilities, continuously offering securities, synthetic issues based on benchmarks, global bonds, extendables, retractables, warrants, multi-currency option bonds, and a variety of reset interest rate obligations" (Rotberg 1994, p. 203). The new Bank brought to the market about one hundred different issues a year—one every three or four days somewhere in the world. By the 1990s, the Bank routinely offered $1–2 billion worth of global bond issues at a time.

14. Other high-income borrowers included the Bahamas, Finland, Greece, Israel, and Singapore. Middle-income borrowers included Brazil, Chile, Fiji, Morocco, Indonesia, and Malaysia. Low-income borrowers include most of sub-Saharan Africa, India, China, Afghanistan, Laos, Yemen, and Vietnam. These are categories and indicators constructed by the Bank, cited in Kapur, Webb, and Lewis 1997.

15. In geopolitical terms, the new strategies follow the shift of the anticommunist crusade from the factory to the field. McNamara's focus on the rural peasantry also reflects U.S. policymakers' discovery that socialism and communism in the third world was not Moscow-directed but rooted indigenously in struggles over land and resources. This point, and superb advice for this chapter, comes from historian Kate Dunnigan.

16. At the same time, McNamara declared to the Bond Club of New York (May 1969) that "the economists at the IBRD have been working on methods for quantifying the economic returns derived from social investment, such as education. Their conclusions demonstrate that the benefits vary enormously. A liberal arts college in a private underdeveloped area can be a dead loss, but a technical high school—in an expanding economy where the available capital is not matched by the requisite skilled manpower—can pay huge dividends. One such project in Latin America brought an annual return of 50 per cent. It is the IBRD's task to determine, in a given situation, precisely what sort of education contributes most to solid economic growth and to invest accordingly. We have not financed in the past, and will not

finance in the future, any education project that is not directly related to that economic growth" (McNamara 1973, pp. 134–35).

17. It should not be forgotten that the Pentagon Papers were published in 1971 (Ellsberg had been a McNamara staffer at the Pentagon) and Halberstam's stunning critique of McNamara and his buddies surrounding Kennedy and Johnson had come out in 1972. Everywhere he went he was castigated for the killing of so many peasants in Indochina. Inside the Bank, apparently no one spoke the word "Vietnam" in front of him even as many saw McNamara's hire, and his legacy, as the "ruin of the Bank" (Shapley 1993).

18. As no loan figures were given, this was presumably a technical assistance grant tied to a possible future loan.

19. In the course of funding its expanded projects, the Bank also invested in, and spurred the growth of, such transnational and national agencies and organizations as the Association of Development Financing Institutions in Asia and the Pacific (ADFIAP), the Pan-African Institute for Development, the Electricity Generating Authority of Thailand (EGAT), the Southeast Asian Regional Center for Graduate Study and Research in Agriculture, and a myriad of UN agencies. Many of these organizations became dependent on the Bank to fund their institutes, seminars, conferences, libraries, research, and projects. Whereas before 1960 hardly any of these organizations existed, by 1980 they were well institutionalized, and the Bank was picking up a large percentage of the bill as well as funding the creation of a network in which these organizations could work collaboratively with the OECD, FAO, UNESCO, UNIDO, WHO, and the European Development Fund (World Bank 1981a). Consequently, a wholly new practice of development became pervasive in multiple arenas—not just in the old Bank style of working only with finance ministries or central banks, charities, or self-help development NGOs, but also with ministries of agriculture, forestry, fisheries, rural development, economic planning, with such quasi-state private entities as EGAT, ICRISAT, and with UN agencies, development banks, and agricultural universities.

20. As John K. Galbraith argued, because the West would supply only capital or technical knowledge to places such as India, where he served as U.S. ambassador under Kennedy, the causes of poverty were then derived from these possibilities. "Poverty," he wrote, "was seen to be the result of a shortage of capital, an absence of technical skills. The remedy included the diagnosis. Having vaccine we invented small pox" (Galbraith 1979, pp. v–vi).

21. Thanks to the Bank's leadership, the international agricultural research institutes greatly expanded their budgets, research agendas, outreach, and successes (Baum 1986). McNamara first created a central secretariat in-

side World Bank headquarters with a technical advisory committee housed in the Food and Agriculture Organization (FAO), which also brought the United Nations into the fold. Next, he financed the Los Banos and El Batan centers, along with the two new institutes in Colombia and Nigeria (Baum 1986; Stakman 1967). Initial pledges from the Bank and other multilaterals, bilaterals, and Northern foundations totaled to more than $160 million at first, and after a few years grants to the CGIARs reached $100 million a year (Baum 1986; Shapley 1993). But for the seeds of these institutes to be utilized in the South required a whole infrastructure of support. Within a decade, the World Bank was investing billions in green revolution infrastructure: dams, irrigation systems, power generators, roads, tractors, fertilizer and pesticide factories (World Bank 1969; World Bank 1981a).

22. Northern firms producing tractors and farm equipment, patented seeds, fertilizers, pesticides, herbicides, turbines, and irrigation equipment benefited most of all. The World Bank not only fueled the lucrative business of selling high-yield variety seeds to third world farmers, it also triggered a global trend in which more than 400 seed companies would be taken over by a handful of rapidly merging firms, so that by the mid-1990s, five firms would control most of the world's commercial seed production and five firms account for almost 80 percent of the world's grain market (Toussaint 1999). In this way, the Bank's green revolution spurred a global commodity chain in which third world farmers became consumers of first world agroindustrial inputs.

23. According to Belgium's executive director at the World Bank, the flow back from the World Bank to industrialized countries was one dollar to seven in 1980, that is, for every dollar invested in the World Bank seven dollars came back to industrialized country firms. By 1996, the flow back rose to $10.50 for every dollar (Toussaint 1999, p. 131).

24. The Baker Plan (Seoul 1985) and Brady Plan (Washington 1990) were crucial levers for transferring enormous power to the World Bank and IMF in exchange for ensuring that Citicorp and other Northern private bankers would be bailed out. For more on this historic conjuncture, see (Gowan 1999; Helleiner 1994; Kapstein 1994).

25. By 1988, half of Thailand's entire land area had been allotted to private logging firms and another tenth of the country to export crop production, largely financed by Bank loans (Rich 1994). World Bank-sponsored Thai agencies went to great lengths to push a narrow export-oriented agenda. Of a Bank-financed Rubber Replanting Promotion Fund, one Thai farmer explained that the fund actually "promotes the destruction of all kinds of plants . . . in 1985, the government regulation actually forbade farmers to have any species of tree on land not being subsidized by the fund. If they find

a mango or jack fruit, they charge people about 250 Baht [ten dollars] per tree" (testimony from the People's Forum of 1991, quoted in Rich 1994, p. 14).

26. Between 1976 and 1986, the World Bank lent $630 million for the Indonesian Transmigration Project. In the name of progress and development, this rural modernization scheme cleared more than 40,000 square kilometers of forest (4 percent of Indonesia's total forest) and 35,000 square kilometers of wetlands and resettled four million people, most of whom were ethnic minorities. The resettled population was promised millions of dollars for agricultural support to produce export crops, such as cacao, coffee, and palm oil, but little of the promised agricultural supports materialized, and the newly resettled were left without resource or government support to eke out a living. The World Bank loans attracted tens of millions of additional dollars from U.S., German, and Dutch governments, as well as from the Asian Development Bank (ADB), UNDP, and the World Food Programme. General Suharto was, strategically, a fierce anticommunist and prime beneficiary of Western aid. (See Caufield 1996; Pincus 2002; Rich 1994).

27. See *The World Bank and the Environment* (World Bank 1990); *Making Development Sustainable* (World Bank Environment Department 1994); and *Mainstreaming the Environment* (World Bank Environment Department 1995).

28. Until recently, the Bank's Environment Department Web site had a running count of EPAs around the world fostered by the Bank. The number of environmental agencies started to rise dramatically after the Rio Summit in 1992 when the Bank made it a priority agenda item and also an informal condition for World Bank loans. For worldwide statistics on EPAs, see Frank, Hironaka, and Schofer 2000.

# Chapter 3.
## Producing Green Science inside Headquarters

1. There are two types of data being discussed here: data on population change, per capita income, etc., which are used widely by academics and other researchers; and "internal" documentation from government budget offices, public officials, and government ministries; internal cost-benefit analyses; and project evaluations, etc.—information that becomes public only in its processed, diluted, and often uncited form in Bank publications. Because the second type of information is only alluded to in Bank reports, readers have no way of knowing how it is being used. See Srinivasan et al. 1994 for a critique of the Bank's heralded database and sources published in a special issue of the *Journal of Development Economics*. They argue that the

data on which most development economists depend, and take for granted—
e.g., income, population, and growth rate figures—originate in extremely
dubious national censuses and surveys. Nonetheless, they become the basis
for many policy-related assumptions and analyses. The models for processing these dubious data sets are also being questioned: the computable general equilibrium (CGE) model, an accomplishment that has placed Bank research on the forefront of economic scholarship, is challenged by many
observers, including Nicholas Stern, the chief economist at the European
Bank for Reconstruction and Development (EBRD) when he wrote his criticism, later to be the chief economist at the World Bank (Stern and Ferreira
1997, p. 46). Such questions about the scholarship of Bank science, however,
do not impede its positive reception by most policy-making institutions.

2. Although the budget is the largest among development agencies
and finance institutions, it is smaller than the European Union's research
budget. The latter, however, has a much broader mandate, and its scientists
serve the member nations as a pan-European academy of science would. Also,
the budget figures for the World Bank fluctuate depending on one's definition of research. Since I include environmental assessments and various routine forms of data collection and analysis that are part and parcel of the job
of loan managers and environmental technicians—because internal reports
and memoranda are utilized as if they represented scientific research findings—I would put the research budget much higher than the official range
of $25–30 million (Pincus 2002; Standing 2000; Stern and Ferreira 1997).

3. Interview, January 1995.

4. See also Tower 1990 and World Bank, "Report on the World Bank
Research Program," Report no. 10153, December 1991, as cited in Stern and
Ferreira 1997.

5. For a discussion of the important role of the Bank in producing and
disseminating information on China, see Stern and Ferreira 1997. On structural adjustment, the Bank invented it; on debt, media, academic, and policy
people depend on the Bank's key publication, *World Debt Tables*, with an annual circulation of 11,000 copies. *World Development Report* has a distribution
run of 120,000 copies a year, which is all the more remarkable when compared
to a brilliant scholarly treatise, with a lifetime press run of maybe 10,000, or
the most prominent economics journals, with a few thousand copies.

6. It is important to distinguish notoriety and accessibility from quality. According to one former high-level Bank official: "If academic development economists were asked to list the thirty most important books or articles on development published in the years since the Bank's research
department was established—very different from the compilation of a read-

ing list for students—we suspect that few would list many articles by Bank researchers" (Stern and Ferreira 1997).

7. Names of departments and divisions change often, such that even Bank staff have confused the exact names of the units with which they work. Because my research covers the Bank for over more than a decade, during which there was at least one major reorganization (and a few minor ones) with unit name changes, I use the name of the unit in which staff whom I interviewed worked at the time of the interview. On a few occasions, I use a simple generic descriptor that identifies the unit's purpose, such as the Mexico Desk or the Policy Research Department.

8. Interviews, April and June 1996. On the organizational chart, the PRD sits under the vice president of development economics, the chief economist (a position that has been filled over the past years by Michael Bruno, Joseph Stiglitz, Nicholas Stern, and François Bourguignon), and the director of development policy, in what is considered "the Center" (rather than "Operations"). PRD consists of the following divisions: Environment, Infrastructure, and Agriculture; Finance and Private Sector Development; Macroeconomics and Growth; Poverty and Human Resources; Public Economics; and Transition Economics. From the World Bank's organizational chart on its Web site.

9. Since most of the Bank's lending money sits with Operations staff, research money often comes from loan support funds. Hence, researchers in the Center depend on bids from Operations staff to support up to half of their work time.

10. McNamara interview conducted by Nicholas Stern, in Stern and Ferreira 1997.

11. World Bank staff training seminar and interviews with Environmental officials, April 1995.

12. Interviews, April 1995.

13. Operational Directive 4.01 paras. 1 and 2, as cited in World Bank Environment Department 1995, p. 2.

14. When I conducted these interviews in the mid- to late 1990s, staff were required to follow these operational directives; since then, President Wolfensohn has made them voluntary but highly advised, much to the dismay of the environmental staff. Bank staff is well aware that public scrutiny is heightened around large-scale loan projects, and this becomes a strong motivating force to conduct comprehensive EAs.

15. A Pandora's box of controversy would burst open if structural adjustment loans, or SAPs, were to be considered for classification. The critical scholarship on SAPs argues that of all the Bank's loans, adjustment loans

have the most deleterious impacts on the poor majority and the natural environments on which they depend.

16. This change reflects the fact that the Bank is shifting its investments to more capital intensive projects; leading the pack are cofinanced investments in China worth $12.9 billion over FY1993, 1994, and 1995. These figures represent the estimated project cost, which includes Chinese government, World Bank, and IDA financing. See World Bank Environment Department 1995.

17. Throughout the day, the specter of the huge Arun 3 Dam in Nepal was everywhere; almost every worst case scenario was dramatized by the Arun case, i.e., if you do not do a good EA, you may end up at the wood shed alongside the Arun managers. This was at the time when Arun 3 had been canceled by the Bank's president in response to the inspection panel's concern about its viability. For a discussion of the controversy, see Fox and Brown 1998; Wade 1997.

18. Our trainer in this seminar observed that: "EAs rarely look into the 'go/no go' option, whether the project should be canned or completely redone. Our counterparts [borrowers] have already made up their minds on the project and don't want to analyze alternatives. They'd rather discuss changing the dam height, 80 feet instead of 82 feet high, rather than engage in the 'no dam' debate. Here is where a 'sectoral EA' of the whole power sector makes more sense, where we can ask if there is actual demand for the dam's power unit, in the first place."

19. Forty percent is a very generous assessment. Most observers conclude that practically no Bank project is satisfactorily supervised, so these desk-top internal reviews are always questionable.

20. Interviews, January and April 1995.

21. A coalition of international organizations lobbied hard to change one small aspect of this huge project—farmer training and seed distribution by extension agents, not state agents but by a private bidder. They felt that a local NGO with ties to a petroleum and chemical company would get the contract for this work and would train farmers in chemical-dependent farming rather than in integrated pest management (IPM). After receiving daily faxes in protest and phone calls from top Bank brass, the task manager relented and gave the contract to a more IPM-sensitive NGO. "If that's what pleases everyone around here, then fine. I'm happy to put 'environmentally sustainable' before every noun in this project report. But I still believe that farmers themselves choose what's best for their own land." The international coalition leader rejoiced at the news, though oddly enough, it was a complete mystery to him and the campaign that this flea-sized farmer outreach program was on the back of a $900-million elephant (interview, 1996).

22. Interview, April 1995.

23. One mid-level Bank official had been invited to participate in a weekend retreat of a highly competitive multinational corporation. He said it took him two days of sitting in meetings and at meals to figure out who was whose boss. "Heck, I wasn't sure who the CEO was until I was introduced to him." By contrast, he said it takes only a few minutes at a Bank staff meeting to learn the pecking order.

24. Interviews with Bank economist, Latin American region, January, April, and June 1995.

25. For example, Fanelli et al. 1992; Stern and Ferreira 1997; David Woodward as cited in George and Sabelli 1994; and Taylor 1993.

26. This remark comes from an interview with the Bank's evaluation expert of NEAPs, January 1995.

27. See World Bank Environment Department 1995.

28. In some countries, Bank task managers' insistence that national officials write their NEAPs themselves has met with strong in-country resistance. In other countries, local officials understand these reports for how task managers treat them, as a "salute to the Bank flag," as one senior economist in the Africa region described them. As of 1996, IDA countries have to have a Bank-approved NEAP before receiving loans, so the incentive for both Bank officials and their clients to patch something together is great.

29. From interviews with Bank consultants from different African countries, conducted at a two-week training seminar in Washington, D.C., 1995.

30. One hundred and four of the 142 citations in Munasinghe's and Cruz's influential report, "Economywide Policies and the Environment" (1995), refer to World Bank documents (114 are to affiliated authors); more than three-quarters of the bibliography to a Bank report on environmentally sustainable development in Africa (68 of 90 citations) refers directly to Bank documents (see AFTES, Toward Environmentally Sustainable Development in Sub-Saharan Africa [World Bank, December 1995 draft]); and almost 60 percent of Frank Convery's citations in his 1995 Bank report, "Applying Environmental Economics in Africa," are to his colleagues' writings. See Convery, "Applying Environmental Economics in Africa," World Bank Technical Paper no. 277, March 1995.

31. Robert Wade (1996) and Alice Amsden (1994) also note these intellectual kinship networks.

32. Interview, April 1995.

33. Interview with a former Bank official, January 1995.

34. Several Bank officials I interviewed were current and past YPs, October and December 1994, January and April 1995.

35. Interview with a former World Bank official who was hired in mid-career.

36. For an insightful portrayal of the Bank's "narcissus," see Amsden 1994, p. 628.

37. One of the leitmotifs in the Morse Report, the independent review of the Bank's catastrophic Narmada dam project in India, is the recognition of how definitions and apparatuses of the development world fail to capture, measure, or explain the complexity of life along the Narmada River and in the Gujarat desert. To discuss the concrete aspects of "resettle and rehabilitate"—shifting real populations—requires an explanation of their present and future. The Morse team—approved by Bank president Barber Conable—can be easily considered a conventional assemblage of professionals institutionally sympathetic to development ideologies: a retired UN technocrat and member of the U.S. Congress, a prominent Canadian supreme court judge, a Canadian hydrologist, and a Canadian anthropologist. Yet they were unanimously appalled at the huge discrepancy between institutionalized assumptions and understandings, that is, how unrealistic it is for a Bank or a centralized governmental agency to think it can "know" a huge, diverse rural population that shows up on the epistemic scanner only because it stands in the way of a dam. The report is a rare gem that documents, in its own small way, the crisis of development. See Morse 1992; also from my interview with the main author, the Honorable Thomas R. Berger, Vancouver, May 1996.

38. In the example described in the preface, one of the world's largest irrigation projects displaced hundreds of thousands of desert dwellers from their land, yet the Bank's final reports never listed them as displaced (Goldman 1998).

39. This is the dilemma that many applied anthropologists face. See, e.g., the Web site of Professor Ted Downing, University of Arizona, and the Development Policy Kiosk Web site, as well as the edited book, Hobart 1993.

40. Daly's books include: *Toward a Steady-State Economy* (editor, 1973); *Economics, Ecology, and Ethics* (1980); *For the Common Good* (1989); *Valuing the Earth: Economics, Ecology, Ethics* (1993); and *Beyond Growth: The Economics of Sustainable Development* (1996). Interview conducted in January 1995.

41. Interview, January 1995, and subsequent conversations.

42. Daly explained: "I was invited to Chile by [eminent economist] Manfred Max-Neff to talk about ecological economics at a conference. I mentioned it to a colleague at the Chile desk, and soon afterwards I was called in by one of my superiors and told that since Chile–World Bank relations were quite sensitive at the time, I was not allowed to give a public talk there. Well, it was near Christmas time and I wasn't so excited about travel-

ing all that way for a talk, but I wasn't going to lie to Manfred either and say my grandmother was ill. He was so upset that he sent back a rush letter to the Bank's top brass saying that after having experienced seventeen years of dictatorship in Chile he was quite surprised that the Bank, the paragon of democratic freedom, would censor its own staff, and that he would read this letter and their response aloud to the conference participants. Well, the guys upstairs immediately called me in and said, 'No, no, no, you misunderstood, of course you can go.' The one condition was that someone from the Bank's Chile desk had to accompany me" (interview, January 1995).

43. Interview, January 1995. A senior economist overseeing a number of African country portfolios explains how there is "absolutely no serious discussion of the environmental impact of privatization of the public sector, which is now the Bank's main business in Africa. Privatization needs a new regulating framework, yet no one does calculations on its environmental impact." Interview, April 1995.

44. Interviews in April 1995, October 1995, and June 1996.

45. See World Bank's Web site on South Asia Environment and Social Development: http://wbln1018.worldbank.org/sar/sa.nsf/a22044d0c4877a3e 852567de0052e0fa/484a44733683f942852567f200585042?OpenDocument# Environment .

46. See Bretton Woods Project Web site (www.brettonwoodsproject .org); and also Fine 2000; Jamison 2001; Mehta 2001; Stone 2000.

## Chapter 4.
## The Birth of a Discipline

1. Interview, Vancouver, British Columbia, 1996.

2. In fact, in anticipation of a negative result, the Indian government cancelled its agreement with the Bank before the directors' vote.

3. Interviews in World Bank headquarters, Washington, D.C., 1995–98, and from a Bank staff training seminar in which I participated.

4. The principal bilateral donor, the German development bank KfW, described Arun 3 as the "best-studied development project ever undertaken by the German government." See Usher 1996.

5. From my participation in a Bank staff training seminar on EIAs, April 1996.

6. Interviews, 1995–96, Washington, D.C., and Vientiane, Laos, 1998.

7. It is important to note that although officially it may be the government or a private investment firm that is responsible for hiring consult-

ants, it is the Bank official in charge who oversees all activities. Although the chief officer in the Lao Hydropower office may sign off on a report or a payment to a consultant, it is not she or he who finds the consultant and sets the terms of reference for the job. In other words, the whole process is governed by the Bank, even if the responsibilities are dispersed among other actors.

8. Some of these engineering firms are actually subsidiaries of builders, whereas others have worked alongside them for years.

9. The term "feasibility study" generally refers to a group of studies that assess the economic and environmental feasibility of a project, its potential social and environmental impacts, and how it measures up against possible alternatives.

10. In early 2001, Transfield sold off its shares of NT2 to a Chicago-based firm but is still heavily invested in energy production in the Mekong.

11. These military helicopters were landing in the same remote densely forested areas where the United States led its largest bombing campaign ever, along the Ho Chi Minh Trail. These anthropologists were asking for more time in part to try to overcome the fear and silence that the presence of such helicopters might evoke.

12. Interviews, Vientiane, January 1998.

13. Interview, May 2001, with a highly regarded U.S. ichthyologist of the Mekong.

14. A few weeks later, the Mekong campaigner for International Rivers Network (IRN) wrote a pointed letter to the ADB director in charge, demanding that the report be released and rebutting the bank's claims that the report failed to produce any clear recommendations. Indeed, since IRN already had the report, it was easy to challenge the ADB's interpretation of its content. The quotation in the text comes from the ADB's response to the hired scientist and to IRN. The scientist was told by a Lao official that his report was suppressed to keep the information from the "environmental lobby."

15. This observation is based on numerous conversations I have had with consultants doing research for the World Bank, as well as public and news reports.

16. The first major study on NT2 fisheries by Hill and Hill (1994) argued that "the central problem with this evaluation, as well as other studies of the Mekong fisheries, is a lack of data and information. Proposed development projects cannot be safely designed or adequately mitigated without a sound and reliable environmental data base." These authors unambiguously warned against acting on any speculation at this point because of the dangers of speculating without data. "There is virtually no body of knowledge upon which to rely in making these decisions." Despite these strong conclusions

and the call for multiple-year and multi-sited studies before any development decisions should be made, these words were not heeded (Hill 1995). Moreover, these conclusions and warnings are missing from subsequent references to this pivotal study; the World Bank and its partners, in both confidential and published reports, put a very different spin on these findings.

17. Personal correspondence, July 2000. See Roberts 1999.

18. Independent of the dam EIAs, Roberts and his colleagues have methodically identified new and potentially rare species of fish and other river fauna. See Roberts and Baird 1995 and Roberts 1995.

19. Understandably sensitive about his treatment, he described the task at hand as extremely complex: "It's not like studying salmon migration in U.S. rivers, where they make one big migratory push before they die. In the tropics, these are feeding migrations, and the fish move when an area dries up. But that includes much more than the big fish—the whole ecosystem packs up and moves with them. And there are absolutely no data on how the whole system holds together"(interview, July 2000).

20. Personal correspondence, July 2000.

21. Interviews, Vientiane, January 1998.

22. IUCN has been negotiating with the World Bank on numerous other high-stakes conservation-development projects elsewhere.

23. Rare species of ox, deer, pig, and frogs recently discovered by Northern conservation scientists may be the necessary "facts" that will help cement the agreement for internationally managed wildlife protection sites, megafauna running corridors, and biodiversity parks in Laos.

24. One high-profile scientific censorship controversy involves the Bank president's independent review of the Pangue project in Chile, a review that was instigated by the Pehuenche indigenous people who claimed the Bank's International Finance Corporation was breaking its own policies on handling of indigenous peoples at development sites. Two separate distinguished panels were commissioned and their reports were summarily censored. See the Web sites of senior anthropologist Theodore Downing (http://www.ted-downing.com/), International Rivers Network (www.irn.org), and the Bank's International Finance Corporation (www.ifc.org/pressroom/Archive/1997/HAIR-E.htm). In this chapter, however, I try to make the point that these high-profile anomalies are built upon a whole set of scientific protocol for which everyday forms of censorship, suppression, and generation are commonplace.

25. Interview, 1997. He is now an official in the Mekong River Commission, Phnom Penh, a funder-driven research and policy institute.

26. For differing views on this project, including the much-touted

participation aspect, see World Commission on Dams (2000), and Web sites for the report (www.damsreport.org), IRN (www.irn.org), and the World Bank (www.worldbank.org).

27. Franklin 1997 as well as author's interviews with people who attended the consultations.

28. These range from the ADB, to the bilateral aid agencies, such as the Swedish aid agency SIDA, and the NGOs, such as CARE.

29. As I note elsewhere, this financial and political pressure encourages a stratification process within borrower states, creating a transnational state sector (e.g., forestry, mining, natural resources) funded to facilitate foreign capital investment, and a domestic state sector (e.g., health, education, welfare) that receives little attention, if it is not bled.

30. By the early 1990s, large transnational conservation groups shifted their stance on the dam project, agreeing with the World Bank that the only way to "save" megafauna or biodiversity was to support the massive dam project and fight to ensure that a portion of the revenues goes for Western-style conservation. In Laos and Cameroon, these conservation groups have negotiated for a share of the revenues from capital-intensive projects (e.g., a major oil pipeline through the Cameroon tropical forest), which would go in an off-shore account supervised by objective and impartial transnational elites, such as their own staff, and be used for conservation efforts.

31. Interview, Vientiane, January 1998.

## Chapter 5.
## Eco-Governmentality and the Making
## of an Environmental State

1. A 1998 map of Laos demarcates about ninety planned dams (see AMRC Web site, Sydney, Australia), and a British consulting firm mapped out thirty-seven different dams on just two rivers of the Mekong River system running through Laos. See Halcrow and Partners Ltd 1998.

2. My emphasis also differs from the perspective of economic geographers who effectively argue that nature is socially produced and under a capitalist regime, produced specifically for commodification (Harvey 1996; Smith 1990). Instead of seeing this process as a fait accomplis, and being hesitant to gloss over the contested terrain from which such transformations occur, I emphasize the heated productive relations out of which new political, economic, and cultural rationalities are born and become institutionalized, resisted, and everything in between. That is, I find it useful to interrogate the process of production from which new hegemonic (and counterhege-

monic) forms emerge, to better understand the actual routes from which the adjective "green" and the noun "neoliberalism" may congeal as naturalized artifact, becoming part of the "there is no alternative" (TINA) state of mind circulating within professional communities across the globe.

3. This name is a pseudonym. This plateau trip took place in January 1998.

4. The way in which the region is being renamed by Northern-based banks and agencies as "the Greater Mekong Subregion," and the way in which the six countries—including the supposed rogue state run by the violent military regime in Myanmar—are being funded as a transboundary region, with major projects, goods, and capital crossing borders as if national sovereignty does not count, is a truly remarkable phenomenon. Socialist, communist, or military junta—politics no longer matters to the forces behind this transformation.

5. See the latest Web sites by the Asian Development Bank, the World Bank, the Greater Mekong Subregion, the Mekong River Commission, the Oxfam Mekong Initiative, the Australian Mekong Region Centre, the International Rivers Network, IUCN, WWF, and many others, to get a sense of the magnitude of these ambitious plans.

6. As one member of the Bank's Panel of Experts commented in response to public statements by ichthyologists that at least one fish species will not survive the dam's construction: "Look, it's between one little fish, on the one hand, and all the poor [people] in the region who would benefit from this project. Which would you choose?" (author interview, Vientiane, January 1998). Many of the experts whom I interviewed in Vientiane adopted this highly reductive TINA perspective.

7. These controversies are well documented by the Bank Information Center (Washington, D.C.), TERRA (Bangkok), and the International Rivers Network (Berkeley), with archived copies of letters, reports, meeting minutes, and emails among the relevant actors.

8. The full letter exchange among IUCN, WCS, and IRN in the 1996–97 period when NGOs were still on the fence in terms of supporting the Nam Theun 2 Dam process, is archived on IRN's Web page (www.irn.org) under Nam Theun 2 campaign.

9. As noted in chapter 4, the plans for NT2 include an ambitious string of conservation and protected areas, megafauna running corridors, watershed conservation sites, eco-tourism projects, biodiversity research and development sites, and indigenous peoples' extractive reserves. Roads, markets, experimental farms, Lao-language schools, health clinics, and workshops in agronomy, resource management, family hygiene and birth control are also part of the project.

10. The fruits of this labor can be found in two publicly circulated data atlases: Asian Development Bank's *GMS Atlas of the Environment*, 2004, and Nordic Institute of Asian Studies and the National Statistical Centre (Vientiane), *The Atlas of Laos*, 2000.

11. The distinction between "in" and "out" is obviously based on one's interpretative framing. For example, as soon as hired anthropologists realized that the Nakai Plateau residents could be moved from their soon-to-be submerged villages to new plots outside the range of the planned dam reservoir but still within the people's "spirit territory," development experts judged this resettlement process as only a minor disruption and easily compensated by the development inputs (e.g., Lao-speaking schools, health clinics, agricultural inputs) rewarded to the displaced. The World Bank applauds such discoveries by its consultants and willingly sets out to preserve a spirit territory, since its success leads to the implementation of another, such as a dam. But this cost-benefit analysis does not take into consideration the effect of a spirit territory once everything the spirit and territory are based on has been radically altered, i.e., forests submerged, rivers dammed, societies put on a development agenda. This exemplifies the ongoing reification process, where pieces of indigenous practices are decontextualized, objectified, and then judged in purely developmentalist terms of commensurability.

12. Although the FOMACOP project is now defunct, the Bank's authority in the domain of "sustainable forestry" remains.

13. Old computers, since replaced with newer models, are stacked behind office doors and a collection of broken-down Volvo station wagons, superseded by newer SUVs, fills a parking lot behind the building. Staff offered two complementary explanations: Vientiane lacked experienced computer and car mechanics, and with each new project comes a new equipment budget.

14. Interview, Vientiane, 1998.

15. Interview, with a STEA staff scientist in Vientiane, 1998.

16. Not a month goes by without Laos being described in the international press as the "little sleepy nation" hidden in the shadows of the rapid growth and prosperity of Southeast Asia.

## Chapter 6.
## Privatizing Water, Neoliberalizing Civil Society

1. In this chapter, I focus exclusively on transnational policy networks supported by the World Bank and not on TPNs unrelated to the Bank. But because the Bank is involved in many global policy issues—from climate

change to Law of the Sea, the war on terrorism, and international trade agreements—the overlap is substantial.

2. Since 1997, in response to external criticism that the Bank itself was neither transparent nor accountable, the WBI decided to establish an external advisory council, one of the first of the major Bank departments to be responsible in some way to outsiders. The WBI's advisory council in 2002 was composed of executives from Sun Micro Systems, the International Herald Tribune, McKinsey and Company, members of the transnational high-end service sector (i.e., key beneficiaries of Bank adjustment loans), the CEO of African Virtual University (a new World Bank-sponsored university), a Peruvian specialist in civil society, and executives from exclusive Southern private universities. In other words, though the WBI is becoming more accountable to the outside world, that world is a highly selective, exclusive, and compatible one, formed largely of the corporate clients that benefit most from Bank loans and activities. See World Bank Institute 2002.

3. The WBI's Water Policy Capacity Building Program alone has trained more than nine thousand professionals from ninety countries since 1994. Almost half of the participants surveyed said that WBI-sponsored activities led to reform of water management policy in their countries (Pitman 2002, p. 10).

4. In 2002, as a result of U.S. pressure on the World Bank to support its post-9/11 agenda, Pakistan received an unprecedented $800 million for adjustment/privatization projects alone (World Bank 2002, p. 150). These loans cut across all institutions in Pakistan, from the courts to parliament, from local state offices, to the insurance, banking, and public-service provision sectors.

5. See "Public Communication Programs for Privatization Projects" downloadable from http://www.worldbank.org/developmentcommunications/Publications/wb%20toolkit%20book%203.6.02.pdf.

6. I thank Nina Laurie for helping me clarify this observation.

7. See www.logincee.org.

8. See www.acbf-pact.org/forums/APIF.

9. See "What Can ACBF Offer Nepad?" ACBF Web site, www.acbf-pact.org/inforResources/briefs/FAQs.pdf.

10. See Laurie et al. 2003.

11. See also Global Water Archive at http://www.platts.com/gwr/081902.html.

12. This report was released during the Second World Water Forum at The Hague.

13. See http://www.worldwatercouncil.org/forum.html.

14. On their concept of relational biographies, see Dezalay and Garth 2002.

15. See http://www.worldwatercouncil.org/forum.html.

16. The terminology here may be confusing in that the commissions, councils, partnerships, and forums discussed are at once networks in and of themselves as well as forming part of a larger network in which these smaller networks interact.

17. See www.worldwatercouncil.org/vision.html.

18. World Bank president Wolfensohn was a founding member of the WBCSD.

19. See www.iccwbo.org. These 160 members of the WBCSD are drawn from more than 30 countries and 20 major industrial sectors. See World Business Council for Sustainable Development 2002, downloaded from http://www.gm-unccd.org/FIELD/Private/WBCSD/Pub1.pdf.

20. In this context, the "new millenium development goals" refer to the goals established at the Millennium Session of the UN General Assembly in 2000 for addressing problems of water access. See World Business Council for Sustainable Development 2002.

21. These figures come from WaterAid's Web site, http://www.wateraid.org/site/in_depth/current_research/157.asp, accessed February 13, 2003.

22. Quoted from WaterAid Web site, "Private Sector Participation" http://www.wateraid.org/site/in_depth/current_research/157.asp, accessed February 13, 2003.

23. Like so many organizations described here, WaterAid has circulated reports that question the argument that privatization is the only or best way to help the poor. Indeed, disagreement and dissensus is a critical element to the making of hegemony. See, e.g., the report "New Rules, New Roles: Does PSP [Private Sector Participation] Benefit the Poor?" (WaterAid and Tearfund 2003).

24. See http://www.wateraid.org/site/in_depth/current_research/400 .asp, accessed February 13, 2003.

25. This information is drawn from WaterAid's Web site, www.wateraid.org, accessed February 13, 2003.

26. From www.wateraid.org, accessed February 13, 2003.

27. Other major funders of these transnational policy actor networks include the bilateral aid agencies of the countries where the world's largest water-service firms reside: DFID, the British aid agency; SIDA, the Swedish aid agency; the French Ministry of Foreign Affairs; the Netherlands Ministry of Foreign Affairs; and U.S. AID. Most of these policy actors have emerged

since 1996 and their agendas hew closely to the Bank's water privatization agenda.

28. See www.worldwaterforum.org/eng/wwf02.html.

29. See www.symposium-h2o.com/symposium.html.

30. See www.worldwatercouncil.org/download/FinPan.Washington.pdf.

31. See www.worldbank.org/wbi/sdwatermedianetwork.

32. See www.wupafrica.org/what.html.

33. See www.iccwbo.org.

34. "The water crisis is a governance crisis, characterized by a failure to value water properly and by a lack of transparency and accountability in the management of water," argues a Global Water Partnership report, for example. "Reform of the water sector, where water tariffs and prices play essential parts, is expected to make stakeholders recognize the true costs of water and to act thereafter" (International Consortium of Investigative Journalists 2002, p. 25).

35. See Web sites, news briefs, and summary reports from all three water forums, which can be accessed through any of these major players' Web sites, including the World Bank's.

36. At the same time, the global water lords were repeating, in the most Victorian-colonial phrasing, that Africa's poor were victims of their own bad habits. Dignitaries exhorted "wash your hands!" as the water campaign's rallying cry during the summit and at the WaterDome.

37. The exceptions are in the United States and Western Europe; however, it could be argued that the world's largest firms can expand into the Northern markets largely because of the heavy Bank/IMF subsidization of the firms' deals in the South.

38. Of course, large borrowers, such as Brazil, Mexico, India, and China, also have the Bank over a barrel since their withdrawal could have devastating effects, and Bank staff act, first and foremost, to avoid conflicts.

39. Debt relief without conditionalities and debt reparations were the most common political demand from African activists at the "anti-summit" forums in Johannesburg during the World Summit meetings (author's personal notes).

40. The Bank's Poverty Reduction Support Credits—the new structural adjustment program for its poorest borrowers, include water privatization as a priority. See World Bank, "Poverty Reduction Support Credits for Uganda and Burkina Faso," at www.worldbank.org.

41. Since structural adjustment loan agreements are often outside the public domain, the information on other Bank/IMF privatization conditionalities in their SAP loans comes through public circulation of so-called

confidential papers as well as from discussions that leak within borrowing countries. See Public Citizen's report of September 2002 (Grusky). Also see the report "Letters of Intent and Memoranda of Economic and Financial Policies" prepared by government authorities with the IMF/WB, available at the IMF Web site, www.imf.org.

42. When these numbers are broken down by year, one finds a continuous increase in privatization as a requirement for access to capital, starting at fewer than 20 percent in 1990 to more than 80 percent in 2002 (International Consortium of Investigative Journalists 2002, p. 17).

43. See also Public Citizen at http://www.citizen.org/cmep/.

44. "Is the Water Business Really a Business?" J. F. Talbot, CEO Saur International, World Bank Water and Sanitation Lecture Series, February 13, 2002, www.worldbank.org/wbi/B-Span/docs/SAURD.pdf.

45. This about-face, of course, has important repercussions on World Bank and IMF lending practices because it becomes more difficult for these institutions to demand privatization if firms are unwilling to provide the services.

46. See also Laurie and Crespo 2002.

47. Author's personal notes from Johannesburg, August-September 2002.

48. In February 2003, lawyers representing the people of Cochabamba requested that the ICSID open its doors to the public and the media, but the ICSID judges refused. See "Secretive World Bank Tribunal Bans Public and Media Participation in Bechtel Lawsuit over Access to Water," Earthjustice press release, February 12, 2003.

49. "Frontline" PBS Web site, Multinational Monitor interview, January 2000, and a presentation by Cochabamba machinist Oscar Olivera, of the Coordinadora de Defense de Agua y la Vida (Coalition in Defense of Water and Life), at the International Forum on Globalization, August 2002, Johannesburg.

50. See http://www.queensu.ca/msp.

51. When I was visiting the area, a busload of World Summit delegates from France, invited by Suez executives, pulled into Orange Farm to see a demonstration of the new French water meters.

52. Interviews in Orange Farm, August-September 2002.

53. One of the strongest voices against privatization is the Southern African Civil Society Water Caucus. Of its members, the South African Municipal Workers Union campaigned against private-sector and NGO-based rural water schemes; the National Land Committee and Rural Development Services network rallied pressure on the government for its failure to provide water to millions of rural South Africans; Earthlife, Environmental Moni-

toring Group, and other environmentalists have protested against the financing of the expensive and corrupt Lesotho Highlands Water Project's Mohale Dam; and numerous civic groups organized a national network of antieviction and antiprivatization campaigns to reverse the government's efforts to strip poor households of their access to water, electricity, and sanitation services (Bond 2003). By the time of the World Summit, these different campaigns had coalesced into a nationwide social movement with "antiprivatization" as its rallying cry and had brought into the fold activists from the rural landless people's movement, the fisherfolk's movement, the trade unions, and AIDS/HIV and human rights campaigns. Finally, these South African groups joined hands with thousands of activists who had traveled from neighboring countries, from across the continent, and from Brazil, South Korea, India, Thailand, Western Europe, Canada, and Northern California.

54. See Bond 2003; Ngwane 2003.

# Chapter 7.
# Conclusion

1. Special thanks to Beverly Bell of the Center for Economic Justice (Albuquerque, N.M.) for her generous help with this interview.

2. Personal communication with the anthropologist Dr. Guillaume Boccara, Buenos Aires, 2004.

# Bibliography

Alex, G. "US AID and Agricultural Research: Review of US AID Support for Agricultural Research." Washington, D.C.: Office of Agriculture and Food Security, U.S. Agency for International Development (USAID), 1996.

Alston, Julian M., and Philip G. Pardey. *Making Science Pay: The Economics of Agricultural R and D Policy.* AEI Studies in Agricultural Policy. Washington, D.C.: AEI Press, 1996.

Amin, Shahid. "'Gandhi as Mahatma.'" In *Selected Subaltern Studies,* ed. Ranajit Guha and Gayatri Spivak. Oxford: Oxford University Press, 1988.

Amsden, Alice. "Why Isn't the Whole World Experimenting with the East Asian Model to Develop?" *World Development* 22, no. 4 (1994).

Anderson, Kay, Mono Domosh, Steve Pile, and Nigel Thrift, eds. *Handbook of Cultural Geography.* Thousand Oaks, Calif.: Sage Publications, 2003.

Anderson, Robert, Edwin Levy, and Barrie Morrison. *Rice Science and Development Politics.* Oxford: Clarendon Press, 1991.

Anderson, Robert S., et al. *Science, Politics, and the Agricultural Revolution in Asia, AAAS Selected Symposium; 70.* Boulder: Westview Press, 1982.

Antholt, Charles H. *Getting Ready for the Twenty-First Century: Technical Change and Institutional Modernization in Agriculture.* Washington, D.C.: World Bank, 1994.

Appadurai, Arjun. "Disjuncture and Difference in the Global Economy." *Public Culture* 2, no. 2 (1990): 1–24.

Arce, Alberto, and Norman Long. *Anthropology, Development, and Modernities: Exploring Discourses, Counter-Tendencies, and Violence.* London: Routledge, 2000.

Arndt, H. W. *Economic Development: The History of an Idea.* Chicago: University of Chicago Press, 1987.

Asian Development Bank. *Rural Asia: Challenge and Opportunity (2nd Asian Agricultural Survey)*. New York: Praeger, 1977.

———. "Indicative Master Plan on Power Interconnection in the Greater Mekong Subregion Countries." 2003.

Australian Mekong Resource Centre. *Accounting for Development: Australia and the ADB in the Mekong Region—Conference Proceedings*. Sydney University, 2000.

Ayres, Robert L. *Banking on the Poor: The World Bank and World Poverty*. Cambridge: MIT Press, 1984.

Babb, Sarah. *Managing Mexico: Economists from Nationalism to Neoliberalism*. Princeton: Princeton University Press, 2001.

Barlow, Maude, and Tony Clarke. *Blue Gold: The Fight to Stop the Corporate Theft of the World's Water*. New York: New Press, 2002.

Barry, Andrew, Thomas Osborne, and Nikolas S. Rose. *Foucault and Political Reason: Liberalism, Neo-Liberalism and Rationalities of Government*. London: UCL Press, 1996.

Bauer, P. T., Gerald M. Meier, and Dudley Seers. *Pioneers in Development*. New York: Oxford University Press for the World Bank, 1984.

Baum, Warren. *Partners against Hunger: The Consultative Group on International Agricultural Research*. Washington, D.C.: World Bank, 1986.

Baviskar, Amita. *In the Belly of the River*. Delhi: Oxford, 1995.

Bayliss, Kate, and David Hall. *Unsustainable Conditions—the World Bank, Privatisation, Water and Energy*. PSIRU, University of Greenwich, UK, 2002. Available from http://www.psiru.org/reports/2002–08-U-WB-WDR2003.doc.

Beckwith, Jonathan R. *Making Genes, Making Waves: A Social Activist in Science*. Cambridge: Harvard University Press, 2002.

Berg, Robert J., and Jennifer Seymour Whitaker, eds. *Strategies for African Development: A Study for the Committee on African Development Strategies*. Berkeley: University of California Press, 1986.

Berger, Luis, Inc. *Economic Impact Study of Nam Theun Dam Project*. Washington, D.C., July 28, 1997.

Berríos, Rubén. *Contracting for Development: The Role of For-Profit Contractors in U.S. Foreign Development Assistance*. Westport, Conn: Praeger, 2000.

Berry, Sara. *No Condition Is Permanent*. Madison: University of Wisconsin Press, 1993.

———. "Claiming Patrimonial Territories in the Era of 'Privatization': Examples from Ghana." Paper presented at the 29th annual spring symposium, African Studies, University of Illinois at Urbana–Champaign, April 2003.

Bhagwati, Jagdish. "The Case for Free Trade." *Scientific American* 265, no. 5 (November 1993): 42–49.

Bird, Kai. *The Chairman: John J. McCloy, the Making of the American Establishment.* New York: Simon and Schuster, 1992.

Black, Stephanie, and Jamaica Kincaid. *Life and Debt.* New York: New Yorker Video, 2001.

Block, Fred L. *The Origins of International Economic Disorder: A Study of United States International Monetary Policy from World War II to the Present.* Berkeley: University of California Press, 1977.

Bonanno, Alessandro, et al., eds. *From Columbus to ConAgra: The Globalization of Agriculture and Food.* Lawrence: University Press of Kansas, 1994.

Bond, Patrick. *Uneven Zimbabwe: A Study of Finance, Development and Underdevelopment.* Trenton, N.J.: Africa World Press, 1998.

———. *African Grassroots and the Global Movement* ZNet, October 19, 2000. Available from http://www.lbbs.org/weluser.htm.

———. "Strategy and Self-Activity in the Global Justice Movements." *Foreign Policy in Focus* 5, no. 27 (August 21, 2001).

———. *Fanon's Warning: A Civil Society Reader on the New Partnership for Africa's Development.* Trenton, N.J.: Africa World Press, 2002.

———. *Against Global Apartheid: South Africa Meets the World Bank, IMF and International Finance.* Cape Town: University of Cape Town Press, 2003a.

———. "Rolling Back Water Privatization." ZNet Commentary, August 4, 2003b. Available from http://www.zmag.org/ZNET.htm

———. "The Politicisation of South African Water Narratives." *Capitalism, Nature, Socialism* 15:1 (2004): 7–25.

Bose, Sugata. "Instruments and Idioms of Colonial and National Development: India's Historical Experience in Comparative Perspective." In *International Development and the Social Sciences: Essays on the History and Politics of Knowledge,* ed. Frederick Cooper and Randall Packard. Berkeley: University of California Press, 1997.

Bourdieu, Pierre, and Loic Wacquant. *An Invitation to Reflexive Sociology.* Chicago: University of Chicago Press, 1992.

Brass, Paul R. *The Politics of India since Independence.* Cambridge: Cambridge University Press, 1990.

Braun, Bruce. "Producing Vertical Territory: Geology and Governmentality in Late Victorian Canada." *Ecumene* 7, no. 1 (2000).

Brenner, Neil. "Beyond State-Centrism? Space, Territoriality, and Geographical Scale in Globalization Studies." *Theory and Society* 28 (1999): 39–78.

Brenner, Neil, and Nik Theodore. "From the 'New Localism' to the Spaces of Neoliberalism." *Antipode* 34, no. 3 (2002): 341–47.

Bretton Woods Commission, ed. *Bretton Woods: Looking to the Future.* Washington, D.C.: Bretton Woods Commission, 1994.

Burawoy, Michael. "For a Sociological Marxism: The Complementary Convergence of Antonio Gramsci and Karl Polanyi." *Politics and Society* 31, no. 2 (2003): 193–261.

Burawoy, Michael, et al. *Global Ethnography: Forces, Connections, and Imaginations in a Postmodern World.* Berkeley: University of California Press, 2000.

Burbach, Roger, and Patricia Flynn. *Agribusiness in the Americas.* New York: Monthly Review Press, 1980.

Burchell, Graham, ed. *The Foucault Effect: Studies in Governmentality.* Chicago: University of Chicago Press, 1991.

Buttel, Frederick. "World Society, the Nation-State, and Environmental Protection." *American Sociological Review* 65 (2000): 117–21.

Calabrese, Daniele. *Public Communication Programs for Privatization Projects: A Toolkit for World Bank Task Team Leaders and Clients.* Washington, D.C.: World Bank, 2002.

Callaghy, Thomas M., Ronald Kassimir, and Robert Latham. *Intervention and Transnationalism in Africa: Global-Local Networks of Power.* Cambridge: Cambridge University Press, 2001.

Canguilhem, Georges. *On the Normal and the Pathological.* Dordrecht: D. Reidel, 1978.

Carty, Bob. Interview with Peter Spillet (head of the Environment, Quality and Sustainability for Thames Water), December 6, 2002. Canadian Broadcasting Corporation, 2002. Available from http://cbc.ca/news/features/water/spillet.html.

Castells, Manuel. *The Rise of the Network Society.* 3 vols. Oxford: Basil Blackwell, 1996.

Caufield, Catherine. *Masters of Illusion: The World Bank and the Poverty of Nations.* New York: Henry Holt, 1996.

Cernea, Michael M., and Scott Guggenheim. "Resettlement and Development: The Bankwide Review of Projects Involving Involuntary Resettlement, 1986–1993." Washington, D.C.: World Bank, Environment Department, 1994.

Cernea, Michael M., and Scott Guggenheim, eds. *Anthropological Approaches to Resettlement: Policy, Practice, and Theory.* Washington, D.C.: World Bank, 1993.

Chamberlain, James R., Charles Alton, and Arthur G. Crisfield. "Indigenous People's Profile: Lao People's Democratic Republic." Vientiane: Report prepared for the World Bank by CARE International, 1995.

Chamberlain, James R., and Charles Alton. "Environmental and Social Action Plan for Nakai-Nam Theun Catchment and Corridor Areas." Report prepared for IUCN, but not released, 1997.

Chape, Stuart. "Biodiversity Conservation, Protected Areas and the Development Imperative in Lao PDR: Forging the Links." Bangkok: IUCN, 1996.

———. "IUCN Programme Focus and Development in Relation to the Forestry Sector." Paper presented at the IUCN donor's meeting, Vientiane, April 1996.

Chenery, Hollis, et al. *Redistribution with Growth: Policies to Improve Income Distribution in Developing Countries in the Context of Economic Growth.* Oxford: Oxford University Press, 1974.

Clark, William. *From Three Worlds: Memoirs.* London: Sidgwick and Jackson, 1986.

Cleaver, Kevin M. "Rural Development Strategies for Poverty Reduction and Environmental Protection in Sub-Saharan Africa." Washington, D.C.: World Bank, 1997.

Clever, Kevin, and Gotz Schreiber. *Reversing the Spiral.* Washington, D.C.: World Bank, 1994.

Cohn, Bernard. *Colonialism and Its Forms of Knowledge.* Princeton: Princeton University Press, 1996.

Colby, Gerard. *Thy Will Be Done: The Conquest of the Amazon, Nelson Rockefeller and Evangelism in the Age of Oil.* New York: HarperCollins, 1995.

Collier, George Allen, and Elizabeth Lowery Quaratiello. *Basta!: Land and the Zapatista Rebellion in Chiapas,* rev. ed. Oakland, Calif.: Food First Books, 1999.

Comaroff, Jean. *Body of Power, Spirit of Resistance: The Culture and History of a South African People.* Chicago: University of Chicago Press, 1985.

Comaroff, John, and Jean Comaroff. *Of Revelation and Revolution.* Chicago: University of Chicago Press, 1997.

———. *Civil Society and the Political Imagination in Africa: Critical Perspectives.* Chicago: University of Chicago Press, 1999.

Conservation Finance Alliance. www.Conservationfinance.org. 2002.

Cooke, Bill, and Uma Kothari. *Participation: The New Tyranny?* London: Zed Books, 2001.

Cooper, F. "Modernizing Bureaucrats, Backward Africans, and the Development Concept." In *International Development and the Social Sciences: Essays on the History and Politics of Knowledge,* ed. Frederick Cooper and Randall Packard. Berkeley: University of California Press, 1997, pp. 64–92.

Cooper, Frederick, and Randall Packard, eds. *International Development and the Social Sciences.* Berkeley: University of California Press, 1997.

The Corner House. *Briefing 19—Exporting Corruption: Privatisation, Multinationals and Bribery.* Dorset: The Corner House, 2000.

Cornia, Giovanni Andrea. *Adjustment with a Human Face.* 2 vols. Oxford: Clarendon Press, 1987–88.

Corrigan, Philip Richard D., and Derek Sayer. *The Great Arch: English State Formation as Cultural Revolution.* Oxford: Blackwell, 1985.

Cosgrove, William J., and Frank R. Rijsberman. "World Water Vision: Making Water Everybody's Business." London: World Water Council, 2000.

Cowen, Michael, and Robert W. Shenton. *Doctrines of Development.* London: Routledge, 1996.

Creed, Gerald, and Janine Wedel. "Second Thoughts from the Second World: Interpreting Aid in Post-Communist Eastern Europe." *Human Organization* 56, no. 3 (1997): 253–64.

Cronon, William. *Nature's Metropolis: Chicago and the Great West.* New York: W. W. Norton, 1991.

Crush, Jonathan, ed. *Power of Development.* London: Routledge, 1995.

CSIS Task Force on the Multilateral Development Banks, and Center for Strategic and International Studies. *The United States and the Multilateral Development Banks: A Report of the CSIS Task Force on the Multilateral Development Banks.* Washington, D.C.: CSIS, 1998.

Cueto, Marcos. *Missionaries of Science: The Rockefeller Foundation and Latin America.* Philanthropic Studies. Bloomington: Indiana University Press, 1994.

Culpeper, Roy, Albert Berry, and Frances Stewart, eds. *Global Development Fifty Years after Bretton Woods: Essays in Honor of Gerald K. Helleiner.* New York: St. Martin's Press, 1997.

Dahlberg, Kenneth A. *Beyond the Green Revolution: The Ecology and Politics of Global Agricultural Development.* New York: Plenum Press, 1979.

Daly, Herman E. *Economics, Ecology, Ethics: Essays toward a Steady-State Economy.* San Francisco: W. H. Freeman, 1980.

———. "The Perils of Free Trade." *Scientific American* 265, no. 5 (November 1993): 50–55.

———. *Beyond Growth: The Economics of Sustainable Development.* Boston: Beacon Press, 1996.

Daly, Herman E., John B. Cobb, and Clifford W. Cobb. *For the Common Good: Redirecting the Economy toward Community, the Environment, and a Sustainable Future.* Boston: Beacon Press, 1989.

Daly, Herman E., and Kenneth N. Townsend. *Valuing the Earth: Economics, Ecology, Ethics.* Cambridge: MIT Press, 1993.

Daly, Herman E., ed. *Toward a Steady-State Economy.* San Francisco: W. H. Freeman, 1973.

Danaher, Kevin, ed. *Fifty Years Is Enough.* Oakland, Calif.: Food First Books, 1994.

Darier, Eric, ed. *Discourses of the Environment.* Malden, Mass.: Blackwell, 1999.

Dasgupta, Biplab. *Structural Adjustment, Global Trade, and the New Political Economy of Development*. New York: Zed Books, 1998.

Dean, Mitchell. *Critical and Effective Histories: Foucault's Methods and Historical Sociology*. London: Routledge, 1994.

———. *Governmentality: Power and Rule in Modern Society*. Thousand Oaks, Calif.: Sage Publications, 1999.

Delphos, William A. *Inside the World Bank Group: The Practical Guide for International Business Executives*. Washington, D.C.: Venture, 1997.

Dezalay, Yves, and Bryant G. Garth. *Dealing in Virtue: International Commercial Arbitration and the Construction of a Transnational Legal Order*. Language and Legal Discourse. Chicago: University of Chicago Press, 1996.

———. *The Internationalization of Palace Wars: Lawyers, Economists, and the Contest to Transform Latin American States*. Chicago: University of Chicago Press, 2002a.

———. *Global Prescriptions: The Production, Exportation, and Importation of a New Legal Orthodoxy*. Ann Arbor: University of Michigan Press, 2002b.

Diouf, Mamadou. "Senegalese Development: From Mass Mobilization to Technocratic Elitism." In *International Development and the Social Sciences: Essays on the History and Politics of Knowledge*, ed. Frederick Cooper and Randall Packard. Berkeley: University of California Press, 1997, pp. 291–319.

Dollar, David. *Globalization, Growth, and Poverty*. Washington, D.C.: World Bank, 2002.

Donini, Antonio. "The Bureaucracy and the Free Spirits: Stagnation and Innovation in the Relationship between the UN and NGOs." *Third World Quarterly* 16, no. 3 (1995): 421–39.

Dove, Michael. "Swidden Agriculture and the Political Economy of Ignorance." *Agroforestry Systems* 1, no. 1 (1983): 85–89.

Duffield, Mark R. *Global Governance and the New Wars: The Merging of Development and Security*. London: Zed Books, 2001.

Easterly, William Russell. *The Elusive Quest for Growth: Economists' Adventures and Misadventures in the Tropics*. Cambridge: MIT Press, 2001.

Eichenwald, Kurt. *The Informant: A True Story*. New York: Broadway Books, 2000.

Emerging Markets. "Agenda." *Emerging Markets*, October 9, 1995, p. 15.

Escobar, Arturo. *Encountering Development: The Making and Unmaking of the Third World*. Princeton: Princeton University Press, 1995.

———. "Constructing Nature: Elements for a Poststructural Political Ecology." In *Liberation Ecologies: Environment, Development, Social Move-*

*ments,* ed. Richard Peet and Michael Watts. New York: Routledge, 1996, pp. 46–68.

———. "Reassessing Development and Modernity: Rainforest Futures." Yale University Program in Agrarian Studies, New Haven, 2002.

Espeland, Wendy Nelson. *The Struggle for Water: Politics, Rationality, and Identity in the American Southwest, Language and Legal Discourse.* Chicago: University of Chicago Press, 1998.

Evans, Grant. *Lao Peasants under Socialism and Post-Socialism.* Bangkok: Silkworm Books, 1995.

Evans, Peter. "The Eclipse of the State? Reflections on Stateness in an Era of Globalization." *World Politics* 50 (1997): 62–87.

Evenson, Robert E., and Carl Pray. *Research and Productivity in Asian Agriculture, Food Systems and Agrarian Change.* Ithaca: Cornell University Press, 1991.

Fairhead, James, and Melissa Leach. *Misreading the African Landscape.* Cambridge: Cambridge University Press, 1996.

———. *Science, Society and Power: Environmental Knowledge and Policy in West Africa and the Caribbean.* Cambridge: Cambridge University Press, 2004.

Falloux, Francois. *Crisis and Opportunity: Environment and Development in Africa.* London: Earthscan, 1993.

Fanelli, Jose Maria, et al. "The World Development Report 1991: A Critical Assessment." CEDES Document #79. Buenos Aires: CEDES, 1992.

Feinberg, Richard E. *Between Two Worlds: The World Bank's Next Decade.* New Brunswick, N.J.: Transaction Books, 1986.

Ferguson, James. *The Anti-Politics Machine: "Development," Depoliticization, and Bureaucratic Power in Lesotho.* Minneapolis: University of Minnesota Press, 1990.

Ferguson, James, and Akhil Gupta. "Spatializing States: Toward an Ethnography of Neoliberal Governmentality." *American Ethnologist* 2 (2002): 981–1002.

Fine, Ben. *Social Capital Versus Social Theory: Political Economy and Social Science at the Turn of the Millennium.* London: Routledge, 2000.

———. "The World Bank's Speculation on Social Capital." In *Reinventing the World Bank,* ed. Jonathan Pincus and Jeffrey Winters. Ithaca: Cornell University Press, 2002, pp. 203–21.

Fine, Ben, et al. *Development Policy in the Twenty-First Century: Beyond the Post-Washington Consensus.* London: Routledge, 2001.

Finnegan, William. "Leasing the Rain: The Race to Control Water Turns Violent." *New Yorker,* April 8, 2002.

Finnemore, Martha. *National Interests in International Society.* Ithaca: Cornell University Press, 1996.

———. "Redefining Development at the World Bank." In *International Development and the Social Sciences: Essays on the History and Politics of Knowledge,* ed. Frederick Cooper and Randall Packard. Berkeley: University of California Press, 1997, pp. 203–27.

Fisher, R. J. "Shifting Cultivation in Laos: Is the Government's Policy Realistic?" In *Development Dilemmas in the Mekong Sub-Region,* ed. Bob Stenholt. Workshop Proceedings of Monash Asia Institute, Australia, 1996.

Florini, Ann. *The Third Force: The Rise of Transnational Civil Society.* Washington, D.C.: Carnegie Endowment for International Peace, 2000.

Forsyth, Timothy. "Questioning the Impact of Shifting Cultivation." *Watershed,* no. 5 (1999): 1.

Foster, John Bellamy. *Ecology against Capitalism.* New York: Monthly Review Press, 2002.

Foucault, Michel. *Power/Knowledge: Selected Interviews and Other Writings.* New York: Pantheon, 1980.

———. *The History of Sexuality: An Introduction.* New York: Vintage Books, 1990.

———. "Governmentality." In *The Foucault Effect,* ed. Graham Burchell, Colin Gordon, and Peter Miller. Chicago: University of Chicago Press, 1991.

———. "Two Lectures." In *Culture/Power/History,* ed. N. Dirks et al. Princeton: Princeton University Press, 1994.

———. *"Society Must Be Defended": Lectures at the Collège de France 1975-1976.* New York: Picador, 1997.

———. *Power.* New York: New Press, 2000.

Fox, Jonathan, and David Brown. *The Struggle for Accountability: The World Bank, NGOs, and Grassroots Movements.* Cambridge: MIT Press, 1998.

Fox, Jonathan, and Eva Thorne. "When Does Reform Policy Influence Practice? Lessons from the Bankwide Resettlement Review." In *The Struggle for Accountability: The World Bank, NGOs, and Grassroots Movements,* ed. Jonathan Fox and David Brown, Cambridge: MIT Press, 1998.

Frank, David J., Ann Hironaka, and Evan Schofer. "The Nation-State and the Natural Environment over the Twentieth Century." *American Sociological Review* 65 (2000): 96–116.

Franklin, Barbara. "A Review of Local Public Consultations for the Nam Theun 2 Hydroelectric Project." Vientiane: Submitted to the World Bank, 1997.

Frey, Bruno, et al. "Consensus and Dissensus among Economists: An Empirical Inquiry." *American Economic Review* 74, no. 5 (1984): 986-94.

Friedmann, Harriet. "The Political Economy of Food: The Rise and Fall of the Postwar International Food Order." *American Journal of Sociology* 88 (1982): 248–86.

Frison, E. A., Wanda W. Collins, and Suzanne L. Sharrock. "Global Programs: A New Vision in Agricultural Research." Washington, D.C.: Consultative Group on International Agricultural Research (CGIAR), 1997.

Galbraith, John Kenneth. *The Nature of Mass Poverty.* Cambridge: Harvard University Press, 1979.

Geest, Willem van der, and Hilary Hodgson, eds. *Negotiating Structural Adjustment in Africa.* London: J. Currey for the United Nations Development Programme, 1994.

Gelb, Alan H. *Can Africa Claim the 21st Century?* Washington, D.C.: World Bank, 2000.

George, Susan, and Fabrizio Sabelli. *Faith and Credit: The World Bank's Secular Empire.* London: Penguin Books, 1994.

Gill, Stephen, ed. *Globalization, Democratization and Multilateralism.* New York: St. Martin's Press, 1997.

Gille, Zsuzsa. "Cognitive Cartography in a European Wasteland: Multinational Capital and Greens Vie for Village Allegiance." In *Global Ethnography,* Michael Burawoy. Berkeley: University of California Press, 2000.

Gills, Barry, ed., *Globalization and the Politics of Resistance.* London: Palgrave, 2000.

Gilman, Nils. *Mandarins of the Future: Modernization Theory in Cold War America.* Baltimore: Johns Hopkins University Press, 2003.

Glaeser, Bernhard. *The Green Revolution Revisited: Critique and Alternatives.* London: Allen and Unwin, 1987.

Global Water Report. "Privatisation, a Question That Just Won't Go Away: Interview with Pierre Giacasso, Director of Water Service of the Service Industriels De Geneve, Uncovers Trends in World Water Supply." *Global Water Report,* September 4, 1996.

Goldman, Michael. "The Rise of the 'Global Resource Managing' Class." In *The Political Development of Nature: New Conflicts over Biological Resources,* ed. Volker Heins and Michael Flitner. Frankfurt: Leske and Budrich, 1997.

———. "The Birth of a Discipline: Producing Authoritative Green Knowledge, World Bank-Style." *Ethnography* 2, no. 2 (2001a): 191–217.

———. "Constructing an Environmental State: Eco-Governmentality and Other Transnational Practices of a 'Green' World Bank." *Social Problems* 48, no. 4 (2001b): 499–523.

———. "Notes from the World Summit in Johannesburg: 'History in the Making'?" *Capitalism, Nature, Socialism* 13, no. 4 (2002).

————. "Tracing the Roots/Routes of World Bank Power." *International Journal of Sociology and Social Policy* 25, no. 1/2 (2005): 10-29.

Goldman, Michael, ed. *Privatizing Nature: Political Struggles for the Global Commons.* New Brunswick, N.J.: Rutgers University Press, 1998.

Gowan, Peter. *The Global Gamble: Washington's Faustian Bid for World Dominance.* London: Verso, 1999.

Gramsci, Antonio, Quintin Hoare, and Geoffrey Nowell-Smith. *Selections from the Prison Notebooks of Antonio Gramsci.* New York: International Publishers, 1971.

Greenough, Paul, and Anna Tsing, eds. *Nature in the Global South.* Durham: Duke University Press, 2003.

Griffiths, Peter. *The Economist's Tale: A Consultant Encounters Hunger and the World Bank.* London: Zed Books, 2003.

Grove, Richard. *Green Imperialism: Colonial Expansion, Tropical Island Edens, and the Origins of Environmentalism, 1600–1860.* Cambridge: Cambridge University Press, 1996.

Grusky, Sara. "Profit Streams: The World Bank and Greedy Global Water Companies." Washington, D.C.: Public Citizen, 2002.

Gupta, Akhil, and James Ferguson. "Beyond 'Culture': Space, Identity, and the Politics of Difference." *Cultural Anthropology* 7, no. 1 (1992): 6–23.

Guyer, Jane. "Spatial Dimensions of Civil Society in Nigeria." In *Civil Society and the State in Africa,* ed. John Harbeson, Donald Rothchild, and Naomi Chazan. Boulder: Lynne Rienner Publishers, 1994.

Gwin, Catherine. "U.S. Relations with the World Bank, 1945–1992." In *The World Bank: Its First Half Century,* ed. Devesh Kapur et al. Washington, D.C.: Brookings Institution, 1997, pp. 195–274.

Halberstam, David. *The Best and the Brightest.* New York: Random House, 1972.

Halcrow, Sir William, and Partners Ltd, UK. "Se Kong-Se San and Nam Theun River Basins Hydropower Study." Asian Development Bank, 1998.

Hall, David. "Financing Water for the World—an Alternative to Guaranteed Profits." PSIRU, 2003 (cited March 2003). Available from http://www.psiru.org/reports/2003–03-W-finance.doc.

Hall, David, Kate Bayliss, and Emanuele Lobina. "Water Privatisation in Africa." Paper presented at the Municipal Services Project Conference, Witswatersrand University, Johannesburg, May 2002.

Hall, Stuart. "Gramsci's Relevance for the Study of Race and Ethnicity." In *Stuart Hall: Critical Dialogues in Cultural Studies,* ed. David Morley and Kuan-Hsing Chen. London: Routledge, 1996.

Haraway, Donna. *Primate Visions.* New York: Routledge, 1989.

Harper, Richard. *Inside the IMF: An Ethnography of Documents, Technology, and Organizational Action.* Computers and People Series. San Diego: Academic Press, 1998.

Hart, Gillian. "Development Critiques in the 1990s: *Culs De Sac* and Promising Paths." *Progress in Human Geography* 25:4 (2001): 649–58.

———. "Developments beyond Neoliberalism? Power, Culture, Political Economy." *Progress in Human Geography* 26:6 (2002a): 812–22.

———. *Disabling Globalization: Places of Power in Post-Apartheid South Africa.* Berkeley: University of California Press, 2002b.

———. "Geography and Development: Critical Ethnographies of D/development in the Era of Globalization." *Progress in Human Geography* 28:1 (2004): pp. 91–100.

Hart-Landsberg, Martin. *The Rush to Development: Economic Change and Political Struggle in South Korea.* New York: Monthly Review Press, 1993.

Harvey, David. *Limits to Capital.* Oxford: Oxford University Press, 1982.

———. *Justice, Nature and the Geography of Difference.* Oxford: Oxford University Press, 1996.

———. *The New Imperialism.* Oxford: Oxford University Press, 2003.

Helleiner, Eric. *States and the Reemergence of Global Finance: From Bretton Woods to the 1990s.* Ithaca: Cornell University Press, 1994.

Hess, David J. *Science Studies: An Advanced Introduction.* New York: New York University Press, 1997.

Hill, Mark. "Fisheries Ecology of the Lower Mekong River: Myanmar to Tonle Sap River." *Natural History Bulletin of Siam Society,* no. 43 (1995): 263–88.

Hill, Mark, and Susan Hill. *Fisheries Ecology and Hydropower in the Mekong River: An Evaluation of Run-of-the-River Projects.* Bangkok: Mekong Secretariat, 1994.

Hirsch, Philip, and Carol Warren. *The Politics of the Environment in Southeast Asia: Resources and Resistance.* London: Routledge, 1998.

Hirschman, Albert O. *Exit, Voice, and Loyalty: Responses to Decline in Firms, Organizations, and States.* Cambridge: Harvard University Press, 1970.

Hirst, Paul, and Grahame Thompson. *Globalization in Question: The International Economy and the Possibilities of Governance.* Cambridge: Polity Press, 1996.

Hobart, Mark, ed. *An Anthropological Critique of Development: The Growth of Ignorance.* London: Routledge, 1993.

Hornick, Robert. *Development Communication: Information, Agriculture and Nutrition in the Third World.* New York: Longman, 1988.

Hoselitz, Berthold Frank. *Sociological Aspects of Economic Growth.* Glencoe, Ill.: Free Press, 1960.

Hulme, David, and Michael Edwards. *NGOs, States and Donors: Too Close for Comfort?* New York: St. Martin's Press, 1997.

Hurni, Bettina. *The Lending Policy of the World Bank in the 1970s.* Boulder: Westview Press, 1980.

Hymes, Dell, ed. *Reinventing Anthropology.* New York: Vintage Books, 1974.

Institutional Investor. *The Way It Was: An Oral History of Finance, 1967–1987.* New York: Morrow, 1988.

International Advisory Group. *World Bank's Handling of Social and Environmental Issues in the Proposed Nam Theun 2 Hydropower Project in Lao PDR.* Vientiane: Submitted to the World Bank, 1997.

International Bank for Reconstruction and Development. *World Development Report 1994: Infrastructure for Development.* New York: Oxford University Press for the World Bank, 1994.

International Consortium of Investigative Journalists. *The Water Barons: How a Few Powerful Companies Are Privatizing Your Water.* Washington, D.C.: Center for Public Integrity, 2002.

International Rivers Network. *Power Struggle: The Impact of Hydro-Development in Laos.* Berkeley: International Rivers Network, 1999.

———. "Trading Away the Future: Mekong Power Grid." Berkeley: International Rivers Network, 2003.

IUCN. *Improving the Capacity of the Lao PDR for Sustainable Management of Wetlands Benefits.* Vientiane, 1993.

———. *Environmental and Social Plan for Nakai-Nam Theun Catchment and Corridor Areas.* Vientiane, 1997.

James, C. L. R. *The Black Jacobins: Toussaint L'Ouverture and the San Domingo Revolution,* 2nd ed. New York: Vintage Books, 1963.

Jamison, Andrew. *Making of Green Knowledge.* Cambridge: Cambridge University Press, 2001.

Jasanoff, Sheila. "NGOs and the Environment: From Knowledge to Action." *Third World Quarterly* 18, no. 3 (1997): 579–94.

Jasanoff, Sheila, and Marybeth Long Martello. *Earthly Knowledge: Local and Global in Environmental Governance.* Cambridge: MIT Press, 2004.

Jennings, Bruce H. *Foundations of International Agricultural Research: Science and Politics in Mexican Agriculture.* Westview Special Studies in Agriculture Science and Policy. Boulder: Westview Press, 1988.

Kapstein, Ethan. *Governing the Global Economy: International Finance and the State.* Cambridge: Harvard University Press, 1994.

Kapur, Devesh. "The Common Pool Dilemma of Global Public Goods: Lessons from the World Bank's Net Income and Reserves." *World Development* 30, no. 3 (2002): 337–54.

Kapur, Devesh, and R. Culpeper. *Global Financial Reform: How? Why? When?* Ottawa: North-South Institute, 2000.

Kapur, Devesh, Richard Charles Webb, and John Prior Lewis. *The World Bank: Its First Half Century.* 2 vols. Washington, D.C.: Brookings Institution, 1997.

Keck, Margaret E., and Kathryn Sikkink. *Activists Beyond Borders: Advocacy Networks in International Politics.* Ithaca: Cornell University Press, 1998.

Khagram, Sanjeev, James V. Riker, and Kathryn Sikkink, eds. *Restructuring World Politics: Transnational Social Movements, Networks, and Norms.* Social Movements, Protest, and Contention, vol. 14. Minneapolis: University of Minnesota Press, 2002.

Kloppenburg, Jack Ralph. *First the Seed: The Political Economy of Plant Biotechnology, 1492–2000.* Cambridge: Cambridge University Press, 1988.

Klug, Heinz. *Constituting Democracy: Law, Globalism, and South Africa's Political Reconstruction.* Cambridge Studies in Law and Society. Cambridge: Cambridge University Press, 2000.

Kneen, Brewster. *Invisible Giant: Cargill and Its Transnational Strategies.* East Haven, Conn.: Fernwood, 1995.

Kolko, Joyce, and Gabriel Kolko. *The Limits of Power: The World and United States Foreign Policy, 1945–1954.* New York: Harper and Row, 1972.

Kraske, Jochen, et al. *Bankers with a Mission: The Presidents of the World Bank, 1949–91.* Washington, D.C.: World Bank and Oxford University Press, 1996.

Krueger, Anne. "The Political Economy of the Rent-Seeking Society." *American Economic Review* 64, no. 3 (June 1974): 291–303.

Kuehls, Tom. *Beyond Sovereign Territory.* Minneapolis: University of Minnesota, 1996.

Kumar, Amitava, ed. *World Bank Literature.* Minneapolis: University of Minnesota Press, 2003.

Kumar, K. "Generating Broad-Based Growth through Agribusiness Promotion: Assessment of USAID Experience." Washington, D.C.: USAID, 1995.

Lancaster, Carol. "The World Bank in Africa since 1980: The Politics of Structural Adjustment Lending." In *The World Bank: Its First Half Century,* ed. Devesh Kapur, John Prior Lewis, and Richard Charles Webb. Washington, D.C.: Brookings Institution, 1997, pp. 161–94.

Lao PDR, Government of. *Socio-Economic Development and Investment Requirements, 1997–2000.* Government Report, Sixth Round Table Meeting. Geneva, 1997.

————. "Project to Stop Shifting Cultivation, Allocate Stabilized Livelihoods and Protect the Environment, 1998–2000." Vientiane, 1998.

————. *Resettlement Action Plan (Rap) Seminar Notes.* Report of meeting held at Lane Xang Hotel, Vientiane, 1999.

Lao PDR, Government of, Department of Forestry. *Development of Policy and Regulations under the Forestry Law for Protected Area Management in Lao PDR.* Vientiane, 1997.

Lao PDR, Government of, State Planning Committee. "Towards a Lao Definition of Poverty." Vientiane, 1997.

Laurie, Nina, Robert Andolina, and Sarah Radcliffe. "Indigenous Professionalization: Transnational Social Reproduction in the Andes." *Antipode* 35, no. 3 (June 2003): 463–92.

Laurie, Nina, and Carlos Crespo. "An Examination of the Changing Contexts for Developing Pro-Poor Water Initiatives Via Concessions." University of New Castle, Department of Geography, SSR Project, 2002.

Laurie, N., and S. Marvin. "Globalisation, Neo-Liberalism and Negotiated Development in the Andes: Bolivian Water and the Misicuni Dream." *Environment and Planning A* 31 (1999): 1401–15.

Le Prestre, Philippe G. *The World Bank and the Environmental Challenge.* London: Susquehanna University Press, 1989.

Levy, Marc, and Robert Keohane. *Institutions for Environmental Aid.* Cambridge: MIT Press, 1996.

Li, Tania. "Compromising Power: Development, Culture, and Rule in Indonesia." *Cultural Anthropology* 14, no. 3 (1999): 295–322.

————. "Government through Community in the Age of Neoliberalism." Paper, Anthropology Department, University of California–Santa Cruz, 2002.

Lie, John. *Han Unbound: The Political Economy of South Korea.* Stanford: Stanford University Press, 1998.

Lobina, Emanuele. *Grenoble–Water Re-Municipalised.* PSIRU, 2000. Available from http://www.psiru.org/reports/Grenoble.doc.

Lohmann, Larry and Marcus Colchester. "Paved with Good Intentions: Tfap's Road to Oblivion." *Ecologist,* no. 2 (1990): 3.

Ludden, David. "India's Development Regime." In *Colonialism and Culture,* ed. Nicholas Dirks. Ann Arbor: University of Michigan, 1992.

Mallaby, Sebastian. *The World's Banker: A Story of Failed States, Financial Crises, and the Wealth and Poverty of Nations.* New York: Penguin Press, 2004.

Markets, Emerging. "Agenda." *Emerging Markets,* October 9, 1995, p. 15.

Mason, Edward S., and Robert E. Asher. *The World Bank since Bretton Woods.* Washington: Brookings Institution, 1973.

McAfee, Kathy. "Selling Nature to Save It? Biodiversity and Green Developmentism." *Society and Space* 17 (1999): 133–54.

McCarthy, James, and Scott Prudham. "Neoliberal Nature and the Nature of Neoliberalism," *Geoforum* 35 (2004): 275–83.

McClelland, David C. *The Achieving Society.* Princeton, N.J.: Van Nostrand, 1961.

McClelland, Donald G. "Investments in Agriculture: A Synthesis of the Evaluation Literature." Washington, D.C.: Center for Development Information and Evaluation, U.S. Agency for International Development (USAID), 1996.

McCully, Patrick. *Silenced Rivers: The Ecology and Politics of Large Dams.* London: Zed Books, 1996.

McDonald, David, and John Pape. *Cost Recovery and the Crisis of Service Delivery in South Africa.* London: Zed Books, 2002.

McMichael, Philip. *Food and Agrarian Orders in the World-Economy.* Studies in the Political Economy of the World-System. Westport, Conn.: Greenwood Press, 1995.

———. *Development and Social Change: A Global Perspective,* 3rd ed. Sociology for a New Century. Thousand Oaks, Calif.: Pine Forge Press, 2004.

McNamara, Robert. *The Essence of Security.* New York: Harper and Row, 1968.

———. *One Hundred Countries, Two Billion People: The Dimensions of Development.* New York: Praeger Publishers, 1973.

———. *The McNamara Years at the World Bank: Major Policy Addresses of Robert S. McNamara, 1968–1981.* Forewords by Helmut Schmidt and Léopold Senghor. Baltimore: Johns Hopkins University Press for the World Bank, 1981.

McNeely, John. "How Dams and Wildlife Can Coexist: Natural Habitats, Agriculture, and Major Water Resource Development Projects in Tropical Asia." *Conservation Biology* 1, no. 3 (1987): 228–38.

Meerman, Jacob. *Reforming Agriculture: The World Bank Goes to Market, A World Bank Operations Evaluation Study.* Operations Evaluation Department. Washington, D.C.: World Bank, 1997.

Mehta, Lyla. "The World Bank and Its Growing Knowledge Agenda." *Human Organization* 60, no. 2 (2001): 189–97.

Meier, Gerald, ed. *Leading Issues in Economic Development.* New York: Oxford University Press, 1995.

Meltzer, Allan and Jeffrey Sachs. "Blueprint for a New IMF." Washington, D.C.: International Financial Institution Advisory Commission, 2000.

Mertes, Tom, ed. *A Movement of Movements: Is Another World Really Possible?* London: Verso, 2004.

Mestrallet, Gérard. "The War for Water: Open Letter." Water Observatory (published first in *Le Monde*), 2001. Available from http://www.waterob servatory.org/news/news.cfm?news_id=210.

Meyer, John , John Boli, George Thomas, and Francisco Ramirez. "World Society and the Nation-State." *American Journal of Sociology* 103, no. 1 (July 1997): 144–81.

Miller-Adams, Michelle. *The World Bank: New Agendas in a Changing World.* Routledge Studies in Development Economics. London: Routledge, 1999.

Mitchell, Timothy. "The Object of Development: America's Egypt." In *Power of Development*, ed. Jonathan Crush. London: Routledge, 1995.

———. *Questions of Modernity.* Minneapolis: University of Minnesota Press, 2000.

———. *Rule of Experts: Egypt, Techno-Politics, Modernity.* Berkeley: University of California Press, 2002.

Mittelman, James, ed. *Globalization: Critical Reflections.* Boulder: Lynne Rienner, 1997.

Mohan, Giles. *Structural Adjustment Theory: Practice and Impacts.* London: Routledge, 2000.

Mol, Arthur. *Globalization and Environmental Reform.* Cambridge: MIT Press, 2001.

———. *The Refinement of Production.* Utrecht: Van Arkel, 1995.

Mol, Arthur P. J., and David Sonnenfeld, ed. *Ecological Modernisation around the World: Perspectives and Critical Debates.* Ilford, Eng: Frank Cass, 2000.

Moore, Donald. "The Crucible of Cultural Politics: Reworking 'Development' in Zimbabwe's Eastern Highlands." *American Ethnologist* 26 (2000): 654–89.

———. "The Ethnic Spatial Fix." Paper, Program in Agrarian Studies, Yale University, New Haven, 2001.

Moore, Donald, Jake Kosek, and Anand Pandian, eds. *Race, Nature, and the Politics of Difference.* Durham: Duke University Press, 2003.

Morley, David, and Kuan-Hsing Chen, eds. *Stuart Hall: Critical Dialogues in Cultural Studies.* London: Routledge, 1996.

Morse, Bradford. *Sardar Sarovar: Report of the Independent Review.* Ottawa: Resource Futures International, 1992.

Mosley, Paul, Jane Harrigan, and John Toye. *Aid and Power: The World Bank and Policy-Based Lending.* London: Routledge, 1991.

Nash, June C. *Mayan Visions: The Quest for Autonomy in an Age of Globalization.* New York: Routledge, 2001.

Nelson, Paul J. *The World Bank and Non-Governmental Organizations: The Limits of Apolitical Development.* International Political Economy Series. New York: St. Martin's Press, 1995.

Neumann, Roderick. *Imposing Wilderness: Struggles over Livelihood and Nature Preservation in Africa.* Berkeley: University of California Press, 1998.

Ngwane, Trevor. "Sparks in the Township." *New Left Review* 22 (July-August 2003): 14–56.

Nietzsche, Friedrich. *The Will to Power.* New York: Random House, 1967.

NTEC (Nam Theun Electricity Consortium). *Social Action Plan.* Vientiane, 1997.

Oasa, Edmund. "The Political Economy of International Agricultural Research: A Review of CGIAR's Response to Criticisms of the Green Revolution." In *The Green Revolution Revisited,* ed. Bernhard Glaeser. London: Allen and Unwin, 1987.

O'Connor, James. *Natural Causes: Essays in Ecological Marxism.* New York: Guilford Press, 1998.

O'Connor, Martin, ed. *Is Capitalism Sustainable? Political Economy and the Politics of Ecology.* New York: Guilford Press, 1994.

Ong, Aihwa. *Flexible Citizenship: The Cultural Logics of Transnationality.* Durham: Duke University Press, 1999.

Organisation for Economic Co-operation and Development (OECD). *Risk Management in Financial Services.* Paris and Washington, D.C.: Organisation for Economic Co-operation and Development, 1992.

Owen, David. "Second Chance for Private Water?" *Privatisation International,* February 14, 2001.

Parnwell, Mike, and Raymond L Bryant. *Environmental Change in South-East Asia: People, Politics and Sustainable Development.* New York: Routledge, 1996.

Paul, Samuel, and Arturo Israel. *Nongovernmental Or    ganizations and the World Bank: Cooperation for Development.* Washington, D.C.: World Bank, 1991.

Payer, Cheryl. *The World Bank: A Critical Analysis.* New York: Monthly Review Press, 1982.

———. *Lent and Lost: Foreign Credit and Third World Development.* London: Zed Books, 1991.

Pearce, David. *The Economic Value of Biodiversity.* London: Earthscan/IUCN, 1994.

Peck, Jamie, and Adam Tickell. "Neoliberalizing Space." *Antipode* 34, no. 3 (2002): 380–404.

Peck, Jamie, and Henry Wai-chung Yeung, eds. *Remaking the Global Economy: Economic-Geographical Perspectives.* London: Sage, 2003.

Peet, Richard, and Michael Watts. *Liberation Ecologies: Environment, Development, Social Movements,* 2nd ed. London: Routledge, 2004 (1996).

Peet, Richard, et al. *Unholy Trinity: The IMF, World Bank and WTO*. London: Zed Books, 2003.

Peluso, Nancy Lee. "Coercing Conservation." In *The State and Social Power in Global Environmental Politics*, ed. Ronnie Lipschutz and Ken Conca. New York: Columbia University Press, 1993.

Peluso, Nancy Lee, and Michael Watts, eds. *Violent Environments*. Ithaca: Cornell University Press, 2001.

Petit, Michel, and Gary E. Alex. "The Emergence of a Global Agricultural Research System: The Role of the Agricultural Research and Extension Group (Esdar)." In *Environmentally Sustainable Development, Agricultural Research and Extension Group Report*. Washington, D.C.: World Bank, 1996.

Phaup, E. Dwight. *The World Bank: How It Can Serve U.S. Interests*. Washington, D.C.: Heritage Foundation, 1984.

Pieterse, Jan Nederveen. *Globalization or Empire?* New York: Routledge, 2004.

Pigg, Stacy Leigh. "Inventing Social Categories through Place: Social Representations and Development in Nepal." *Comparative Studies in Society and History* 34, no. 3 (1992): 491–513.

Pincus, Jonathan. "State Simplification and Institution Building in a World Bank-Financed Development Project." In *Reinventing the World Bank*, ed. Jonathan Pincus and Jeffrey Winters. Ithaca: Cornell University Press, 2002, pp. 76–100.

Pincus, Jonathan, and Jeffrey Winters, eds. *Reinventing the World Bank*. Ithaca: Cornell University Press, 2002.

Pithouse, Richard. "Producing the Poor: The World Bank's New Discourse of Domination." *African Sociological Review* 7, no. 2 (2003).

Pitman, George Keith. "Bridging Troubled Waters: Assessing the World Bank Resources Strategy." Washington D.C.: World Bank Operations Evaluation Department, 2002.

Polanyi, Karl. *The Great Transformation*. Boston: Beacon Press, 1957.

Porter, Theodore. *Trust in Numbers: The Pursuit of Objectivity in Science and Public Life*. Princeton: Princeton University Press, 1995.

Purdue, Derrick. *Anti-Genetix: The Emergence of the Anti-GM Movement*. Aldershot, Eng.: Ashgate Publishing, 2000.

Rabinow, Paul. *French Modern: Norms and Forms of the Social Environment*. Cambridge: MIT Press, 1989.

Ray, Debraj. *Development Economics*. Princeton: Princeton University Press, 1998.

Rayack, Elton. *Not So Free to Choose: The Political Economy of Milton Friedman and Ronald Reagan*. New York: Praeger, 1987.

Reed, David. *Structural Adjustment and the Environment.* Boulder: Westview Press, 1992.

"Relocation in Sight for Hill People." *The Nation* (Bangkok), August 4, 1996.

Rich, Bruce. *Mortgaging the Earth: The World Bank, Environmental Impoverishment, and the Crisis of Development.* Boston: Beacon Press, 1994.

———. "The Smile on a Child's Face." Paper for Environmental Defense, Washington, D.C., 2002.

Riles, Annelise. *The Network Inside Out.* Ann Arbor: The University of Michigan Press, 2000.

Roberts, John. "The Role of the Media in Reporting on Water Issues in the Middle East and North Africa." Paper presented at the Fourth International Symposium on Water, Cannes, France, June 5, 2002.

Roberts, Tyson. "Mekong Mainstream Hydropower Dams: Run-of-the River or Ruin-of-the-River?" *Natural History Bulletin of Siam Society* 43 (1995): 9–19.

———. *Fluvicide: An Independent Environmental Assessment of the Nam Theun 2 Hydropower Project in Laos, with Particular Reference to Aquatic Biology and Fishes.* Bangkok, 1996.

———. "A Plea for Proenvironment EIA." *Natural History Bulletin of Siam Society* 47 (1999): 13–22.

Roberts, Tyson, and Ian Baird. "Traditional Fisheries and Fish Ecology on the Mekong River at Khone Waterfalls in Southern Laos." *Natural History Bulletin of Siam Society* 43 (1995): 219–62.

Rockefeller, David. "What Private Enterprise Means to Latin America." *Foreign Affairs* (April 1, 1966).

Rockefeller, Nelson. "Widening the Boundaries of National Interest." *Foreign Affairs* (October 1951).

Rose, Nikolas S. *Powers of Freedom: Reframing Political Thought.* Cambridge: Cambridge University Press, 1999.

Rostow, W. W. *The Stages of Economic Growth: a Non-Communist Manifesto,* 2nd ed. Cambridge: Cambridge University Press, 1971.

Rotberg, Eugene. "Financial Operations of the World Bank." In *Bretton Woods: Looking to the Future,* ed. Bretton Woods Commission. Washington, D.C.: Bretton Woods Commission, 1994.

Ryder, Grainne. "The Political Ecology of Hydropower Development in the Lao People's Democratic Republic." Environmental Studies Program, York University, Toronto, 1996.

Sachs, Wolfgang, ed. *Development Dictionary.* London: Zed Press, 1992.

Sachs, Wolfgang, ed. *Global Ecology: A New Arena of Political Conflict.* London: Zed Press, 1993.

Sahn, David E., Paul Anthony Dorosh, and Stephen D. Younger. *Structural*

*Adjustment Reconsidered: Economic Policy and Poverty in Africa.* Cambridge: Cambridge University Press, 1997.

Said, Edward. *Orientalism.* New York: Vintage, 1978.

Saldana-Portillo, Josefina. *The Revolutionary Imagination in the Americas and the Age of Development.* Durham: Duke University Press, 2003.

Sanderson, Steven E. *The Transformation of Mexican Agriculture: International Structure and the Politics of Rural Change.* Princeton: Princeton University Press, 1986.

Sassen, Saskia. *Losing Control? Sovereignty in an Age of Globalization.* New York: Columbia University Press, 1996.

————. *Globalization and Its Discontents: Essays on the New Mobility of People and Money.* New York: New Press, 1998.

Sauer, Carl Ortwin, and John Leighly. *Land and Life: A Selection from the Writings of Carl Ortwin Sauer.* Berkeley: University of California Press, 1963.

Sayer, Derek. *The Violence of Abstraction: The Analytic Foundations of Historical Materialism.* New York: Blackwell, 1987.

————. "Some Dissident Remarks on 'Hegemony.'" In *Everyday Forms of State Formation,* ed. Gilbert Joseph and Daniel Nugent. Durham: Duke University, 1994.

Schapsmeier, Edward L., and Frederick H. Schapsmeier. *Prophet in Politics: Henry A. Wallace and the War Years, 1940–1965.* Ames: Iowa State University Press, 1970.

Schofer, Evan, Francisco Ramirez, and John Meyer. "The Effects of Science on National Economic Development, 1970 to 1990." *American Sociological Review* 65, no. 6 (December 2000): 866–87.

Scott, David. "Colonial Governmentality." *Social Text,* no. 42 (1995): 191–220.

Scott, James C. *Seeing Like a State: How Certain Schemes to Improve the Human Condition Have Failed.* New Haven: Yale University Press, 1998.

Scudder, Thayer, et al. *Third Report of the International Environmental Social Panel of Experts.* Vientiane: Government of Lao PDR, 1998.

Shapin, Steven, and Simon Schaffer. *Leviathan and the Air-Pump: Hobbes, Boyle, and the Experimental Life.* Princeton: Princeton University Press, 1985.

Shapley, Deborah. *Promise and Power: The Life and Times of Robert McNamara.* Boston: Little, Brown, 1993.

Shenton, Robert, and Michael Cowen. "The Invention of Development." In *Power of Development,* ed. Jonathan Crush. London: Routledge, 1995.

Shihata, Ibrahim F. I., Franziska Tschofen, Antonio R. Parra, Margrete Stevens, and Sabine Schlemmer-Schulte. *The World Bank in a Changing World.* Dordrecht: M. Nijhoff, 1991.

Shrybman, Steven. "Thirst for Control: New Rules in the Global Water Grab." Ottawa: Blue Planet Project, 2002.

Sivaramakrishnan, K. "A Limited Forest Conservancy in Southwest Bengal, 1864–1912." *Journal of Asian Studies*, no. 56 (1997): 75–112.

Skidelsky, Robert. *John Maynard Keynes*, vol. 3. New York: Viking, 2002.

Smith, David A., Dorothy J. Solinger, and Steven C. Topik, ed. *States and Sovereignty in the Global Economy.* London: Routledge, 1999.

Smith, Jackie G., Charles Chatfield, and Ron Pagnucco. *Transnational Social Movements and Global Politics: Solidarity Beyond the State.* Syracuse: Syracuse University Press, 1997.

Smith, Neil. *Uneven Development: Nature, Capital and the Production of Space.* Oxford: Oxford University Press, 1990.

Sonnenfeld, David, and Arthur P. J. Mol, eds. *Ecological Modernisation around the World: Perspectives and Critical Debates.* Ilford, Eng: Frank Cass, 2000.

Southavilay, Thongleua and Tuukka Castren. *Timber Trade and Wood Flow-Study, Lao PDR.* Report prepared for the Mekong River Commission, 2000.

Spaargaren, Gert, and Arthur Mol. "Sociology, Environment, and Modernity: Ecological Modernization as a Theory of Change." *Society of Natural Resources* 5 (1992): 323–44.

Sparkes, Stephen. *Public Consultation and Participation on the Nakai Plateau.* Vientiane, 1998.

Spivak, Gayatri. "Can the Subaltern Speak?" In *Selected Subaltern Studies*, ed. Ranajit Guha and Gayatri Spivak. New York: Oxford University Press, 1988.

Srinivasan, T. N., et al. "Database for Development Analysis: An Overview." *Journal of Development Economics* 44, no. 1 (1994): 3–27.

Stakman, E. C., Richard Bradfield, and Paul Manglesdorf. *Campaigns against Hunger.* Cambridge: Belknap Press, 1967.

Standing, Guy. "Brave New Words? A Critique of Stiglitz's World Bank Rethink." *Development and Change* 31, no. 4 (2000): 737–64.

Stern, Nicholas, and F. Ferreira. "World Bank as 'Intellectual Actor.'" In *The World Bank: Its First Half Century*, ed. Devesh Kapur et al. Washington, D.C.: Brookings Institution, 1997, pp. 523–610.

Stiglitz, Joseph. *Globalization and Its Discontents.* New York: Norton, 2002.

Stokes, Eric. *The English Utilitarians and India.* Oxford: Oxford University Press, 1959.

Stoler, Ann Laura. *Race and the Education of Desire: Foucault's History of Sexuality and the Colonial Order of Things.* Durham: Duke University Press, 1995.

Stoler, Ann Laura, and Frederick Cooper, eds. *Tensions of Empire.* Berkeley: University of California Press, 1999.

Stone, Diane. *Banking on Knowledge: The Genesis of the Global Development Network.* London: Routledge, 2000.

Strathern, Marilyn, ed. *Audit Cultures: Anthropological Studies in Accountability, Ethics, and the Academy.* London: Routledge, 2000.

Taylor, Lance. "The World Bank and the Environment: The World Development Report 1992." *World Development* 21, no. 5 (1993): 869–81.

Tendler, Judith. *Inside Foreign Aid.* Baltimore: Johns Hopkins University Press, 1975.

Thukral, Enakshi Ganguly, ed. *Big Dams, Displaced People.* New Delhi: Sage, 1992.

Toussaint, Eric. *Your Money or Your Life! The Tyranny of Global Finance.* London: Pluto Press, 1999.

Traisawasdichai, M. *Rivers for Sale.* Reuters Foundation: Oxford University Paper, 1997.

Tropical Rainforest Programme. *Aspects of Forestry Management in the Lao PDR.* Amsterdam, 2000.

Turok, Mary, ed. *The African Response—Adjustment or Transformation.* London: Institute for African Alternatives, 1992.

Udall, Lori. "The International Narmada Campaign: A Case of Sustained Advocacy." In *Toward Sustainable Development: Struggling over India's Narmada River,* ed. William Fisher. New York: M. E. Sharpe, 1995.

Umali-Deininger, Dina, and Charles Maguire. *Agriculture in Liberalizing Economies: Changing Roles for Governments: Proceedings of the Fourteenth Agricultural Sector Symposium.* Washington, D.C.: World Bank, 1995.

UNDP. *Report of the Sixth Round Table Meeting for Lao PDR.* The Roundtable Meeting for the Lao PDR, June 19–20, 1997, Geneva.

United States Congress. Senate. Committee on Foreign Relations. *Multilateral Development Banks: Hearing before the Committee on Foreign Relations, United States Senate, Ninety-Sixth Congress, First Session, on S. 662 . . . March 12, 1979.* Washington, D.C.: Government Printing Office, 1979.

United States Congress. Senate. Committee on Governmental Affairs. *U.S. Participation in the Multilateral Development Banks.* Washington, D.C.: Government Printing Office, 1979.

United States Department of State. *Proceedings and Documents of the United Nations Monetary and Financial Conference, Bretton Woods, New Hampshire, July 1-22, 1944,* vol. 2. Washington, D.C.: Government Printing Office, 1948.

United States Department of the Treasury. *United States Participation in the*

*Multilateral Development Banks in the 1980s.* Washington, D.C.: Department of the Treasury, 1982.

———. *The Multilateral Development Banks: Increasing U.S. Exports and Creating U.S. Jobs.* Washington, D.C.: U.S. Department of the Treasury, 1995.

United States Department of the Treasury. Office of the Assistant Secretary for International Affairs. *The Multilateral Development Banks: Increasing U.S. Exports and Creating U.S. Jobs.* Washington, D.C.: Department of the Treasury, International Affairs, 1994.

United States Department of the Treasury. Office of International Energy Policy. "An Examination of the World Bank Lending Program." Washington, D.C.: Department of the Treasury, 1981.

United States General Accounting Office. *Low U.S. Share of World Bank-Financed Procurement: Multiagency: Report to the Congress.* Washington, D.C.: General Accounting Office, 1974.

United States General Accounting Office, and United States Congress. Senate. Committee on Small Business. *Multilateral Development Banks: U.S. Firms' Market Share and Federal Efforts to Help U.S. Firms.* Washington, D.C.: General Accounting Office, 1995.

Upton, Barbara. *The Multilateral Development Banks: Improving U.S. Leadership,* The Washington Papers; 178. Westport, Conn.: Praeger, 2000.

Usher, Ann Danaiya. "The Race for Power in Laos." In *Environmental Change in South-East Asia,* ed. Michael Parnwell and Raymond Bryant. London: Routledge, 1996a.

———. *Dams as Aid.* London: Routledge, 1996b.

Wade, Robert. "Globalization and Its Limits: Reports of the Death of the National Economy Are Greatly Exaggerated." In *National Diversity and Global Capitalism,* ed. S. Berger and R. Dore. Ithaca: Cornel University Press, 1996a.

———. "Japan, the World Bank, and the Art of Paradigm Maintenance: The East Asian Miracle in Political Perspective." *New Left Review* 217 (May–June 1996b): 3–36.

———. "Greening the Bank: The Struggle over the Environment 1970–1995." In *The World Bank: Its First Half Century,* ed. Devesh Kapur et al. Washington, D.C.: Brookings Institution, 1997, pp. 611–734.

———. "Showdown at the World Bank." *New Left Review* 7 (January–February 2001): 124–37.

———. "U.S. Hegemony and the World Bank: The Fight over People and Ideas." *Review of International Political Economy* 9, no. 2 (2002): 201–29.

Walker, Andrew. "The Timber Industry in Northwestern Laos: A New Regional Resource Economy?" Paper presented at the conference, Development Dilemmas in the Mekong Subregion, Melbourne, 1996.

Wapenhans, Willi. "Effective Implementation: Key to Development Impact." Report of the Portfolio Management Task Force. World Bank, 1992.

WaterAid, and Tearfund. "New Rules, New Roles: Does PSP (Private-Sector Participation) Benefit the Poor?" 2003. Posted on WaterAid Web site.

Watershed. "Why the Nam Theun 2 Dam Won't Save Wildlife." *Watershed* (Bangkok) 1, no. 3 (March-June 1996).

———. "Special Forum on Swidden Cultivation." *Watershed* (Bangkok) 5, no. 1 (July-October 2000).

Watts, Michael. "A New Deal in Emotions." In *Power of Development,* ed. Jonathan Crush. New York: Routledge, 1995 pp. 44–62.

Wegner, David. "Review of the Nam Theun 2 Environmental Assessment and Management Plan." Paper presented at the Ecosystem Management International, Arizona, 1997.

Weisbrot, Mark, et al. "The Emperor Has No Growth: Declining Economic Growth Rates in the Era of Globalization." Washington, D.C.: Center for Economic and Policy Research, 2001.

Weiss, Linda. *The Myth of the Powerless State.* New York: Cornell University Press, 1998.

Wilkes, Garrison. "Maize and Its Wild Relatives." *Science* 177 (1972): 1071–77.

Williams, Eric. *Capitalism and Slavery.* Chapel Hill: University of North Carolina Press, 1944.

Williamson, John. "Democracy and the Washington Consensus." *World Development* 21, no. 8 (1993): 1329–36.

Wolf, Edward C. *Beyond the Green Revolution: New Approaches for Third World Agriculture,* Worldwatch Paper 73. Washington, D.C.: Worldwatch Institute, 1986.

Wood, Robert Everett. *From Marshall Plan to Debt Crisis: Foreign Aid and Development Choices in the World Economy.* Studies in International Political Economy 15. Berkeley: University of California Press, 1986.

Worby, Eric. "'Discipline without Oppression.'" *Journal of African History* 41 (2000): 101–25.

World Bank. World Bank Annual Report, 1961–62. Washington, D.C., 1962.

———. World Bank Annual Report, 1969. Washington, D.C., 1969.

———. World Bank Annual Report, 1981. Washington, D.C., 1981.

———. World Bank Annual Report, 1986. Washington, D.C., 1986.

———. "The World Bank and the Environment: Annual Report." Washington, D.C., 1990.

———. "Agricultural Biotechnology: The Next 'Green Revolution'?" World

Bank Technical Paper no. 133. Agriculture and Rural Development Department. Washington, D.C., 1991.

———. *World Development Report*. Washington, D.C., 1992.

———. "Lao PDR Forest Management and Conservation Project, EA Category B. East Asia and Pacific Regional Office." Washington, D.C., 1993.

———. "Lao PDR Forest and Conservation Management Project. East Asia and Pacific Regional Office." Washington, D.C., 1994.

———. World Bank Annual Report, 1995. Washington, D.C., 1995.

———. "World Bank News: The Bank's Presidents," 1995.

———. "Lao PDR Public Expenditure Review." East Asia and Pacific Regional Office. Washington, D.C., 1997.

———. *World Development Report, 1998/99: Knowledge for Development*. New York: Oxford University Press, 1998.

———. "Country Assistance Strategy for Lao PDR." East Asia and Pacific Regional Office. Washington, D.C., 1999.

———. World Bank Annual Report, 1999. Washington, D.C., 1999.

———. *World Development Report*. Washington, D.C., 1999.

———. "Dams for Development in Laos." Washington, D.C.: External Affairs Department, 2001.

———. "FY01 Annual Report on Portfolio Performance, Report R2001–0216." Washington, D.C., 2001.

———. World Bank Annual Report, 2002. Washington, D.C., 2002.

———. "Public Communications Programs for Privatization Projects: A Toolkit for World Bank Task Team Leaders and Clients." Development Communications Unit. Washington, D.C., 2003.

———. *World Development Report*. Washington, D.C., 2003.

World Bank, Environment Department. "Making Development Sustainable." Washington, D.C., 1994.

———. "Evaluation Report." Washington, D.C., 1994.

———. "Mainstreaming the Environment." Washington, D.C., 1995.

———. "The Impact of Environmental Assessment: Second Environmental Assessment Review of Projects Financed by the World Bank (July 1992–June 1995)." Washington, D.C., 1995.

———. "National Environmental Strategies: Learning from Experience." Washington, D.C., 1995.

———. "Evaluation Report." Washington, D.C., 1996.

World Bank Institute. Annual Report. Washington, D.C., 2002.

World Business Council for Sustainable Development (WBCSD). "Water for the Poor." Geneva: World Business Council for Sustainable Development, 2002. Available from http://www.gm-unccd.org/FIELD/Private/WBCSD/Pub1.pdf.

World Commission on Dams. *Dams and Development*. London: Earthscan, 2000.

World Commission on Water for the 21st Century (WCW). "The Africa Water Vision for 2025: Equitable and Sustainable Use of Water for Socioeconomic Development." Marseille, France. Available at http://www.worldwatercouncil.org.

World Rainforest Movement. "Notes from a NGO/Bank Consultation." London, 1993.

Worldwide Fund for Nature (WWF). "Building Conservation Capital for the Future." 2002. Available at www.worldwildlife.org.

Worster, Donald. *Rivers of Empire: Water, Aridity, and the Growth of the American West*. New York: Pantheon Books, 1985.

Wright, Angus. *The Death of Ramón González: The Modern Agricultural Dilemma*. Austin: University of Texas Press, 1990.

Young, Zoe. *A New Green Order: The World Bank and the Politics of the Global Environmental Facility*. London: Zed Press, 2003.

Zinn, Howard. *A People's History of the United States*. New York: Harper and Row, 1980.

# Index

academia: reliance on WB publications, 102;
vs. World Bank, 101, 106, 130
activism, 19th-century, 27–28
activism, 20th- and 21st-century. *See* opposition to water privatization; opposition to World Bank
ADB. *See* Asian Development Bank
Afghanistan, 275–76, 296n14
Africa: capacity building in, 230–31; debt crisis (1980s), 89 (*see also* debt of borrowing nations); early WB loans, 296n14; inapplicability of WB models/assumptions, 2–3; internationalized imperialism, 270; NEAPs, 131–32, 303n28; postcolonial development, 28–29; public opposition to WB/IMF, 278; structural adjustment's effects, 90; training in neoliberal policies, 228; water privatization, 41, 245, 252–55, 256–57t, 260–61; WB knowledge production in, 3–4, 230–32; WB publications on, 131–32. *See also* South, global; *and specific countries*
African Capacity Building Foundation (ACBF), 230–31
African Development Bank, 222, 230
African National Congress (ANC), 264–65, 288
agriculture: employee exchange program, 38; farmer credit, environmental ramifications of, 123–24; green revolution, 70–71, 84–87, 297–98n21, 298n22; integrated pest management vs. chemical-dependent farming, 302n21; in Laos, 205; 1961 loans, 79; 1981 loans, 81

Aguas de Portugal (water company), 255, 256t
Alberts, Bruce, 49
Alexandra township, Johannesburg, South Africa, 263–64
Amazon, 35–36, 95–96. *See also* Brazil
Amsden, Alice, 147
ANC (African National Congress), 264–65, 288
Angola, 253t
anthropologists, 136–39, 304n37; and the NT2 dam project, 165–67, 194, 310n11. *See also* social impact assessments
antiprivatization movement. *See* opposition to water privatization; opposition to World Bank
Argentina: anti-neoliberal politics, 44, 289; default on WB loans, 277–78; electric power project loan (1961), 78; water privatization opposition/termination, 41, 258, 259t
Aristide, Jean-Bertrand, 282
Arndt, H. W., 72
arrogance of World Bank, 19
Arun 3 dam project, 153, 302n17, 305n4
Asher, Robert E., 295n7
Asia: CGIAR wheat varieties, 86; public opposition to WB policies, 261, 278; structural adjustment's effects, 90. *See also* South, global; *and specific countries*
Asian Development Bank (ADB): Indonesian Transmigration Project investment, 299n26; and Laos/Mekong region, 154, 164, 192–93, 201, 306n14